Prisoners of War
at Dartmoor

Prisoners of War at Dartmoor

American and French Soldiers and Sailors in an English Prison During the Napoleonic Wars and the War of 1812

TREVOR JAMES
Foreword by John Lawrence

McFarland & Company, Inc., Publishers
Jefferson, North Carolina, and London

LIBRARY OF CONGRESS CATALOGUING-IN-PUBLICATION DATA

James, Trevor, 1934–
    Prisoners of war at Dartmoor : American and French soldiers and sailors in an English prison during the Napoleonic Wars and the War of 1812 / Trevor James ; foreword by John Lawrence.
       p.   cm.
    Includes bibliographical references and index.

    ISBN 978-0-7864-7407-3
    softcover : acid free paper ∞

    1. Dartmoor Prison — History — 19th century.
2. Prisons — England — Princetown — History.
3. Napoleonic Wars, 1800–1815 — Prisoners and prisons, British. 4. United States — History — War of 1812 — Prisoners and prisons, British. 5. Prisoners of war — France. 6. Prisoners of war — United States.
7. Prisoners of war — Great Britain. I. Title.
HV9650.P752D375 2013
940.2'77 — dc23   2013024528

BRITISH LIBRARY CATALOGUING DATA ARE AVAILABLE

© 2013 Trevor James. All rights reserved

No part of this book may be reproduced or transmitted in any form or by any means, electronic or mechanical, including photocopying or recording, or by any information storage and retrieval system, without permission in writing from the publisher.

Cover art by Paul Deacon, *Detailed Representation of Dartmoor Depot in 1810*, watercolour, 12" × 12"; *The Massacre Scene*, oil on canvas, 30" × 15"

Manufactured in the United States of America

McFarland & Company, Inc., Publishers
  Box 611, Jefferson, North Carolina 28640
  www.mcfarlandpub.com

The story you are about to read is dedicated to the memory of those brave men of two nations, namely the French and the Americans who suffered and died in captivity at Dartmoor. My admiration for the French relates to their undying loyalty to Napoleon, who possessed an unrivaled charisma, and leadership qualities of a rare kind. The Americans on the other hand were, to a man, loyal to a cause, namely their independence and freedom.
May they never be forgotten.

Table of Contents

Acknowledgments ix
Foreword by John Lawrence 1
Preface 3
Introduction 7
Prologue: A Sad Corner of England in 1812 9

1. The Saga Begins 13
2. A Start Is Made 24
3. The Prison Is Built 33
4. The Militia 44
5. How the Depots Were Run 48
6. Life Inside the War Depot 56
7. French Freemasons at Dartmoor 68
8. Ways Out of Dartmoor and the Hulks 74
9. The Americans Arrive 82
10. Yankee Ways 91
11. More Tribulations, Then Better Times 100
12. Dartmoor Becomes an American Depot 108
13. Escapes 114
14. Frustration and a New Regime 121
15. The Princetown Massacre 129
16. The Inquiries into the "Melancholy Occurrence" 140

Table of Contents

17. Privateers 153
18. Voices from Dartmoor Prison 158
    - Benjamin Brown 158
    - Benjamin Palmer 162
    - Charles Andrews 166
    - George Little 171
    - Perez Drinkwater 175
    - Other Journals 178
19. Survivors 183
20. The Depot's Final Days 186
21. Mortality Rates and the Price of Victory 194
22. Princetown Church and Memorials 199

Epilogue 213
Appendix 1: Those Who Died 215
Appendix 2: Chronology of Dartmoor Prison 222
Chapter Notes 224
Bibliography 228
Index 231

Acknowledgments

I owe much of the content of this book to Cyril Stringer, former Strode College Manager/Offender's Learning and Skills Service at Dartmoor Prison. For the last ten years of his life he devoted all his spare time to a study of Americans imprisoned at Dartmoor during the War of 1812. Sadly, he died before completing his aim of publishing his findings to coincide with the bicentennial of the start of that war. His collection of documents and data was very generously placed at my disposal by his widow, Christine Stringer, and they have been invaluable in compiling this book. I am privileged to have partly succeeded in his plan and wish to pay tribute to a man who devoted his energies on such a wide scale — far wider than this humble offering — to place on record a full and accurate account of events. Had Mr. Stringer lived he would have produced a very thorough and lengthy description not only of a prisoner's fate and sufferings under the often brutal regime that prevailed at Dartmoor Depot, but their backgrounds and activities. Such a work would have at least equaled if not surpassed anything else written to date.

Ron Joy, author of *Dartmoor Prison: A Complete Illustrated History*, a historian and former principal officer at the prison, assisted Cyril Stringer in several ways, and his contribution is appreciated and acknowledged.

The late Ira Dye, author *The Fatal Cruise of the Argus*, also made several valuable contributions. Author and historian, he was without doubt one of the foremost authorities on the War of 1812. His enthusiasm for matters relating to that war began by chance. He was a World War II U.S. Navy submarine commander and evidently an officer of exceptional ability because at the end of hostilities he was entrusted with a special project. The German Navy had developed an advanced type of submarine which was far ahead of anything the Allies had. Three vessels were captured by the Americans and brought to Plymouth. Captain Dye was selected to take an experienced crew to Plymouth to get acquainted with the technical equipment to take the submarines to the

United States. This took several weeks, during which time he got to know the city pretty well. One day while on a stroll he found himself at St. Andrews Church, where he came across a headstone in memory of Lt. Allen and Midshipman Delphey of the U.S. brig *Argus,* who died after a battle at sea during the War of 1812. He was determined to find out how these two officers came to be buried there. His search became an obsession, culminating in his amassing a huge collection of documents, books relating to that period, microfilms, letters, etc., which together constituted one of the most extensive databases on the war. His priceless collection was donated to the USS Constitution Museum in Boston after his death in 2005. Every researcher and writer on that war owes him a huge debt, and due acknowledgement is rendered here.

It has been my privilege to employ the information referred to above in order to present the reader with what I hope they will accept as a sober description of the sufferings the men endured and their brave defiance in adversity.

Among others who kindly helped with this book were John Lawrence, former governor of Dartmoor Prison; Terry Witton, governor of Dartmoor Prison; Dartmoor Prison Museum, Princetown, Devon; former Dartmoor Prison officer Mike Chamberlain; former Dartmoor Prison officer and artist Paul Deacon, Auckland, New Zealand; Betty Thomson, researcher, Public Records Office, Kew, Surrey; Commander "Nobby" Clegg, R.N., retired; Duchy of Cornwall Office, Princetown, Devon; James Stevenson, photographer; William Saxton, Taunton, Somerset; Robert Martin, Versailles, France; the late Dr. R. Taverner, Exeter, Devon; the late Col. F. Theobold, Moretonhampstead, Devon; the late James Barber, Plymouth City Museum, Plymouth; R. Wood, Plymouth City Library, Plymouth, Devon; the late Ron Chudley, Exmout, Devon; Devon and Exeter Institution Library, Exeter, Devon; Exeter Central Library, Exeter, Devon; Plymouth City Museum and Art Gallery, Plymouth, Devon; Moretonhampstead History Society, Moretonhampstead, Devon; Freemasons Hall of Research, Leicester; United Grand Lodge of England, London; Westcountry Studies Library, Exeter, Devon; Public Record Office, Exeter, Devon; West Devon Record Office, Coxside, Plymouth, Devon; Devon Library Services, Okehampton and Tavistock, Devon; Regimental Museum (Duke of Cornwall Light Infantry), Bodmin, Cornwall; Archives Office, Diocese of Exeter, Devon.

There are many others too numerous to mention, and I express my sincere gratitude to them all.

Foreword

by John Lawrence

Dartmoor Prison is world famous, but few know of its origins and early history. This book is a fascinating journey from the decision to build through to its occupation by prisoners of war, both French and American.

Trevor James has used many primary sources to illustrate this book, and under his skilled hands the prison buildings teem with life. An ex-journalist and a colleague of mine at the prison in the 1990s, he has written many readable booklets with pictures on this subject over the past 20 years.

You will be informed and perhaps surprised by some of the firsthand stories within. You will certainly get a glimpse of life in the very early nineteenth century, and learn something of the feelings of those incarcerated in these grim buildings on an isolated area of land liable to sudden mists and with poor roads.

John Lawrence joined the English Prison Service in 1973. He served at various prisons around the country and was sent to Dartmoor Prison in 1990 as deputy governor. He was promoted to governor in 1994 and remained so until 2001. He now lives in Wales with his wife of forty years.

Preface

I grew up in Tavistock just seven miles from Dartmoor Prison and became familiar with its past from an early age, but it was just the convict era that was featured in the stories that were told to me — tales of daring escapes, bread and water punishments, solitary confinement and manacles applied to those who broke the rules or otherwise rebelled. Yet the full history of that infamous place includes the French and American prisoners of war who were held there, the French for most of six years and the Americans for a little over two.

It was not until I attained manhood that I became aware of the French connection and even later in life that I first heard about the Americans. You may be surprised to know that even today there are people living in the surrounding towns who are astonished when told of the prison's origins and purpose (most American visitors are also surprised to learn about their countrymen being imprisoned there). I was employed in the Works Department at Dartmoor Prison for the last ten years of my working life. History has always been my main interest and when I began my job at the prison I formed a fascination for it and its sad but colorful past, which never left me. Every working day I trod the very ground occupied by those foreign captives of long ago and saw at close quarters the remaining buildings they lived in. This led to my reading everything I could get hold of relating to that period and the many accounts written by the prisoners themselves.

My inspiration for writing about the prison was the sight of visitors to Princetown congregating at the entrance and surrounding vantage points to take photos. I talked to many of them and was impressed by the fact they were intensely interested in the place and wanted to learn more. There were some little-known publications available but they were long out of print and out of date. One of the best-known books is *The Story of Dartmoor Prison* by Basil Thompson, a previous governor. It covers the entire history of the prison and was obviously well researched. However, there is so much more that could have been recorded, and I have learned that the more we discover about Dartmoor's past the more there is to learn. For myself I determined to produce a similar volume but in more detail and relating exclusively to the Napoleonic Wars and the War of 1812. It took ten years, during which time I not only read all I could find about the place but made notes about certain significant events. These were confirmed in other books written by former prisoners of war. Unfortunately, I failed to record all the sources of the information I gathered which explains the shortage of footnotes in this volume, but I believe most of my readers will agree there can be no more authentic evidence than that related by those who were there.

As an Englishman my loyalty to my country is resolute, but I am not blind to the often arrogant and cruel manner in which prisoners of war were treated, both French and American. History is past and cannot be changed; certain things happened and cannot be disguised; only time can heal the hurts and sometimes the hurts are still felt — the so-called "Princetown Massacre," for example. My tale deals initially with the French prisoners; they were the first, they were more numerous and they were there the longest. A pattern of everyday prison life was therefore firmly established when the first Americans were admitted in April 1813, and because their incarceration was (and often still is) generally unknown, and because I have several American friends whose friendship I value greatly, I have concentrated my story around their countrymen.

Those "Yankees," as they were called, were said to have caused more trouble than twice their number of Frenchmen would have done. There can be no doubt they were defiant and rebellious throughout their imprisonment. Can this be a bad thing though? I think not, for their continued resistance to the often unjust treatment they suffered and despite the extreme hardships they endured, they displayed bravery of a rare kind. Their country had been independent for just over 35 years, and among the British officers were veterans from the war that brought it about and who still regarded Americans as rebels. The "rebels" were proud of their hard won independence and the liberty they inherited. That alone helped sustain them during their stay.

I do not presume to teach Americans their history because in my experience the average American knows far more about his country's past than the average Britisher knows about his. Furthermore, this is not a learned treatise on the early days of Dartmoor Prison, but an effort is made to correct some misconceptions about that era. For example, just nine men were killed in the "Massacre" and thirty or so wounded; I will quote the Public Record Office references for the transcripts of the inquiries held as a result. This in no way diminishes the horror of what happened, but it has to be said there is no truth in some accounts which allege many more were killed and that there were secret burials.

It is my fervent wish that what I have written will present an accurate and revealing glimpse into what really took place at Dartmoor all those years ago.

Introduction

This book provides the early history of Dartmoor Prison from its inception to the building of it and the reasons for creating such a place on a wild and stormy moor, but perhaps its greater purpose is to present an account of certain events that occurred during the War of 1812 and the incarceration of thousands of American war prisoners. It includes accounts of the lives led by those held on the prison ships (known as the "hulks") at Plymouth and in the depot during the wars with France (1803–1815) and the United States War of 1812.

To fully understand the tribulations endured by the "Yankees," as they called themselves, the reader needs to be acquainted with the origins of Dartmoor Depot and the way of life led by the French prisoners who were the first to be imprisoned there and of whom more than 1100 died, mainly of diseases. The conditions they lived under were inherited by the Americans who came later and who generally suffered the most.

The year 1812 was a significant one for France and for Europe. Emperor Napoleon Bonaparte was at the height of his power and his "Grand Army" was poised at Boulogne for the invasion of Britain. His faithful followers held in British prisons fully expected the invasion to take place and patiently awaited that fateful day. It never came because the Royal Navy maintained a blockade of the French ports, preventing the remaining French fleet from putting to sea (after their devastating defeat by Admiral Lord Nelson at Trafalgar in 1805) and escorting the barges that would carry the invaders to British shores. Subsequently Napoleon sent the Grand Army to Russia instead, where disaster overtook them and a mere remnant of that fine body of men survived and got back to France.

In England there was rioting over food shortages after bad harvests. To cap it all, King George III was suffering another bout of madness[1] and the Prince of Wales (the future King George IV) ruled in his place as prince regent. He and his government stood alone in defiance of the French Empire.

It might be thought things could not get worse but a severe setback occurred on June 18, 1812, when the United States declared war after a series of disputes and unresolved grievances with Britain. The British now faced conflict on two fronts — the French on the continent of Europe and another in America, where the war spread to parts of Canada (U.S. President James Madison's administration claimed certain territorial rights there) and on the Great Lakes. Sea battles also took place worldwide from British home waters and the Atlantic to the Pacific Oceans.

At Dartmoor Depot, overcrowding was becoming severe and the previous year (1811) two extra prison blocks were constructed[2] to help alleviate an already serious problem. But it wasn't enough. The Duke of Wellington began winning victory after victory in the Peninsula and sending more captives to Britain despite negotiating exchanges wherever possible. The congestion was as bad as ever and getting worse. Many Frenchmen at Dartmoor had been prisoners for nine years (including their initial confinement on the hulks), disease was rife and morale was getting low. It was into this maelstrom of unhappiness and deprivation the first American prisoners were thrust in April 1813, which is where their story begins.

A narrative of this kind relies heavily on the writings of the prisoners themselves, making allowances for national pride and the bias against their enemy, the British. The data and correspondence gleaned from the libraries and public record offices often make dull reading and are limited here to a few examples of special interest. The historical notes are for continuity and to provide a chronological sequence of events.

Prologue

A Sad Corner of England in 1812

It was a wild winter night on Dartmoor. Rain and sleet embroiled in a roaring gale from the Atlantic Ocean beat against the walls of the Prisoner of War Depot. The swinging oil lamps suspended from each corner of the prison buildings barely relieved the darkness of the night and formed weird shadows that raced to and fro across the empty yards. The dim light lent a silvery glint to the water that streamed down the outside of the prison blocks. It seeped through every cranny of the stonework and trickled down inside where thousands of prisoners of war, Napoleon's soldiers and sailors, were trying to sleep. The lucky ones were in their hammocks, side by side and one above the other four and five high; others were on straw mattresses on the floors. In winter the often terrible cold froze their breath in layers on the walls and condensation ran over the floors making them permanently wet. The tiny barred windows had wooden shutters but no glass and the prisoners stuffed rags and bits of wood and other objects into the apertures to stop the howling draught. As a result a warm fusty odor permeated the dormitories from the mass of bodies, a poor substitute for the lack of proper heating, and a breeding ground for disease.

Outside the sentries were changed and the old guard doubled away to their stone barracks hoping to find something hot to drink as they splashed through the freezing puddles, while their comrades on the walls cursed their luck at being on duty on such a night. The wind shrieked around the wooden platforms they occupied, causing the alarm bells, strung on wires around the perimeter walls to warn them of any escape attempt, to jingle continuously. One might think only a madman would venture forth in weather like this, yet one of the most determined (and unsuccessful) escapes ever attempted occurred on just such a night by a group of French prisoners who hoped the

The famous arch and main entrance to Dartmoor Prison. The overhead inscription reads, "Parcere Subjectis," which relates to a quotation by the Roman poet Virgil and means "Spare the Vanquished" (instead of killing them and taking their wives and children as slaves). This picture was taken about 60 years after the war depot closed and depicts armed warders who were responsible for guarding convicts when working outside the boundary wall (courtesy Dartmoor Prison Museum).

terrible weather would shield them from the sentries' eyes. They were spotted and recaptured, every one of them, a tribute to the vigilance and stoicism of the military guards on that occasion.

Inside the prison blocks, seven in number, there was no furniture other than the bedding, and the men of many nations (Napoleon recruited as he conquered and his armies included at various times a number of Danish, Italian, and other Europeans) were awake. Some sobbed quietly from hunger and despair; others sought pathetic comfort from one another in embraces of an unnatural kind. Angry men whispered in the darkness, plotting escape or vengeance on the guards and there were young boys, bold lads by day, trembling and frightened in the night as scavengers prowled silently among their comrades looking to steal an unguarded crust of bread. Hunger and cold and foul air were the cause of killer diseases. In the hospital were men writhing with dysentery and fevers which were the curse of every jail — typhus for example, known then as "gaol [jail] fever." Others died from exposure, having gambled away their clothing and often their rations too. Most prisoners had spent three years here unaware they were only a little more than half way through their term of imprisonment and that worse was to come when in 1813 American prisoners would begin arriving, making conditions unbearable in an already overcrowded establishment. This was Dartmoor Depot for Prisoners of War, the most dreaded prison in the land.

The sleet turned to hail which rattled against the granite buttresses, startling the horses in the stables. Beyond the prison walls Prince Town folk snuggled into their straw beds and sighed at the noise the storm made outside. Early next morning the supply wagons rumbled through the streets, the drummers' call roused the troops in the barracks and across the moor cattle and sheep were herded to their doom in the slaughterhouses. The bakeries were already busy.

Meanwhile, the tiny hamlet that once housed a handful of agricultural workers and their families had prospered with the opening of the prison, and was now a thriving township. The story of those times is one of brave endeavor on the part of Sir Thomas Tyrwhitt (pronounced "Tirrit"), who founded a colony on the open moor, and of the braver spirit of Britain's foes, who suffered and died to make it possible.

1

The Saga Begins

On the western quarter of Dartmoor above the present day town of Princetown, a high hill dominates the landscape. From the summit on a fine day the view is breathtaking: beyond the fringes of Dartmoor the rolling Devonshire landscape of fields and river valleys stretches to Plymouth Sound and the pale blue hills of distant Cornwall. The opposite slope faces northeast to the heart of the moor. Take but a few steps towards it and the patchwork scenery behind you is blotted out and in its stead a huge landscape of undulating heath, enclosures, plantations of conifers, rivers and bogs confronts the onlooker, surrounded by other distant hills. Below this windswept and isolated spot lies HM (Her Majesty's) Prison Dartmoor. The grey granite buildings retain a high degree of notoriety from the stark convict days, attracting sightseers like a magnet, most of whom are unaware of the facility's history and beginnings as a prisoner of war depot.

When the war against Napoleon recommenced following the Treaty of Amiens (March 1802–May 1803), Britain soon had the advantage in the number of prisoners taken, mostly sailors. Before long the existing prisons and the dreaded hulks (prison ships) were full and a problem then arose as to where to house them. Dartmoor Depot, as it was first called, was one of several specially built nationwide for that purpose. In addition to the Frenchmen, it housed Dutch and Danish prisoners (although nearly all the Danes were held on board one of the Plymouth hulks), Germans and Italians, in fact men from all the European nations which were either allied to, or had been conquered by, France.

The depot was opened in 1809 and quickly filled to its capacity of just over 5,000. By 1813, after the two extra prison blocks were added, there were around 10,000 men imprisoned here. And then the Americans came. They too were mostly sailors taken at sea during the War of 1812 (often referred to in the United States as the "Madison War" or alternatively the "Second War of Independence"). Among them were large numbers of Negroes. They were guarded by units of the militia, originally 500 strong, increased to more than 1200 as the prison population swelled, and who were almost as cramped in their barracks as the captives in the prison.

Inside the prison walls a legend was in the making and of a most tragic kind. From May 1809 when the first prisoners of war arrived, to February 1816 when the very last of them left for home, diseases, self-neglect, suicides and the very nature of their confinement — the wet, the cold and the often inadequate clothing killed more than 1100 French and 271 Americans. Some men were shot or bayoneted while trying to escape. In the winter they froze, and when the fine summer weather prevailed, they endured the baking heat inside the prison walls and the anguish of being forcibly confined. French and Americans reacted in different ways to their imprisonment.

In general, the main body of Frenchmen settled down to make the best of things. They are remembered today for the intricate bone models and ornaments they made and sold at the daily market, for their many talents in the arts and their ability to entertain themselves. The Yankees, on the other hand, were defiant and resentful to the end and not without good cause, it must be said, because they were neglected by their government's representative here, unwanted by the French and scorned by their captors. The little town where the momentous events about to be described took place was first called Prince's Town, later shortened to Prince Town and ultimately Princetown, by which name it is known today. But first some explanation is necessary concerning Dartmoor.

Until the final quarter of the 18th century, it was a wilderness in every sense. The moor was a barren, treeless land, over which roamed wild ponies, foxes, deer, and buzzard hawks. Apart from the spoil heaps left by the tin miners, the turf-ties of the peat cutters, and a few farmsteads, there was little trace of human activity. The lonely moor was and still is, criss-crossed by ancient tracks along which pack horses (in reality donkeys and ponies), the only means of transport on the moor at that time, carried goods like tin ingots and peat to the border towns. News spread slowly in these isolated places and superstition was rife among the farmers and peasants who lived on the moor in harsh conditions. When the winter gales shook the rafters of their tiny huts at night and the rain swished across the desolate landscape, they kept close to their crackling firesides, barred the doors and went to bed early. Ghosts and pixies[1] were very real to them.

"The Moor" is an upland area of 368 square miles that has changed little since medieval times. It comprises open moorland, a mixture of heath and gorse and rocks and streams interspersed with granite outcrops called "tors," which are the remaining cores of ancient volcanoes. There are many of them, all with names; the tallest is High Willhays, whose peak is just over 2,000 feet above sea level. There are some small towns and hamlets amid the wilderness and farms raising sheep and cattle (the land is wet, cold, and barren — unsuitable for crops). There are several rivers, one of which, the River Dart, lends its name to the moor. At the head of these rivers are mires or bogs, some of them dangerous and dubbed "Dartmoor Stables" on account of the many animals which have disappeared into their depths over the years. Then there are Neolithic remains — stone rows, hut circles, ancient burial sites — more in fact than anywhere else in Europe. The longest stone row in the world is among its thousands of years old artifacts. Finally there are traces of tin mining. All over the moor there are gulleys and pits that were excavated by miners seeking the rich lodes of ore hundreds of years ago and more recent ruins associated with underground workings from the 19th century and beyond. In 1772 the building of a highway was approved by an act of Parliament and a road was constructed across the most desolate parts of Dartmoor from Tavistock to Moreton Hampstead and Ashburton. It changed the face of the moor forever, bringing in pioneering "improvers," gentlemen of means who saw Dartmoor as a land ripe for exploitation, a fertile country they thought, ready to be cultivated and make fortunes for them. Alas for their dreams! Working the poor moorland soil has long since given way to grazing cattle and sheep and no fortunes were made.

Into this wild and largely unpopulated land came an aristocratic figure who was determined to create an agricultural community on one of the most remote and exposed parts of Dartmoor. Meet Sir Thomas Tyrwhitt, who played a prominent part in the development of Princetown and the war depot in particular. In fact, if it were not for him, Princetown would not exist and the depot would have been built elsewhere. Sir Thomas came from an eminent family who for generations were Lords of the Manor at Cameringham near Lincoln in the north of England. He was also a close friend of the Prince of Wales, the future King George IV, whom he first met at Oxford University. He left Oxford in 1794 and the following year he was appointed personal secretary to the prince, then in 1796 he became auditor and secretary to the Duchy of Cornwall. The latter term will require some explanation:

The term *Duchy* of Cornwall does not mean the *County* of Cornwall. The sovereign's eldest son and heir is always created Prince of Wales, but in addition assumes the title *Duke of Cornwall* (the county) and as such he (daughters are not eligible) also inherits the *Duchy of Cornwall*, which consists of vast estates, land and mineral rights in several different parts of England, the rents and leases providing a private income until he succeeds to the throne. If and when there is no son and heir, the duchy lies dormant. The largest area of duchy land lies on Dartmoor in that portion of the moor known as the "Forest of Dartmoor," which dates from 1337 when King Edward III created it for his eldest son Edward the Black Prince. The term *Forest* implies a royal hunting ground, which it originally was. At this writing, the duke is Prince Charles, and when he becomes king, his eldest son, Prince William, will be Duke of Cornwall.

Sir Thomas Tyrwhitt arrived in 1785 as plain Mr. Tyrwhitt (he was knighted in 1812) and built a house he named "Tor Royal" just a mile or so from Princetown. Here he hoped to cultivate the moor, attract settlers and establish a thriving estate despite the fact that on his own admission he knew nothing about agriculture. Like several other enterprising pioneers on Dartmoor, he made the mistake of believing all he had to do was plough the land and plant crops. Although he had some success at first, as previously mentioned the moor does not lend itself to cultivation and his dream began to fade. There was an inn, the Plume of Feathers (still a thriving business today), a few miserable cottages, one or two mills and quarries, and that was all in the little settlement he called Prince Town in honor of his royal friend.

Sir Thomas Tyrwhitt. He was a friend of the Prince of Wales (the future King George IV) who influenced the location of a prison on the moor and founded the settlement that was to become Prince Town, named in honor of his royal friend (courtesy Paul Rendell, Dartmoor News).

Thomas Tyrwhitt had acquired the lease of 2,500 acres of moorland, about two miles south of where the new road passed through a small community known today as Two Bridges. He was undaunted in the fight against adverse conditions and is rightly remembered now as the Father of Prince Town. He was 23 years old, wealthy, and ambitious. The amazing story of the war depot and the development of Princetown is entirely due to this man, one of the least known but more influential figures of his time. Being well educated and from a distinguished family whose members included two sheriffs of the County of Lincolnshire and high ranking ecclesiastics, Thomas Tyrwhitt was high on the list of potentially powerful men in England—a rising star. It was undoubtedly his friendship with the prince that brought him to Dartmoor and a succession of important posts that included:

> 1795, private secretary to the Prince of Wales.
> 1796, auditor and secretary to the Duchy of Cornwall.
> 1803, Lord Warden of the Stannaries.[2]
> 1805, Vice Admiral of the Counties of Devon and Cornwall.
> 1812, Gentleman Usher of Black Rod (having previously been knighted).[3]
> 1812, keeper (ranger) of His Majesty's Little Park at Windsor.

He was also member of Parliament for Okehampton, Devon (1796–1802), Portarlington, Cornwall (December 1802–February 1806), and Plymouth, Devon (March 1806–June 1812).

Tyrwhitt was still determined to found a colony on Dartmoor. At first he did have some success when he produced a crop of flax to a standard which earned him a medal from the Bath Agricultural Society. Mills were established at Bachelors Hall and the Oakery, both places close by Tor Royal, thus laying the foundations for what Tyrwhitt hoped would be a thriving agricultural community. The inn he built for his workers and the packhorse drovers was named the Prince's Arms and can still be seen plying its trade in the center of modern Princetown. Its new name, The Plume of Feathers, is a reference to the Prince of Wales' coat of arms, which is surmounted by a plume of ostrich feathers. It is the oldest building in the town. The tiny cottages that housed the first residents have long since disappeared.

A beginning had been made and Thomas Tyrwhitt, full of optimism, enjoyed happy times at Tor Royal, entertaining many of his friends there. As for the settlement, a new road was constructed from the inn to a local landmark known as Rundlestone, where it joined the Tavistock–Two Bridges road, thus saving several miles on a journey to Tavistock. It was named Tyrwhitt Road and it was adjacent to this road further development took place including the prison, after which it was named Prison Road (Tavistock Road today). At the commencement of the 19th century the prison was undreamed of, the intention being to focus every effort on agricultural matters and attract new settlers, but "Old Dartymoor" brought ruin to many a bold venture and Thomas Tyrwhitt's plans were to be no exception, despite his affluence and enthusiasm. His estate was situated high up on a cold moor, 1400 feet above sea level, where growth of anything other than ferns and heather is restricted. The soil is acid and stony and by the turn of the century things were not going well. Because he was absent for long periods on his official duties, Tyrwhitt probably did not realize things were not turning out as he had hoped and that his dreams were beginning to fade. The war with France was to be his salvation.

As already noted, in May 1803 the Treaty of Amiens was terminated when Britain once again declared war on France after just over a year of peace. Agents had reported French carpenters were working night and day at Calais and Boulogne-sur-Mer building huge barges (more than 2,000 had been planned) to transport a 200,000 strong "Grand Army" in an invasion of Britain's shores. Napoleon realized his plans to expand his European influence could only be consolidated by subjugating Britain first. The security of this country now became entirely dependent on the Royal Navy, whose job was to blockade French ports, contain France's navy (without which the invasion could not take place) and prevent trade. The scale of the navy's success was reflected in the vast numbers of prisoners taken, especially after the Battle of Trafalgar in 1805, and Britain was faced with the enormous problem of where to confine them. The gaols (jails) were full. There were some prisons from previous wars: Normans Cross near Peterborough, first opened in 1797, could accommodate 7,000 men; Stapleton near Bristol (1782) held 5,000, the oldest being Mill Prison in Plymouth dating from 1695 and capable of containing another 5,000 or so. All three establishments were soon filled. Old castles were then pressed into service — Edinburgh in Scotland and Forton near Gosport for example; even country houses and dockside warehouses were used for a short while. At Plymouth, French prisoners were confined in the Citadel (a military fortress on the Hoe) and the China House at Cattedown, and Thomas Cookworthy's old porcelain factory (now a popular public house and restaurant). Devonport Dockyard held many hundreds of captives, and a brief description may assist the reader in realizing how desperate the situation was and how it led to the building of Dartmoor prison.

Situated in the South Yard at Devonport is the 1,000 foot long Old Ropery where ropes for British warships were made since before Admiral Nelson's time. A part of this complex known as the West Ropery was destroyed by enemy bombing during World War II, but under the foundations there are more than 40 stone "cells" (formerly storehouses) which were used for the confinement of French prisoners of war. Each cell is about 20 feet long and 8 feet high, the width being about 9 feet. There are no windows so light and ventilation must have been limited to what entered via the barred gates that shut the prisoners in. Altogether these cells held around 1,000 men. The Ropery also had an execution chamber, situated in a room originally used for tarring rope. Today the lever-operated trap and "drop" is in perfect working order and the heavy wooden beam from which the noose was suspended is still there. Mounted on the walls are the candle holders which provided light for the grisly business of hanging the 149 men who died in this room between 1793 and 1815. On the stone paved floor below there would have been a lead covered mortuary slab on which the bodies were laid out to enable Plymouth surgeons to remove internal organs (for instruction purposes), after which the remains were thrown into a lime pit outside.

Commander "Nobby" Clegg, R.N., who very kindly showed the author around several years ago, said a nail was knocked into the wall for every victim but only one is still in place, the rest having been removed by an overzealous painter who did not realize their significance. The gallows was erected at the insistence of the French themselves who wanted the ultimate penalty to be available to them for murder and severe breaches of discipline. "The French acted as arbitrators and judges on their countrymen and probably provided the executioner as well, because the British had nothing to do with it whatsoever," declared Commander Clegg. Prisoners convicted of capital offenses elsewhere were tried and convicted in British courts and hanged in British jails.

As more prisoners arrived the ill-famed hulks were commissioned. They had been used in earlier wars and were dreaded by the foe. They comprised dismasted, derelict men o'war converted to prison ships, where hundreds of men were confined below decks in an atmosphere so fetid that when the ports were opened in the mornings after being battened down for the night the guards often fainted from the stench that exuded from within. The foul air, lack of exercise and poor sanitary arrangements led to outbreaks of fatal diseases and chest complaints. As the war progressed the hulks were used for the confinement of the very worst of men — troublemakers from the shore depots, for example. In addition to the problems associated with overcrowding and illness, there were several desperate attempts to escape. Holes were cut in the sides through which numbers of men were to emerge, overpower the guards and make a getaway. On at least one occasion fires were deliberately started in the hope of making off in the confusion. A major concern was the possibility of a mass escape which could endanger the huge naval arsenal (including ammunition ships filled with gunpowder and shot situated just a short distance away).

Above all, the hulks were expensive to run and maintain compared to shore establishments, and consequently the time was ripe for another shore prison to be built. That requirement was about to be met by Thomas Tyrwhitt (referred to from now on as Sir Thomas because he is better known by that title), who saw an opportunity to retrieve a difficult situation at Prince Town. The Prince of Wales, as Duke of Cornwall, indicated he was willing to help, being prepared to release a portion of duchy land on which to build the new depot.

The responsibility for prisoners of war then lay with the Commissioners of the Sick and Hurt Office, whose jurisdiction, as the name implies, was over sick and wounded seafarers. In 1799 this was changed when the Transport Office (or board) took over the supervision of prisoners. Both of these offices were departments of the British Admiralty and subject to its authority. Thus in 1805 the following letter was written to the Admiralty by the Transport Office:

> Sir;   26 June 1805
>
> Considering the impropriety of keeping a great body of prisoners in the immediate neighborhood of the naval arsenals, and the very great expense unavoidably attendant on prison ships, we have long been desirous of providing as much accommodation as possible in the interior of the country; but having only two inland depots of Stapleton and Norman Cross, there is still a considerable number of prisoners kept from necessity at Plymouth, occupying six prison ships at a yearly expense of the whole of not less than £18,000 [the new prison was expected to incur an annual running cost of less than £3,000]. With a view to reduce this expense, we request you will inform the Right Honourable Lords Commissioners of the Admiralty that we have proposed to erect a prison to contain not less than 5,000 men in the County of Devon at a convenient distance from Plymouth which would save us the expense of 7 or 8 third rate ships. And having judged Dartmoor to be a most eligible and healthy situation for such a purpose, we thought it proper to enquire whether a part of that extensive district could be procured, and in consequence of our application to Mr. Tyrwhitt, the Lord Warden of the Stannaries in Cornwall and Devon has signified to us the entire consent of His Royal Highness the Prince of Wales to our having whatever quantity of the moor we may find necessary for a prison, without any charge to the public other than an Act of Parliament to transfer the property from the Duke of Cornwall to the Crown.[4] We now therefore beg leave to submit the matter to their Lordship's consideration and if for the reasons above stated they should approve of the proposed measure being carried into execution we request you will inform us whether it is their Lordship's pleasure that one of the Commissioners of this Board with a surveyor should proceed to Dartmoor for the purpose of selecting a fit situation for the intended buildings in order that we may forthwith procure plans and estimates of the expense to be laid before their Lordships for their ultimate determination.

The Prison Ships

During the war against France and the U.S., there were more than 40 prison ships or "pontons," as the French called them, on the South Coast. They included the following.

1. The Saga Begins

AT PORTSMOUTH

Prothea	Suffolk
Crown	Assistance
San Tomaso	Ave Princessa
Vigilant	Kron Princessa
Guildford	Waldemar
San Antonio	Negro
Vengeance	Diamond
Veteran	

Hospital ships *Caton*, *Pegasus*, *Marengo*, and *Princess Sophia*

AT CHATHAM

Cornwall	Southwick
Brunswick	Irresistible
Buckingham	Nassau
Sampson	Belligueux
Bahama	Vryheid
Canada	Hero
Bristol	Eagle
Glory	Camperdown
Crown Prince	Gelykheid
Rochester	Sandwich

Hospital ships *Freyer* and *Trusty*

Prison Ships at Plymouth

Before the construction of Dartmoor Prisoner of War Depot at Princetown, prisoners were kept aboard ships moored in the Hamoaze, the inner landlocked waterway at Plymouth formed by the estuaries of the rivers Tavy and Tamar. In 1808 those in commission included the following.

- The *Brave*, formerly the 80 gun French vessel *Formidable*, captured in November 1805 after escaping the Battle of Trafalgar. This ship could properly accommodate 800 prisoners.
- *El Firme*, an ex–Spanish vessel captured by Sir Robert Calder in July 1805 off Ferrol. It was commissioned at Plymouth on February 23, 1808, and could accommodate 750.
- *San Ysidro* and the *San Nicolas*, both Spanish vessels captured by Sir John Jarvis in February 1797 off Cape St. Vincent. These two could hold 750 prisoners each.
- *San Rafael*, a Spanish 80 gun ship captured by Vice Admiral Sir Robert Calder's squadron July 22, 1805.
- *Hector*, a French vessel captured by Lord Rodney on April 12, 1782. It could hold 700 prisoners.

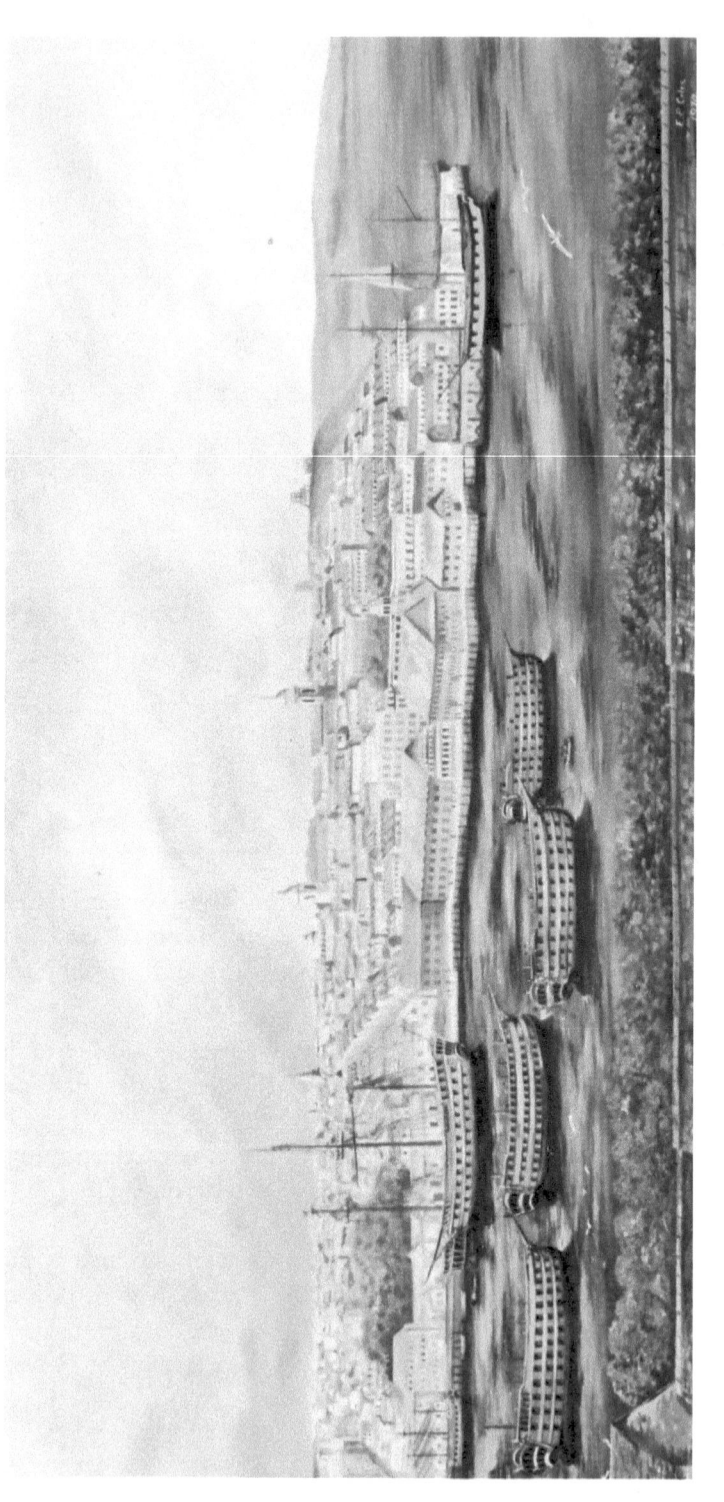

The hulks at Plymouth, an oil painting on canvas (about 3 feet by 2 feet) by a prisoner who was in custody during World War II. Depicted are the naval dockyard with the town of Devonport behind, but the picture is historically incorrect as the "Hamoaze" is farther up the estuary to the left of the picture (courtesy Dartmoor Prison Museum).

- *Generaux*, another French vessel Rear Admiral Lord Horatio Nelson captured in the Mediterranean on February 18, 1800. It could accommodate 750 prisoners.
- *L'Oiseau*, formerly the 36 gun French frigate *Cleopatra*, captured on June 18, 1793, off Start Point by Captain Edward Pellew in command of HBMS[5] *Nymphe*. It was small and could only take 300 prisoners.
- *Bienfaisant*, *Europe* and *Panther*, all British ships, each accommodating around 300 prisoners.
- The hospital ship *Le Caton* was a French vessel captured by Lord Hood in April 1782 in the Mona Passage. It was moored off Saltash.

Thus something like 6,200 prisoners of war could be held on board these ships. The *Panther* was taken out of service on December 24, 1811, having been replaced by the *Ganges*, which was commissioned on December 12. On December 26, the *Bienfaisant* was also taken out of service.

In 1812 only the *Brave, San Ysidro, San Nicolas, Europe* and the hospital ship were in commission. The *Europe* was taken out of service on December 28, 1812. On January 1, 1813, the prison ships in commission were the *Brave, El Firme, Hector, Generaux, L'Oiseau, San Ysidro, San Nicolas, Ganges* and *Le Caton*. The *Europe* was brought back into service in September 1813 and the *Bienfaisant* the following month.

W. Branch Johnson tells in *The English Prison Hulks*, "During the War of American Independence two prisoners swam from the *San Rafael* at Plymouth to a lighter full of powder, overpowered the man in charge and got away safely with her to France where they sold the powder at a very handsome profit!"[6]

John Harris' "Essay Toward a History of Plymouth" (1806) relates this bit of information: "On 21 September 1810 the *San Rafael* was undocked and towed round to Plymouth (Sutton Pool). Purchased by John Hawker, Esq. of Plymouth for the purpose of being made into a dry dock capable of receiving a ship of 800 tons burthen."[7]

During all this time some hulks were taken out of service and other old warships were converted to replace them. No one list is therefore complete. In addition, there were hulks at Cape Town, Bermuda, and Nova Scotia. The suffering endured by their occupants below decks in extremes of cold and tropical heat without heating or adequate ventilation was acute. The temperate English climate must be the only redeeming feature of the hulks in English harbors.

2

A Start Is Made

Sir Thomas Tyrwhitt, as we have seen, was well placed to influence what was intended with regard to a prisoner of war depot on Dartmoor and would have known those persons most influential in making decisions. On July 9, 1805, the Transport Office, having received approval from the Admiralty to proceed, wrote to Daniel Alexander, the surveyor and architect they had selected, and directed "that you will be at Mr. Tyrwhitt's Tor Royal between Moreton Hampstead and Tavistock on the 18th. of this month where you will meet with the Hon. E. Bouverie, one of the members of this Board. The intended building at Dartmoor is to be for 5,000 prisoners with an hospital and the necessary accommodation for the officers to be employed in the superintendence of the prisoners and the military guard."[1]

The cat was out of the bag, as the saying goes, and the *Bristol Mirror* gave this report a few days later on July 13, 1805: "The Prince of Wales is about to erect at his own expense a chapel at Prince Town in the Forest of Dartmoor under the direction of Thomas Tyrwhitt, Esq., Lord Warden of the Stannarie. Mr. Tyrwhitt has suggested to the government the propriety of erecting a building near the above for depositing such prisoners of war as may be brought into Plymouth who can without any difficulty be conveyed up the River Tamar and landed a few miles from the spot."

The article must have been a scoop for the paper, as the initial survey on which everything depended had not yet been carried out and the Transport Office had certainly not made a decision about it. Some interesting conclusions may be drawn:

1. Sir Thomas's ambitions for Prince Town and a war prison there were already known.
2. A settlement was already established and the number of occupants, including those in the surrounding area, justified the expense of a chapel

Tor Royal, the country estate of Sir Thomas Tyrwhitt as it is today — little has changed over the years. His original intention was to found an agricultural settlement on the moor, but it was not to be. The cold and wet climate and the barren soil were not conducive to growing crops. He turned his energies to founding the prisoner of war depot instead. It was the main factor that created the community which was to become Prince Town. A memorial plaque to this remarkable man can be seen in Princetown Parish Church of St. Michael and All Angels, a unique edifice built by French and American prisoners. The house is still on lease from the Duchy of Cornwall and is now a bed and breakfast (author's photograph, reproduced courtesy the Duchy of Cornwall).

(the chapel was not completed until 1815, having been built by French and U.S. prisoners of war).
3. The Prince of Wales was aware of developments. It seems the entire project and the location had already been decided upon.

Five days later, the three men — Tyrwhitt, Bouverie, and Alexander — duly met at Tor Royal and Sir Thomas conducted his visitors to various parts of the moor, one of which, the site of the present day prison, was chosen. We can be sure Sir Thomas's opinions were crucial, bearing in mind his position and the fact his companions, who were strangers to Dartmoor, would have relied heavily on his advice. It is generally recognized there were other sites suitable for the war prison, but he was determined it would be built close to his quarries and mills which would fulfill its needs, ensuring a handsome return on his investments as well as furthering his ambitions. It transformed the moor in the way Tyrwhitt had hoped. When the war depot was established the quiet hamlet that had arisen on a bare landscape expanded to form a thriving township. A slaughterhouse and two bakeries were built. All other essential supplies for the thousands of prisoners and the garrison had to be transported by wagon from Plymouth and towns throughout the west. Above the creaking of the cartwheels the ring of the blacksmith's hammer was heard amid the shouts of the drovers and the military in the barracks. The quarries must have been worked to capacity as additions were made to the town, and the "Capital of the Moor," as it is often called, reached its zenith.

Alexander's expertise should not be overlooked. His task was to assess what could be done with the materials at hand, the manpower that would be required, and of course the cost, which had to be kept as low as possible. Daniel Alexander was one of the foremost surveyors of his day and a brilliant

The prison leat is four miles long and took water from the nearby River Walkham. It is still there, winding its way across the desolate moorland, but stagnant now because the water for the prison comes from the district mains supply. The leat remained in service until 1993 with a water treatment plant at the point of entry to the prison. Princetown's water once came from boreholes on the moor and was collected at a pumping station which transferred the water to the township. It, too, is now supplied from the mains (author's photograph).

designer from early on in his career, his ability having won him a silver medal at the Royal Academy when he was a student there. He was born in London in 1768, and after attending St. Paul's School was apprenticed to Samuel Robinson, a well known and much sought after builder of warehouses and docks. Young Alexander did so well that on completing his apprenticeship he was immediately hired to build a large house at Highbury Hill (a rapidly growing area of London at that time), an unprecedented event for a recently qualified person. He went on to construct warehouses, harbors and lighthouses for the Admiralty and the London Dock Company, and was at the top of his profession when he was chosen to plan and execute the building of Dartmoor Prison.

In many ways the choice of site was ideal. It was 17 miles from Plymouth and therefore secure, but close enough for reinforcements to be quickly on the scene should the need arise. Most importantly, plenty of stone was available on the moor and at the nearby quarries, including Herne Hole, the present day prison quarry (no longer being worked). Wood for building purposes was scarce and expensive. Norman Cross near Peterborough had been built entirely of wood, but with the Baltic ports now blockaded by Napoleon there were no further imports of timber at that time, and in any case most available stocks had been used to construct the Royal Navy's "wooden walls." Therefore, Britain's most famous prison was built of stone, despite the fact it was intended to be a temporary place of confinement for war prisoners. Another consideration was the enormous quantity of water required for the 5,000 prisoners, the military guards, and the workmen. The springs in the locality were inadequate, but ample supplies were at hand from the upper reaches of the River Walkham, from where water was extracted and conveyed by gravity along the contours of the hills via a four mile long leat (a shallow manmade stream) to a reservoir adjacent to the prison.

Finally, the climate was judged to be healthy, which it certainly was compared to the stinking hulks, but the inspection was made on a summer day in July and experience later revealed (Sir Thomas must have known) that this particular spot is notorious on Dartmoor as being subject to the full fury of winter's icy blasts. Apart from the frightful cold and snowstorms that often occur in winter, there are the thick wet mists which frequently linger for days. Even during the summer months if there is bad weather North Hessary will get the worst of it.

The Transport Office was anxious to get the best possible value for its money and for good reason: the war was getting costly and the number of captives to be provided for was an ever increasing burden. Up until 1799 the French and British governments each provided fixed sums for the subsistence of every officer and man held prisoner by the other side, to be used for clothing as well as food. The French then repudiated their commitment, with the express intention of weakening Britain financially by forcing it to provide for the prisoners on both sides. The French were short of funds because of the restrictions on trade brought about by the Royal Navy's blockade, and the fact that its vast armies were a tremendous drain on the exchequer. Nevertheless, it was a callous decision by the French, who abandoned their countrymen to the mercy of the enemy. In Mill Prison at Plymouth, for example it was reported the French prisoners were reduced to skeletons who picked out snails to eat from crevices in the walls. The expense of running and maintaining the hulks was worrying too. It was estimated that the annual cost of a 74 gun vessel holding 700 men was £5,869, whereas Dartmoor Depot housing 5,000 men (initially) would cost an estimated £2,600 per annum. Alexander submitted his first proposals, with costs, on September 18, only two months after seeing the ground for the first time. The area allocated for the prison proper was to be 23 acres with accommodation for 5,282 prisoners and capable of being enlarged at a later date to house up to 8,370. The total costs were presented as follows:

	£	s.	d.
For 5,282 men	£86, 423	13s.	4d.
Cost of increase to 8,370 men	£17, 901	3s.	4d.
TOTAL =	£104, 24	16s.	8d.

Note: £ = pounds sterling. s. = shillings. d. = pence (no. of pennies).
12 pence = 1 shilling. 20 shillings = 1 pound.

It was not accepted by the Transport Office because, while recognizing the relatively small cost of increasing the prison's capacity to over 8,000, they felt unable to afford the initial figure of £86,000-plus and called for another plan (yes — it *was* Plan B). The second plan was approved and is worth recording. From Alexander's report:

> Prison of War Dartmoor.   London Sept. 26, 1805
> To the Honourable the Commissioners of the Transport Service, and for the Care and Custody of Prisoners of War.
>
> Honourable Sirs,
>
> In obedience to your direction of the 20th. inst. to see, in what manner, and to what degree, the Plan proposed to your Hon. Board on the 18th. inst. could be reduced, in regard to extent and cost, and so as to be built in the least possible time I beg leave further to report that I have made another plan, with accommodation for 5,158 men but without any means of increasing the depot at any further time: and have reduced the area of ground from 23 acres to 15 acres and a quarter, shortening the length of the boundary walls proportionately.[2] The quantity of rough masonry is thus reduced from 29,706 perches[3] to

18,632 perches, and the time required to build such a quantity of walling, the only difficulty to be foreseen in the whole work, is consequently shortened. If possible we should use more masons from the Moors in Yorkshire, in addition to the Cornish and Devon Moor Men, I think, that the major part of the scheme might be completed by the end of the year 1806 containing 3,374 men, and at an expense of:

	£	s.	d.
Internal Boundary Wall, water courses, etc.	13,756	10	1
Three prison buildings	16,664	18	6
Hospital	7,951	5	1
Cook rooms, etc.	995	18	2
Offices for Management	9,994	5	6
Expense first year — 3,374 men	49,362	17	4

and that the remainder of the prison would be finished in the year 1807 at an expense of:

	£	s.	d.
Barracks for 500 men early in the year	5,004	7	0
Two prison buildings	8,868	5	7
Four sheds	3,070	4	0
Petty Officers Prison	3,107	7	11
External boundary wall	733	8	0
Expense second year	20,783	7	6
TOTAL =	70,146	4	10

I have the Honour to be Gentlemen,
Your Most Obedient and Humble Servant,
Daniel Alexander[4]

Several points are worthy of note. The calculations are to the nearest *penny*, presumably based on an accredited formula much the same as that used by estimators today, and in much the same way does not always work out in practice! As always, there were unforeseen circumstances which will be considered presently. Note the optimism regarding the timetable — twelve months to complete the first stage (conditions on the moor were vastly different to those in the capital, as Alexander was soon to discover). As for the masons, in a later communication, he said, "The masons in the country are beginning to 'rouze' and by information received at Calstock, Truro, Penryhn, and Helston in the West, that a great many Moor Masons may be procured at prices below what I have estimated," indicating the Yorkshire men were no longer needed. Penryn in Cornwall was known in those days as the "Granite Borough" on account of the large quantity of that stone to be found there. Following the stone mason's trade ("always work with your back to the wind") was a family tradition. We know some men from that area did come to Dartmoor to help build the prison, and many of them walked back home when they learned how poor the pay was.

Both plans were submitted to the Admiralty on October 9, 1805, by the Transport Office, which had been advised by Alexander that still further savings could be made by making use of the moor stone (granite boulders) lying around on site, saving the time and expense of quarrying. Then a local surveyor, engaged by him to examine the place more closely, advised that the layers of peat were not as thick as had been thought, and "could be removed by running off with water," thus saving £5,000 on excavation work. As expected, Plan B was approved and advertisements appeared in the newspapers in October, including one in the *Exeter Flying Post*, part of which reads:

> Buildings and boundary walls will cover about 15 acres; they are to be constructed of moorstone to be broken from scattered rocks on the spot, where there is also fine gravel, sand and water. They are to be floored with timber and slate. Plans and specifications will be laid out at this office and Tor Royal. Tenders are to contain proposals for executing the work, including every trade or for any separate trades with the names of sufficient sureties for fulfilling the contracts.

The contract would at once be cancelled if the war should end. As it happened, the floors were not laid with timber for the reasons previously given and concrete was used instead. Furthermore, the quantities of sand and gravel were not as great as had been supposed, and ultimately these two items alone added considerably to the final cost. Four tenders were received, all of them from Plymouth, and details of three survive:

Messrs.	Fowell and Company	£115,377
"	Sheppard and Company	£84,828
"	Isbell Rowe and Company	£66,815

The lowest tender was of course accepted and Alexander was appointed to personally supervise the work. Far from completing the first phase by the end of 1806, it was not finished until the following year, and it was May 1809 before the first prisoners arrived, by which time the costs escalated to £135,000. Not only that, but by 1811 the capacity had to be increased and the Admiralty must have rued the day they turned down Alexander's first plan.

There were problems from the start. As late as January 16, 1806, the Transport Office advised their lordships that "in consequence of a communication from Mr. Tyrwhitt on the part of His Royal Highness the Prince of Wales as Duke of Cornwall, stating that a lease for 99 years of the ground amounting to 390 acres, being the quantity marked out by the surveyor upon which the prison is to be built on Dartmoor ... we request you will transmit to us as early as possible that no hindrance may occur in the prosecution of our works for which we are making the necessary preparations."[5]

2. A Start Is Made

The first French prisoners march under escort to the depot in May 1809. The scenery depicted in this oil painting on canvas is unchanged since those times. Note the baggage carts and the officers on horseback. The 17 mile trek was a real hardship for the prisoners, some of whom were barefooted and all of whom had been confined on the hulks with no exercise and fed on a poor diet. One man in this first intake at Dartmoor died on the march (courtesy artist Paul Deacon).

This was a delay not bargained for, but at last all was arranged, the foundation stone was laid on March 20, 1806, by Sir Thomas Tyrwhitt and work commenced.[6]

It was to be more than three years before the first prisoners of war were admitted. On May 22, 1809, the first French prisoners, nearly 500 of them, marched up to Dartmoor Depot from Mill Prison, Plymouth, many of them from the *Bienfaisant* hulk, which was in such a bad state of repair it was never used as a prison ship again. Or did they? That date and numbers of French prisoners admitted to Dartmoor that day contradict what has been recorded in the past by nearly every writer on the subject. One or two have simply said they arrived in May 1809; all the others (including the author) have alleged that 2,500 prisoners were landed from the Plymouth hulks and marched to the Depot on May 24, 1809. It was generally accepted this was the case, but fresh evidence came to light when the consul for France at Plymouth, M. Alain Sibirl and his wife Monique, were researching these events at the Public Record Office at Kew. They examined the General Entry Book No. 1 for Dartmoor Depot and to their surprise discovered 496 Frenchmen were taken into custody there two days earlier than commonly supposed. Confirmation (as if any were needed) was obtained later from the Public Record Office at Clare Place, Plymouth, when they were shown a letter dated May 23, 1809, from Captain James Rogers of the Royal Navy (agent for Mill Prison) addressed to Captain Hawkins, Royal Navy (superintendent of prison ships), advising him that " the prisoners who set off for Dartmoor Prison yesterday morning [22 May] arrived safe at their place of destination just past 3 o'clock in the afternoon."

It is now apparent that the mostly widely accepted date for the entry to of those first prisoners of war into Dartmoor is inaccurate, the numbers are wrong, and the men did not land that day from the hulks but stayed overnight at Mill Prison before setting off. The true figures from the Public Record Office at Kew are:

> 22 May: 496, one of whom was dead on arrival[7]
> 23 May: 2
> 24 May: 999
> 25 May: 982

The lesson to be learned is that recorded history is never complete; new evidence and discoveries are constantly emerging.[8]

3

The Prison Is Built

Daniel Alexander, the surveyor engaged to design and supervise the building of Dartmoor Depot, had written: "I think that the major part of the scheme might be completed by the end of the year 1806," and "The remainder of the prison would be finished in the year 1807," referring to Plan B.

How was it, then, that completion was delayed for nearly a year and a half? It was a combination of many factors, not the least of which was simply Dartmoor weather. There must have been unimaginable difficulties hewing stone on the open moor in freezing fogs or sleet showers and on soggy ground. Working on Dartmoor in summer heat can be equally trying; there were no trees and no shade. No tradesman was prepared to endure such conditions without an adequate reward for his labors, and there must have been a large turnover of workmen. Then there was the Transport Office, a parsimonious employer who quibbled over every penny and who must have been appalled when the tender it accepted at about £3,000 below the estimate ran to more than twice as much before the job was done. This, together with the fine margins the contractors set themselves, resulted in such hurried and poor workmanship that much of it had to be done again.

Another problem arose from the sheer scale of the project. The mighty edifice surpassed anything previously seen in the West of England and the spectacle attracted a constant stream of official and unofficial visitors, often accompanied by their families and friends, expecting guided tours. It had to be stopped and it was. *Trewman's Exeter Flying Post* for July 2, 1807, reported: "Whereas great hindrance and delay is being experienced by the men employed on the works of the said prison in consequence of visitors going through the same: it is ordered that no persons be admitted but such as apply to the clerk of works who will give proper directions accordingly, and then none to be admitted on Sundays."

It had been expected the depot would receive its first inmates by Christmas 1807, but it was May 1809 before it was ready for occupation, with construction still in progress and only two prison blocks available. Alexander and his men must have had their patience and endurance tried to the limit. To add to the contractor's difficulties, the price of timber (of which some quantity was necessary for the roofing, for example) rose to a level beyond their resources, and the Admiralty was obliged to provide timber from discarded ships at Plymouth dockyard to help out. Some of that wood is still in place in the roof space of the "Old Chapel" (formerly No. 4 block for prisoners of war), the best preserved remaining building from that time, about which more will be said presently.

The boundary wall that remains now was the outer one of two walls, enclosing an area of roughly 15 acres. Mounted at intervals on the inner wall were wooden platforms overlooking the interior and manned by armed militia soldiers. The 20 foot wide gap between the walls was known as the Military

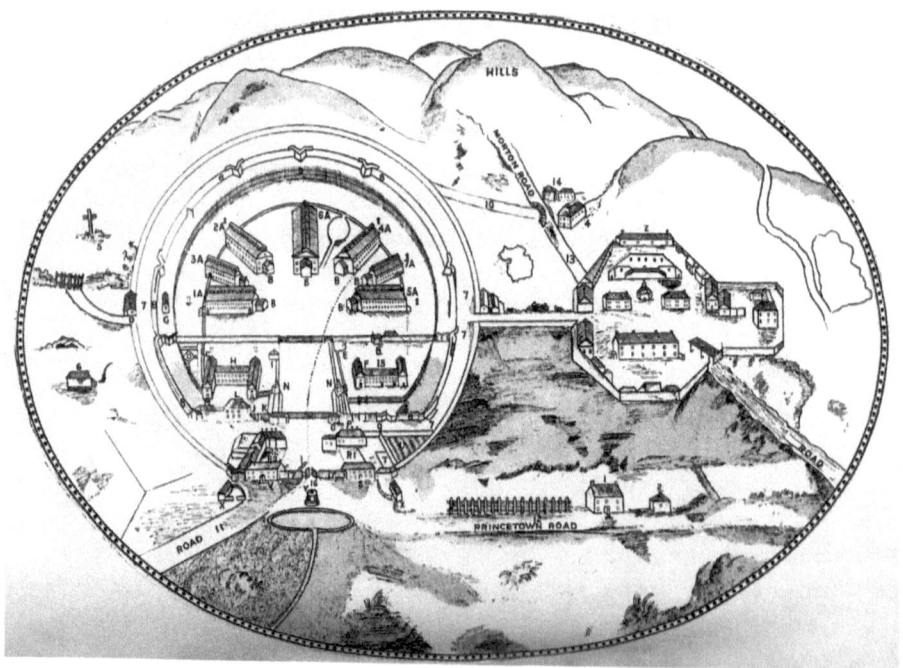

Dartmoor prison in 1812. The basic layout has not changed and the modern prison blocks occupy the same ground where the old war prisons were situated. This old print gives a realistic picture of what the prison and surrounding area looked like — grim, lonely and remote. Note the cemetery outside the boundary wall (left) and below it the little building known as the "Dead House" where bodies were stored before burial (courtesy Dartmoor Prison Museum).

3. The Prison Is Built

Dartmoor Prison under construction. Samuel Prout was a Plymouth born artist of renown remembered today for his brilliant portrayals of country scenes both in the Westcountry and later on the Continent. Plymouth Museum and Art Gallery has drawings he did of Dartmoor Prison under construction, the only known pictures of their kind of this subject. They were specially photographed for the author several years ago. This picture shows the railway built to transport some of the stones from nearby Herne Hole (Herne is the name of a Saxon god), which later became the prison quarry (now redundant)(courtesy Plymouth Museum and Art Gallery).

Walk, a "no man's land" for potential escapees with guardrooms positioned within for the sentries to rest and take shelter in very bad weather. The inner wall was extended across the diameter of the circular interior, leaving a half-moon shaped area on the lower part (the ground slopes from the front to the rear of the prison), where the main body of prisoners were accommodated in five blocks, each three stories high and radiating from a common center in a fan-like formation. This design ensured the maximum amount of light and air between each block, as well as giving the guards a wider view of the interior. The ground areas, or yards as they were called, were surrounded by a palisade of iron railings to prevent the inmates from approaching the walls and fraternizing with the guards. The yards were lit at night by oil lamps suspended from the corners of each block, and were surfaced with macadam, a type of hard surface invented by John Macadam (1756–1836), mainly for use in road building. His method was to use stone broken into small pieces about 6 ounces in weight. When these were compressed and the gaps filled with powder ground from the stones, it formed a solid surface, very strong and enduring. To this day such surfaces are said to be "macadamized" (not to be confused with "tarmacadam," which did not appear until after 1869, when Trinidad bitumen was discovered).

The accommodation blocks had granite steps with granite pillars inside to support the upper floors, no straw or covering of any kind being provided. There was no furniture. Rows of iron posts were installed to enable the prisoners to sling their hammocks one above the other in tiers. At a later stage, as a result of the overcrowding, men slept on the floors as well, a daunting prospect in winter without heating and with 2 foot square windows having no glass to stop the freezing draught, just wooden shutters which could be closed but which would not have been draught-proof by any means.

Each block was designed to accommodate 1,000 men, 500 on each floor. The top floors were laid with wood and were called cocklofts, areas where the men could exercise when the weather was bad. Ultimately they were pressed into service as extra dormitories, resulting in 1500 men being crammed into each block, eating and sleeping in hideously cramped conditions. By the year 1812 the number of blocks had increased to seven, two more having been built by the prisoners themselves, not by forced labor (which was forbidden by mutual agreement on both sides) but by volunteers who were paid a daily rate. These last two blocks had wooden floors throughout made of stout planks caulked and seamed as on board ship; as a result they were warmer and much sought after. Daniel Alexander designed one main kitchen to serve the entire prison population, but by the time the two extra blocks were built, each of the seven blocks had an extension added for that purpose, quaintly marked *cookeries* on the surviving drawings. Cooks and helpers were recruited from among the prisoners and received a daily wage.

Three of the original seven blocks stand today. One of them is in use for modern inmates who occupy individual cells and unlike the war prisoners of old, enjoy the benefit of central heating. The roof of this building was restored in the late 1980s, the original wooden rafters made with timber saved from redundant 18th century warships finally showing signs of distress. Of course the entire block has been renovated throughout and proper windows fitted. Another war prison was converted for kitchen use in the 1940s, but is now redundant (a fine new kitchen was commissioned in 1993) and is a derelict reminder of those far off days. The other remaining accommodation block from the war depot days is referred to by the prison staff as "The Old Chapel," although it has long ceased to be used for that purpose, alternative premises having been provided. This old building is far from derelict and was the notorious No. 4 block, about which more will be told later. From the outside you can still see the original granite window sills, and the outlines of the now blocked up apertures are clearly visible. The roof area (the cockloft of old) is sound, the timbers are dry and a few rusty nails are embedded in the timbers that form the roof supports, some of which may have been used to sling hammocks (although we know from some of the written accounts of those who lived here that most of them slept on the floor). Many of the overhead beams carry scorch marks, almost certainly the scars left from the candle holders fixed to them at that time.

The place has a somber appearance and an atmosphere very much in keeping with its sad history, for it was in this building two French fencing masters settled a quarrel by dueling with improvised swords, resulting in one of them being "run through" and killed. It seems this was the place where arguments were concluded, out of sight and earshot of the prison authorities who would certainly have put a stop to such goings on. The despicable "Romans" were kept in this building, separate from the main body of prisoners. They were degenerate outcasts, so filthy and vice-ridden their fellow prisoners couldn't stand them and in the end they were removed from Dartmoor to finish their captivity on the hulks. American Negroes who were segregated for different reasons afterwards took over No. 4 block.

These were the arrangements for the main body of men. The upper half of the depot was for the supervisory staff, the hospital, and the so-called Petty Officers' Prison. Contrary to what the name implies, the last named was a separate enclosed prison specially provided for ships' captains, chaplains, surgeons, army officers, and "persons of respectability" who were captured as passengers — planters in the West Indies, officials, and the like. The term *petty* was probably a corruption by the British of the proper French term, *le petit cautionnement.*

Among those confined here were the *detinues,* French civilians who had taken advantage of the period of peace during the Treaty of Amiens to visit England. Many Britishers had done the same thing, having traveled to France in large numbers after years of warfare had made such visits impossible. On the very day that war was again declared (May 18, 1803), the Royal Navy captured two French warships in the English Channel. This action so angered Napoleon he promptly retaliated by ordering the arrest of all British subjects who happened to be on French territory at the time. Around 1,000 British nationals were detained and this single act was to harden British resolve in the years of conflict that lay ahead. The British reacted by arresting all visitors to this country — hence the presence of *detinues* in our war prisons. Women and children were repatriated but many wives on both sides chose to remain near their prisoner husbands outside prison walls.

The personnel in the Petty Officers' Prison were those who had violated, or refused to take, their parole. Under this system certain officers were permitted to reside in nearby towns in complete freedom, provided they gave their word of honor not to try to escape and to observe the conditions for parole laid down by the authorities. Those who broke these terms or attempted to escape, together with those who refused to accept parole, were held in this separate prison which still stands above and to the right of the main prison blocks (looking from the entrance). The present day chapel, prison hospital and various other offices are integral parts of it now. The hospital for prisoners of war stood opposite and to the left of the entrance to the prison. It was run by a Royal Navy surgeon, a matron, and three attendants, assisted by nurses recruited from the fit and healthy prisoners. This building now houses training workshops.

Between the Petty Officers Prison and the hospital was an open space called the Market Square, where a market was held every day except Sundays from 9 A.M. until noon to enable prisoners to buy or barter for food and clothing to supplement what was issued to them. The goods were brought in by country folk from the surrounding farms and traders from Plymouth and Tavistock. Entrance to the square was via two stout gates, one for the prisoners at the lower end, and an upper gate for those coming and going. Also at the higher end of the market square were two roughly circular buildings which were used as storehouses. Originally emergency rations were kept there for when the prison might be cut off by snow during the winter and the daily bread ration was stored here too prior to being issued. These buildings are in use today after extensive renovation work — one is for the reception of inmates' visitors and the other is now an office block.

The Military Walk completed its circuit at the upper gate of the market square. Initially all access to the square and the prisons were through the main entrance, but in 1813, probably for security reasons, a postern gate was built in the outer wall at a point adjacent to the soldiers' barracks. The market people and the military personnel then entered and left by this gate (it was blocked up after the convict prison opened in 1850). The stone pillars and lintel are clearly visible today, as is the overhead inscription cut by the French mason who constructed it, which reads: *Henri Prisonniere Journee 1813*.

The administration and supervisory staff lived in the upper part of the prison near the road. The governor, or "agent" as he was called (the term indicates he was the agent for the Transport Office whose written orders for the care and supervision of the prisoners he was expected to enforce), lived with his family in the house to the right of the archway. It was also home to the governors who administered the convict prison in later years. To the left of the arch was the surgeon's house and living quarters for the medical staff and the clerks. Today they are used for offices and stores.

The giant archway, which has become a symbol of Dartmoor prison, is remarkably well preserved, as are the words "Parcere Subjectis" ("Spare the

Vanquished") engraved overhead. These words are taken from Virgil's *Book 6* of the *Aenid:* "Be These Your Arts: Pacisque Imponere Morem Parcere Subjectis et deballare Superbus." It translates as, "To Impose the Rule of Peace Spare the Vanquished and Abase the Proud." Sparing the vanquished meant refraining from killing prisoners and taking their wives and children as slaves.

Thousands of unhappy war prisoners and the convicts who came afterwards have entered into captivity under its grim visage. The sightseers who tend to congregate here on summer days often fail to notice the low stone tower which stands above the wall on the opposite side of the road. This wall is in fact part of the reservoir that was supplied by the leat and was the source of the water supply to the entire prison. Sluice gates within the tower controlled the flow of water by gravity to the various prison buildings via slate-lined open channels. In the prison blocks it first of all passed through the cookeries, then a washing area before exiting under the latrines. All the waste from the prison was directed to a "foul water" leat that conducted it to the wild moorland beyond Tor Royal. At the lower part of the prison compound was a bathing pond described by American prisoner of war John Mellish as "a plunge bath of great comfort to the prisoners," which no doubt it was. The water supply sometimes froze solid and during one severe winter the prisoners were compelled to eat snow to alleviate their thirst. One of the principal appointments listed when the depot first opened was that of "navigator," and it has caused much speculation; in fact the post was an essential one. The men who dug Britain's canals were called navigators, a colloquial term later shortened to "navvies" when applied to the manual workers who constructed roads and railways. The navigator's job at Dartmoor was a simple but very necessary one — he maintained the leat and was therefore a key figure who fully merited a mention on the list of staff.

A short distance from the main entrance where the boundary wall curves to the left towards the rear of the prison, there was a stone hut called the Dead House where in the war depot days corpses were placed prior to burial. There was no consecrated ground for those who died and no religious rites; a shallow pit on the open moor (now occupied by farm buildings[1]) was their last resting place. Many hundreds of prisoners were interred there and in a manner we would consider callous and inhuman today. All the same, it was no different from the way in which British soldiers who died anywhere in the world were simply "spaded under"; the practice was extended to those in captivity.

Over 50 years later the burial ground was disturbed by farm animals, the wild moorland creatures and the action of wind and rain. The graves were exposed and the area was littered with human bones. Rachel Evans of Tavi-

The American Memorial Obelisk. There are two mass graves on open ground behind the prison, one for the French who died here and the other for the Americans. Each grave is covered by a cairn surmounted by an obelisk. The American one, easily identified by the single bronze badge affixed to it, is shown here before renovation work took place. The wording is the same on both memorials (author's photograph, reproduced permission of Dartmoor Prison Governor T. Witton).

stock, whose well known account *Home Scenes, or Tavistock and Its Vicinity* was published in 1846, wrote: "Without the walls of the prison is the burial place of the unfortunate captives, which has of course been sadly neglected; the horses and cattle have broken up the soil and left the bones of the dead to whiten in the sun."

This shocking state of affairs came about during a period of decline at Princetown between the closing of the war prison in 1816 and the opening of the convict establishment in 1850. In 1866 the governor of the convict prison, Captain W. Stopford, ordered the bones to be collected and as many of the graves as could be found exhumed. The skeletal remains were then divided, one heap being designated French and the other American. Two communal graves were then dug, each in a separate area, and the bones respectfully interred with full religious ceremony. Over the mass graves cairns were built, and on each cairn identical granite obelisks were erected, each bearing the following inscription: "In Memory of the American (French) Prisoners of War Who Died Between the Years 1809 and 1814 and Lie Buried Here." A quotation from the *Odes* (written by Horace in 23 B.C.) was added: "*Dulce Et Decorum Est Pro Patria Mori*" ("It is Dutiful and Honorable to Die for One's Country").

A discerning observer might question the dates, which are identical on each obelisk and honor Americans from the year 1809, three years before the War of 1812 began. This may have been an oversight by the stone mason who inscribed them, but technically they are correct, bearing in mind there were American sailors captured while serving on French ships who were interned with them, some of whom died in prison.

This bronze badge is the official symbol of the National Society of United States Daughters of 1812, whose members are direct descendants of those who took part in the War of 1812. Representatives have in the past been regular visitors here and at Princetown Parish Church of St. Michael and All Angels, which was constructed by French and American prisoners of war (author's photograph, reproduced permission of Dartmoor Prison Governor T. Witton).

The cemeteries are situated on prison land outside the prison wall and to the rear of the main buildings. They overlook the moors, sheltered from the worst of winter storms, and the dead lie in solitude amid birdsong and moorland beauty. The view from here has hardly changed since those times. Regular visitors used to be representatives of the National Society of United States Daughters of 1812, an organization whose members have a direct family connection with the men who fought in that war and are committed to revering their dead and keeping alive the best traditions of that time (their visits have been less frequent in recent years). They provided a replica of the prison archway which now serves as a separate entrance to the American graveyard and which bears a metal memorial plaque inscribed: "To the Glory of God and in Loving Memory of the Two Hundred and Eighteen American Sailors and Soldiers of the War of 1812 Who Died Here. This Memorial Gateway is Erected by the National Society of United States Daughters of 1812."

The gateway was dedicated in May 1928 by the president of the society, Mrs. Samuel E. Shope, and the memorial was unveiled by the chairman, Mrs. Earle. Many years later a circular bronze badge was added to their obelisk, which distinguishes it from the French monument at a glance. The badge is inscribed: "In Honour of Service in the War of 1812 Americans N.S.U.S.D. 1812." The French sent a message of gratitude to Capt. Stopford for his humanitarian act.

The late Ira Dye, author and historian of Mill Valley, California, who was a respected authority on the War of 1812 and related subjects, produced a number of papers containing carefully compiled data, and through his generosity several official statistics are quoted here and later in this book. Here is what he had to say about his countrymen who died at Dartmoor:

> The latest figures obtained by modern research reveal a total of 271 American dead and there may be more. The official British records of American Prisoners of War at Dartmoor show 267 men as having been "Discharged Dead" ... [This] may not be an exact number as a few men were transferred to Plymouth and may have died in the hospital there.... Dartmoor (and the prison ships at Plymouth and Chatham) were obviously a fertile ground for diseases to spread. However, during the 19 months between early April 1813, when the first Americans arrived at Dartmoor, and October 1814, only 40 Americans died. The next ten months were the killer months, from October until the last Americans left in July 1815. About 225 died during this period. It is especially tragic that about 160 of these men died after the signing of the peace treaty in Ghent on 24 December 1814. During that fall and the winter of 1814/15 there was a smallpox epidemic in the prison, and typhus, and a malignant version of measles. These diseases plus colds that turned to pneumonia, accounted for most of the deaths, of which 236 were rated as seamen.

This initial look at the prison concludes with mention of the *cachot*, which means *dungeon* in French, but cannot be considered as such in the English context because it was situated above ground. The British always called it the Black Hole. It was a place of confinement for prisoners who committed punishable offences, such as selling or buying another man's rations, assaulting the guards, or attempting to escape. The first Black Hole at Dartmoor was near the hospital and was simply a barricaded stone hut where offenders were locked up for periods of up to ten days (the maximum an agent could award a miscreant). Because there were a number of escapes, it was decided to build a more secure place of confinement.

This was done by a gang of prisoners who cut and dressed huge granite blocks and transported them to a spot below the hospital, between the inner wall and the metal railings. Here they constructed what can best be described as a stone igloo with stone blocks forming the floor, the walls, and the roof. The heavy door was reinforced with metal plates, leaving a small aperture through which rations could be passed (the punishment included a reduction to two-thirds normal rations). Ventilation was via a single grill under the roof measuring a mere six inches by four. Inside this frightful place transgressors (up to a maximum of 60 at a time) lived in almost total darkness, stifling in summer and freezing in the winter months when many a man was carried from it to the hospital in the final stages of hypothermia. Rachel Evans, who toured the prison in 1845, wrote a vivid description of it, concluding with the words: "Walls are so thick that the instrument of release could never pierce them: the light comes dimly through a small iron grating, and the doubly plated door closes with a thundering sound which reverberates through the vaulted cell. It would be cold heartless misery to sojourn in such a place, even for a short time."

4

The Militia

To appreciate how certain unpleasant events occurred at Dartmoor, a short description of the militia forces and their role is necessary. When Britain again declared war on France in May 1803 its defenses were at an all-time low, having been drastically reduced following the Treaty of Amiens, which temporarily ended hostilities. The realization that Napoleon was planning an invasion called for urgent action, the immediate problem being how to raise a sufficient force in time to defend the country.

It took many months to recruit and train regular soldiers, and therefore great reliance was placed upon the reserve forces — the militia. A proclamation had already been announced to bring their strength up to 75,000 but it was quickly evident more would be needed. The militia was a kind of reserve army, with the important difference that whereas our present day reservists are volunteers, the militia units were raised by compulsory ballot. In general those who were balloted were expected to drill for 20 days (later increased to 28 days) a year. When war came the commitment was for three to five years, later amended to service through the end of the war. Many of the problems that lay ahead were because of the system of substitution. For a fee of £10 a man could buy exemption and the money would pay for a substitute to serve in his stead. The sum varied from place to place and got more expensive as the war progressed so that in less than a year it more than doubled.

As a result most militia soldiers were recruited from the very poor and illiterate classes who were unable to afford the substitution fees and joined the ranks alongside those who were themselves substitutes. The majority of them, coming as they did from the very lowest level of society, were a mixture of rascals and alcoholics who in most cases outnumbered those who were balloted or volunteered. Their pay was a pittance, from which deductions were made for food and necessary cleaning materials. Uniforms and discipline were much in line with the Regulars—flogging was freely employed as a punishment and death was the penalty for serious offences either by hanging or a firing squad. In addition men were away from home for long periods because the militiamen were expected to serve anywhere in Britain and deserters were energetically pursued. As the war went on the increasing number of dead and wounded required an act for recruiting direct from the militia to the regular army with a bounty being offered as an inducement. It had the desired effect. The *Historical Records of the Notts Militia*, for example, tells us that in May 1805 "the Regiment was called upon to furnish its quota of volunteers for the line. The number being stated on parade by the commanding officer, more men than were required at once stepped forward for active service, and this, be it remembered, was at a time when a fierce and bloody war was raging."

The payment to those who volunteered was around £12 (an enormous sum for a common man at that time), which soon found its way into the hands of the tavern keepers when the recipients celebrated their new found wealth in drunken sprees. Those who

A British "Redcoat" soldier. The prisoner of war depots and some of the hulks were guarded by soldiers, a mixture of regulars, some wounded veterans, and regiments of militia. Royal navy sailors manned most hulks, supplemented by Marines, but at Plymouth the militia soldiers were the main guardians. The latter were raised by ballot but for those who could afford it there was a way of avoiding service; payment of a "substitution" fee exempted them and their places would be taken by a man who could not pay. Thus many of the militiamen were drunkards, layabouts and scallywags, most of whom were without scruples or morals, all of which goes a long way to explaining the erratic and often cruel manner in which they treated the prisoners. The picture is of a grenadier of the 32nd (Cornwall) Regiment of Foot in 1812 (courtesy Cornwall's Regimental Museum, T.W. Stipling, curator).

Guardhouse for the soldiers' barracks. This building stands in the aptly named Barrack Road opposite Princetown Church and is the only remaining one of five guardhouses for the soldiers' barracks, nearly all of which have now been demolished. It was for many years used as a recreation room for prison officers but is now empty (author's photograph).

transferred to the regulars had to be replaced in turn, and the resulting manpower shortage starved many counties of sufficient manpower for the harvest. The food shortages that then occurred caused riots, which were terrible affairs with looting and murder commonplace. Hunger led to a dramatic increase in stealing and poaching, which in turn led to the death penalty being introduced for the latter offense. Most militiamen sympathized with the rioters and in many cases were reluctant to do their duty.

At first militia officers were recruited exclusively from the landed gentry. Later in the war the shortage of officer recruits compelled the authorities to accept lower standards. Wounded regulars, ordinary householders and tradesmen were permitted to join the officer ranks with occasional dire consequences. In many cases discipline lapsed because shopkeeper officers could not afford to upset their customers in the ranks. In the Lancashire Militia several officers were indicted for keeping taverns and selling illicit alcohol, and there were instances where the county officials actually requested their own men be posted as far away as possible because they were so unreliable and troublesome. The picture that emerges from all this is of a low set of ruffians in uniform masquerading as soldiers, but the real problem was most certainly the brutal lives they led and being treated like brutes.

During the war against Napoleon the militia duties were to repel an invasion, act as coastal lookouts, help control smuggling, suppress riots, and guard prisoners of war. This was not a popular duty, especially at Dartmoor, a remote posting where conditions were notoriously bad.

When we consider the unsavory characters who formed the substitutes in the militia ranks doing guard duty, we can appreciate how the temptations afforded through bribery (to assist in an escape, for example) was often difficult for them to resist. Callousness and sheer cruelty was widespread, particularly on the hulks where conditions were unbearably hard for them as well as the prisoners. An escape attempt was often a welcome diversion (there are accounts of the guards gleefully taking "pot shots" at escapees on the run who more than likely would have been recaptured). Unlike the regular army, whose men were trained and disciplined over long periods, the militiamen were part-time soldiers, many of whom lacked even basic training, because when war broke out they were needed at once for their various tasks. A distressing consequence of all this occurred at Dartmoor Depot twelve years later when free Americans were fired on by the militia in what became known as the Princetown Massacre.

5

How the Depots Were Run

The center of Princetown is dominated by a building of almost regal appearance and with a long history. It was built at the same time as Dartmoor Depot as living quarters for the officers commanding the military forces guarding it. After the wars with France and the U.S. it was refurbished to become the Duchy Hotel with a history going back to the mid–1800s, when there was a small brewery at the back. Later still when the hotel closed down, the prison acquired it. The prison officers' mess occupied the ground floor and there was accommodation for bachelor warders. When that facility was no longer required the place was extensively refurbished and now accommodates the High Moorland Visitor Center (opened by Prince Charles in 1990). The Duchy of Cornwall occupies offices in the same building. Its present appearance dates from 1908 when massive alterations were made and the rough stone walls were rendered as you see them now.

The main body of troops lived in the huge barracks nearer to the prison and on the other side of the road. One of the principal entrances to the barracks was opposite the church and aptly named Barrack Road, where one of the old guardhouses once stood (there were seven of these), a portion of which still remains. By 1812 the garrison of 500 officers and men had swollen to more than 1200 as the prisoner population increased and the Petty Officers' Prison was requisitioned to accommodate the extra soldiers. The officer prisoners, much to their disgust, were relegated to the prison blocks to live among their men. They rigged heavy curtains to screen them from the rank and file prisoners so as to continue living aloof and in privacy.

The county regiments of militia who were stationed at Dartmoor are household names in Britain: Staffordshire, Nottinghamshire, Cheshire, Lancashire, Roscommon (Irish) and many others, including some Scottish contingents. Bearing in mind the appalling conditions under which the laboring classes, who formed the bulk of the soldiery, lived at that time, it is not surprising that every man was out to fend for himself by whatever means were at hand. Bribery and corruption were rife among the militia, and many an escapee owed his freedom to their help — at a price of course. It was partly for this reason and because of Dartmoor Depot's remote location that the garrison was changed roughly every three months. The punishments for helping a prisoner to escape were severe. In 1809 four soldiers of the Nottinghamshire Militia were charged at Plymouth with aiding the escape of some French prisoners who, when they were recaptured, revealed they had paid the militiamen eight guineas each for their assistance. The culprits were court-martialed and two of them were shot. The honor of the Nottingham men was redressed the following year when, on October 10, they arrived at Dartmoor to take over guard duties from the Shropshire Militia. The French assumed their new guards would not at first be as vigilant or effective and planned an escape for the following night. Under cover of a heavy rainstorm they gained the outside of the walls before being discovered, but the sentries were so prompt in turning out, some of them clad only in breeches and shirtsleeves, every prisoner was caught and detained.

The prison's position on a bleak moor was deterrent enough for most men contemplating escape. If they did manage to get away, the nearby residents were only too glad to earn a reward for apprehending them. The agents were authorized to pay a reward of one guinea (£1, 1s) over and above expenses to anyone capturing and returning an escaped prisoner, the fugitive being "rewarded" with a spell in the Black Hole. Add to this the cold and mists so prevalent on the moor and one can appreciate that a prisoner on the run was in for a hard time.

Princetown's prosperity and that of the various suppliers of goods relied on the continuance of the war and the war depot. The ultimate cost was at the expense of Britain's captive foes who languished in their stone prison for years, making do on their meager rations and whatever they could scrounge, barter or buy. The agents of the depots everywhere were mostly volunteers, and the commanding officers of some militia units actually applied for guard duties at these establishments. On the hulks, which were commanded by Royal Navy lieutenants, there was a waiting list of applicants and it became necessary to limit them to officers with at least ten years' service (Dartmoor Depot's first agent was Captain Isaac Cotgrave, a Royal Navy post captain with ten years of seniority).

The reasons were simple: nearly everyone was "on the make" at the expense of the prisoners. There were honest officials, of course, but the temptations were strong and in all too many cases contracts were awarded to certain suppliers of food and clothing in return for hidden favors. "Corruption in disguise" was an accepted practice in high and low places in Georgian times, when family connections and wealth were essential qualifications for advancement. The going rate for members of Parliament buying votes for example was £100 per vote, openly bought and paid for. Commissions in the Army were purchased by men of "gentle birth" regardless of their suitability for command, and Royal Navy captains relied heavily on prize money to supplement their pay, when the salvage value of captured enemy ships was shared among officers and crew.

It is not difficult to see how the confinement of thousands of prisoners presented an opportunity not to be missed by unscrupulous men whose duty

The external appearance of the officers' mess is unchanged since the war depot days. Note the rough stonework — the work of the masons who built it by breaking up and using the boulders lying around on the open moor. This building stands nearly half a mile from the prison, and it was here the army and militia officers were dining when the Princetown Massacre took place. Extensive alterations were made internally when the place was converted to the famous Duchy Hotel in the mid–1800s (the name can be seen at right). Notable visitors included Prince Albert (Queen Victoria's consort), Alfred Lord Tennyson (poet laureate), and author Sir Arthur Conan Doyle of Sherlock Holmes fame (courtesy Dartmoor Prison Museum).

5. How the Depots Were Run

The former officers' mess today. In 1908 the hotel building was completely refurbished externally and in 1914 extended (right of the picture) to accommodate the Duchy of Cornwall offices. In 1941 it was taken over by the prison and became the prison officers' mess with accommodation for bachelor officers. In 1993 it again changed hands and is now Dartmoor National Park Authority High Moorland Visitors' Center, as shown (author's photograph).

it was to administer and provide for them. In 1812 a newspaper article alleged that certain high ranking officials entrusted with large amounts of money invested it in short term speculations on the stock markets instead of forwarding it at once to the depots. Likewise, private sums advanced (with permission) by friends and relatives to officer prisoners of war were often delayed for the same reason and there were cases where local agents charged a "commission" for delivering sums of money to officers living on parole. Instructions issued to agents by the Transport Office specifically stated: "If money be remitted for a prisoner to you for his use you are to take charge of it and deliver it to him without any charge for commission."[1] It is obvious the practice of illegally taking a "commission" was known about and officially forbidden. Consider the clothing allowance, which stipulated prisoners' clothing should be renewed every 18 months though it very often was not. With the vast number of prisoners to be provided for, the potential gain from fraudulent practices was colossal. The standard of clothing and bedding was often very poor — accounts of depot life mention blankets so thin they were almost transparent, and shoes that fell to pieces in weeks.

As for the food, the quality laid down in the regulations was not always observed by the contractors; if it had been the men at the depot would have fared better because their rations, the scale of which was based on those laid down for the Royal Navy, would have been very good and not of the dubious quality they sometimes got.

The *West Briton* reported on June 10, 1814: "Owing to the general shortage of flour, adulteration with foreign matter in order to increase its bulk was not uncommon. The first case of this kind in Cornwall was discovered a few weeks earlier at the Treyew Grist Mills, Truro (Cornwall), where china clay was being incorporated with the flour produced. Its consumption had caused illness, not only in Cornwall but also amongst the French prisoners at Dartmoor, and Wellington's Peninsula Army."

Feeding thousands of Dartmoor prisoners must have been a tremendous task, and to learn that flour was brought from so far away indicates how great that task was (and how one of the "tricks of the trade" worked). The regulations drawn up for the proper treatment of prisoners of war were precise and very fair, but of course their implementation was entirely in the hands of those in charge. Happily, there was another side to the coin. There were Americans at the depot who, prior to the War of 1812, had served in the Royal Navy and were entitled to prize money. These men had aroused the Navy's wrath because they elected to go to prison rather than fight against their countrymen, yet their back pay and prize money was paid to them in full during their captivity.

How the Depots Were Controlled

Written instructions were issued to every agent by the Transport Office, whether at the depots, on the hulks, or in the parole towns. They were similar in content but with variations according to the locations. In general the regulations were fair and took into consideration certain agreements made with the enemy to be observed on both sides; for example no corporal punishment was to be employed; no slave labor was allowed; conditions for exchange of prisoners was spelled out.

The actual treatment of prisoners depended on the individual agent. At Dartmoor, Captain Cotgrave was far more severe than his successor Captain Shortland, although both men operated within the rules laid down. Good supervision always allows for a little moderation and this was the difference between the two men. However, the Transport Office maintained strict control over their agents by insisting that movements of prisoners, numbers of sick, disciplinary matters, and other issues be reported to them in writing as they

5. How the Depots Were Run

occurred. The following is a sample list of conditions which agents were expected to adhere to (capitalization and spelling from the original document):

> The original number of each prisoner is to stand invariably against his Name during the Time he may remain in your Custody. Whenever Prisoners shall have been received into your Custody, you are to transmit to this Office by the first post, a correct List of them.
>
> If any Women or Girls, or boys under Twelve Years of Age should accompany the prisoners, at any time, delivered into your Custody, you are, by the first Post, to transmit to us a List of them, in order that we may give such Directions as we may judge proper or their disposal ... you are not to receive any Women or Girls into your Custody ... as such Persons are not meant to be treated as Prisoner of War; but if they have no other Means of Subsistence, they are to be victualler by you.
>
> The Prisoners are to be mustered regularly by Name twice in every week in your Presence; and also to be mustered or counted over daily, at the Time of Locking up the Prisons and Hospital, by the Clerks or Turnkeys.
>
> The Surgeon will visit the Prisons every Day in order that such Prisoners as shall, in his Judgement ... be removed to the Hospital. A Sick Ticket, signed by you, is to be delivered to him of all the Prisoners sent to the Hospital, and he will deliver to you Hospital Discharge Tickets, signed by him, for such Prisoners as shall have been returned to your Charge from the Hospital.
>
> You are to permit the Prisoners every Day, in fair weather, to go into the Airing Ground of the Prisons for the benefit of the air, but not to remain after sunset[2].... Once a Week at least in fair weather, all Hammocks, Bedding etc. are to be brought into the Airing Ground for the purpose not only of being aired, but also of being Examined in order to ascertain whether any article be missing or wilfully damaged.
>
> The prisoners are forbidden to strike, menace or insult, any Officer, Turnkey, or other person employed in the prisons or prison Ships, under pain of losing their Turn of Exchange, of being closely confined in the Black Hole, and forfeiting one third of their rations ... are forbidden to fight, quarrel or excite any Tumult or Disorder in the Prisons, or in the places where they shall be allowed to take the Air, under pain of being confined in the Black Hole and forfeiting one third of their ration for a time proportional to the offence.
>
> Any prisoner who shall be taken attempting to escape shall be put in the Black Hole for ten days, and shall lose his Turn of Exchange.
>
> Any prisoner who shall be retaken after having escaped from the Prison or prison Ships, and shall by this means have occasioned Expense, shall not only lose his Turn of Exchange, and be put in the Black Hole, but shall, with the whole of the Prisoners kept on the same deck or room from which he has escaped, be reduced to one third of their Ration until, by such reduction, the Expenses shall be made good, and even if he should not be retaken, the whole of the Prisoners in the same manner to reimburse the Expenses of attending such escape.
>
> A Market is allowed ... but the Prisoners are forbidden to buy or introduce

into the prison, Liquor, Knives or Weapons of any kind under pain of being confined in the Black Hole for Ten Days for such offence.

The prisoners are allowed during market hours to sell articles of their own manufacture, except Mittens, Woollen Gloves, Straw Hats, or Bonnets, Shoes, Plaited Straw, Obscene Pictures, or Images, and articles formed of the Prison Stores which are strictly forbidden, and any Prisoner selling or making any of these Articles ... shall be confined in the Black Hole, and reduced to two thirds of his Ration for three days ... and such Articles shall be destroyed.

Any prisoner who shall have bought, sold, or disposed of his Ration by gambling or otherwise, or shall have sold or made away with any article of clothing, even though such Articles belong to him, shall be confined in the Black Hole, and shall only receive two thirds of his Ration during such time as the Agent may direct, and lose his Turn of Exchange.

Given under our Hands at the Transport Office (Day and Date)
To Agent for Prisoners of War[3]

Black Hole Offenses

Some examples of offenses for which prisoners of war were placed in the Black Hole are taken from Basil Thomson's account in *The Story of Dartmoor Prison*. In 1812:

- 24 February. Louis Constant and Olivier de Camp, for striking a sentinel on duty.
- 20 May. Jean Delchambre, for throwing a stone at a sentinel and severely cutting his head.
- 14 June. F. Rousseau, for striking Mr. Bennet, the storekeeper, when visiting the prisoners.
- 15 August. A. Creville, for drawing a knife on the hospital turnkey.
- 25 August. A. Hourra, for attempting to stab William Norris, one of the turnkeys, with a knife.
- 24 September. S. Schamond, for throwing down a sentinel and attempting to take away his bayonet.
- 16 October. G. Massieu, for attempting to stab one of the turnkeys.
- 23 October. B. Marie, for knocking down a Turnkey and attempting to seize the arms of a sentinel.
- 30 November. N. Moulle and B. Saluberry, for having daggers concealed on their persons.

And in 1813:

- 13 March. P. Boissard, for striking a turnkey and threatening to murder him at the first opportunity.

- 23 March. F. Bilat, for striking a prisoner named B. Marie, who died shortly afterwards, and taking away his provisions by force.
- 28 March. J. Beauclaire, for threatening to stab Mr. Moore, because he could not procure employment for him on the buildings.
- 6 April. F. Le Jeune, for being one of the principal provision buyers in the prison, and for repeatedly writing blood-thirsty and threatening letters.
- 10 April. M. Girandi and A. Moine, for being guilty of infamous vices.

6

Life Inside the War Depot

Most accounts of the prisoners' way of life at Dartmoor Depot divide them into specific groups according to a class system and the mode of living they adopted. With the exception of the officers in the *Petit Cautionnement* and the "Romans," who were the lowest form of depot life, they will be examined collectively here.

The rule of the Emperor Napoleon was dominated by continuous warfare, not always of his making but all the same calling for ever increasing numbers of soldiers and sailors. Some of them were raised by ballot, others by conscription, and of course there were volunteers, not only in France but from every nation under French rule and from all manner of men — craftsmen, writers, artists, as well as professional soldiers. The "Grand Army" was probably the first citizens' army, hence the diversity of men in the depots, on the hulks and on parole (the British only employed the lower classes in the ranks).

At Dartmoor the prisoners soon formed individual groups to which other like-minded men gravitated, a process of natural selection which can be observed in every society. The "aristocracy" were those who lived in the *Petit Cautionnement* and were referred to as *les lordes*. The better off ones regularly received money sent by relatives and friends from France, enabling them to buy everything they needed to live in style. Not for them, the humble rations provided by the Transport Office; they bought fresh vegetables at the market, poultry, coffee, tobacco, fruit, and succulent delicacies to suit their discerning palates. Furthermore, they were permitted to employ servants from the ordinary prisoners to cook and wait upon them and launder their clothes. Tailors maintained their wardrobes and provided them with new outfits made from materials bought at the market. Among these privileged ranks were professors of music, fencing masters, language experts and artists, to name but a few. It comes as a surprise to many people to learn of the many artistic activities they engaged in. The French are renowned as a cultured people, yet to discover

6. Life Inside the War Depot

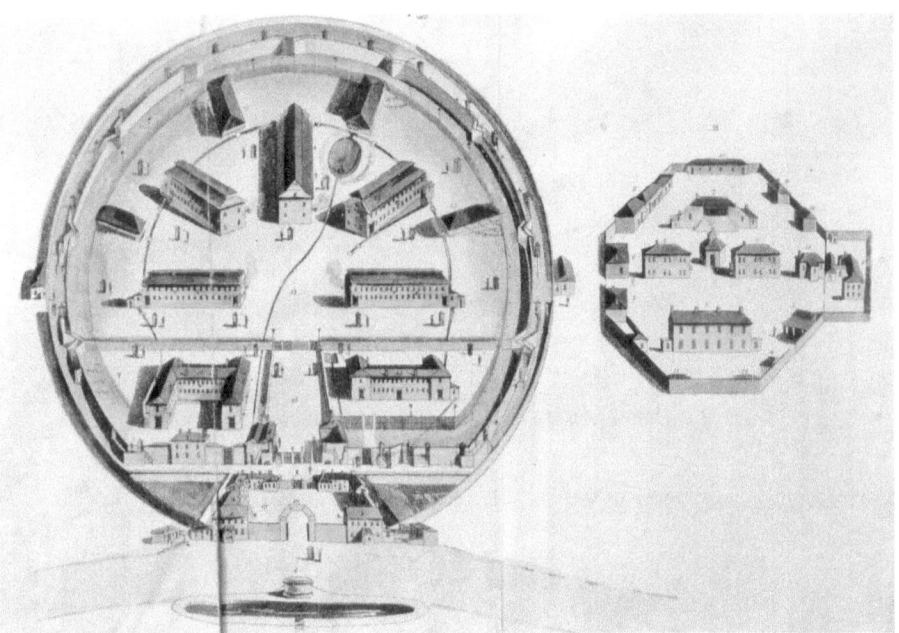

Prison and barracks. This illustration from an old print shows the relevant position of the barracks to the depot. At first the soldiers entered and left by the prison's main entrance, but in 1811 a portal was made in the wall adjacent to the barracks to enable a more satisfactory flow of traffic (courtesy Dartmoor Prison Museum).

that among the internees of a war prison there were theatricals, fencing lessons, art classes and music performed to the highest standards taught by experts is truly remarkable.

For the majority things were not so cozy. As the war progressed and more prisoners arrived, they were crammed into their stone prisons and left to cope as best they could with rough conditions, scanty clothing and a boring diet. The official scale of rations yielded approximately 2,400 calories a day per man, probably less after allowing for the bone content of the meat. Yet at a later date one American prisoner declared the Dartmoor ration was better than what he'd received on board ship and it was certainly better fare than that of the average British laborer. The exception as far as the "Yankees" were concerned was the Scotch barley which was issued. They called it "burgoo," and because they fed it only to animals at home, considered it an insult to be expected to eat it themselves.

The prisoners' rations were surrendered to the cooks who prepared the beef and vegetables in communal cauldrons and served it up in wooden bowls as soup, to be collected by representatives from each mess of 6 men. The

INSTRUCTIONS

FOR

AGENTS

UNDER

The Commissioners for conducting His Majesty's Transport Service, for taking Care of Sick and Wounded Seamen, and for the Care and Custody of Prisoners of War,

RESPECTING THE

MANAGEMENT OF PRISONERS OF WAR

AT HOME;

AS PROPOSED BY

The Commissioners appointed for Revising the Civil Affairs of His Majesty's Navy,

AND ESTABLISHED BY

HIS MAJESTY'S ORDER IN COUNCIL,

Dated the 14th of September, 1808.

LONDON:

PRINTED BY THE PHILANTHROPIC SOCIETY,
ST. GEORGE'S FIELDS.

1809.

Official cover of the booklet issued to agents for guidance in the supervision of prisoners of war. These were generally adhered to, but much depended on the integrity of agents. Some bent the rules to suit a certain situation either for personal gain (charging a commission for delivering money sent by officers' families, for example), or for disciplinary reasons (courtesy Dartmoor Prison Museum).

bread was baked and issued by outside contractors in nine pound loaves, one for each mess per day, one and a half pounds per man. The authorities, recognizing the hardships resulting from a restricted diet, allowed an extra five pounds per hundredweight (112 pounds) of beef and two pounds per hundredweight of bread to compensate for the wastage in dividing it (exactly how this was done is uncertain). Substitutions were not allowed without the special order of the board.

French and American Prisoners of War – Table of Daily Ration

Days	Bread	Beef	Codfish	Herrings	Potatoes	Greens	Scotch Barley	Onions	Salt
	lb.	lb.	lb.	lb.	lb.	lb.	oz.	oz.	oz.
Sunday	1.5	0.5	-	-	-	0.5	1.0	qtr	third
Monday	1.5	0.5	-	-	-	0.5	1.0	qtr	third
Tuesday	1.5	0.5	-	-	-	0.5	1.0	qtr	third
Wednesday	1.5	-	-	1.0	1.0	-	-	-	-
Thursday	1.5	0.5	-	-	-	0.5	1.0	qtr	third
Friday	1.5	-	1.0	-	1.0	-	-	-	-
Saturday	1.5	0.5	-	-	-	0.5	1.0	qtr	third
TOTAL	10.5	2.5	1.0	1.0	2.0	2.5	5.0	1¼	1⅔

N.B. Bread. To be made of Wheaten Meal, wherein the whole Grain is to be reserved, except such Part as will not pass through the London and Bristol Seam Cloth No. 7, usually called an Eleven Shilling Cloth, or what is considered equal to No. 6 of the Patent Cloth of Fifteen Shillings Price.
Beef. To be good and wholesome fresh Beef, not Bull Beef, and delivered in clean Quarters, a Fore and Hind Quarter alternately.
Cod-Fish. To be the produce of the Fishery at Newfoundland, or the Coast of Labrador and to be delivered in whole Fish.
Herrings. To be good and sound; and Red and White Herrings to be issued alternately.
Potatoes, Greens, Turnips, and Onions. To be good in their respective Kinds. The Greens to be stripped of outside Leaves, and fit for the Copper. **When Greens or Turnips, or Onions, cannot be procured, the following are the Substitutions to be made:** For Half a Pound of Greens, or Turnips — Two Ounces of Scotch Barley.

The hospital diet, more generous and sustaining, was shared by the prisoner nurses and helpers, a welcome perk in addition to the sixpence a day they were paid ("in money" to quote the official phrase). Helpers included washermen, cleaners, barbers, and others chosen by the depot surgeon from the fit and healthy men. Attention was also paid by him to the well-being of all the prisoners, it being stipulated for example that their bedding should be regularly aired and that the men should stow their hammocks and other belongings when absent from their prison blocks so as to permit maximum circulation of fresh air. Bedding was supposed to be inspected regularly and renewed every two years, although it is now known this was not always done. On admission to the depot every man was issued a palliasse with straw (the straw to be "regularly changed") and damages or losses were the responsibility of each prisoner; the punishment for any loss was to be put on two-thirds rations until the value was made good. Loss of clothing was more seriously dealt with. For this offense the culprits were placed in the Black Hole and on two-thirds rations until the Transport Office decided otherwise. At first the men were given a woolen or straw hat, jacket, trousers, two shirts, two pairs

The Market Square is depicted in an oil on canvas painting (about 3 feet by 2 feet) by a prisoner who was in custody during World War II. A market was held here every day except Sundays from 9 A.M. until noon. Traders came from the surrounding villages and farms as well as Tavistock and Plymouth to sell or barter clothing, tobacco, poultry, and little luxuries the prisoners might desire. Many prisoners who had no money made models and trinkets of every kind to barter with; today they are rare objects and highly valued all over the world. A man in the foreground is making something to sell, and behind him a boxing match is held for entertainment. Note the open water channels where the water flowed by gravity through the yards to individual prison blocks (courtesy Dartmoor Prison Museum).

of stockings, and canvas shoes with wooden soles, all of which were supposed to last 18 months. The rising cost of the war forced the authorities to trim back on expenses; at a later stage all incoming prisoners were examined and a list made of their clothing needs with the exception of what they already possessed. Then a ticket was handed to them signed by the agent or his deputy listing the articles they were given. No article was replaced unless the prisoner produced his ticket, and everything he was issued with had to be returned when he was either transferred or released.

The severity with which these rules were enforced was cruelly illustrated in 1814 when the French war ended and men were being released, in some cases after a total of 11 years in captivity. One Frenchman who could not produce his bedding intact was prevented from joining his comrades for the march home and killed himself by cutting his own throat in despair.

Try and imagine what it must have been like to be taken prisoner and to find yourself confined within gray stone walls, without heat or light and with nothing to do. The loss of personal freedom has a devastating effect on some men; this is borne out by the surgeons in the depots and more especially on the hulks, who in their reports concerning chest infections and the like said death was often brought about by "moral despair" as much as the foul air and conditions generally. Nevertheless, the first prisoners to arrive at Dartmoor soon settled in and the talented ones quickly found ways to earn a little money with which to improve their lot. Most Frenchmen

"Spinning Jenny." This delightful object made by a French prisoner from meat bones saved from his rations was for sale several years ago in a saleroom at Tavistock. It was a mere 4½ inches high and in working order. Turning the small handle at the bottom set the cog wheel in motion; it in turn operated the loom; the lady's arms moved to and fro and her head turned from left to right, thus creating a realistic imitation of a weaver at work. It was sold, appropriately, to representatives from a French museum (author's photograph).

This beautiful bone ship model of the *San Pareil* was bought at auction by Mr. and Mrs. R. Brandon of Chudleigh in Devon, England, in the 1960s. It has an interesting history linking it to Dartmoor Depot. The model carries a plaque dedicating it to a Major C.J. Alexander from his son and daughter, Major C.W. Alexander and Mrs. C. Watson. After the model appeared on British television there was an inquiry from Major C.W. Alexander's family, who recognized it, and after some correspondence during which a photo was forwarded to them, his widow was able to confirm it had belonged to the Alexander family for as long as anyone could remember. The Alexander family home was at Yarmouth, Isle of Wight (the large island off Portsmouth), where they lived for generations. It was also where Daniel Alexander, the architect who designed and supervised the building of Dartmoor Depot, once lived and was buried in the churchyard. Is it too much of a coincidence to suggest he acquired the model during the period between the first prisoners being interned at Dartmoor Depot and the completion of the building work? (courtesy Roger Brandon).

certainly tried to make the best of things and there was no shortage of men willing to work. As a result money began to circulate inside the prison in a variety of ways. In addition to those who served les lordes, there were the men paid by the authorities for working as previously mentioned, the barbers being employed to save the expense (not to mention the hazards) of issuing the prisoners with scissors or razors of their own. By the time Americans began arriving in 1813 there were more than 500 men in work. The cash that was earned soon passed into other hands, mainly through gambling, the curse of every depot and which was referred to as the "French disease" (an unkind phrase when in fact British captives in France were equally addicted). The problem was worse on the hulks, where there was not even a market held.

In the market, many prisoners, probably those without money, traded or sold models of ships,[1] wooden cabinets, workboxes, ornaments and all kinds of novelties in return for little luxuries. There soon developed a huge demand for these articles, which were manufactured to a high degree of perfection from leftover meat bones and odds and ends. Examples of the Frenchmen's skill can be seen today in museums all over Britain, exquisitely made and beautiful to behold.

The guards, besides checking for fair prices, were expected to prevent "bad books" and obscene toys from being exchanged. Straw hats and articles made of wool by prisoners were also forbidden on the grounds; it would have encouraged the men to tear up their blankets and extract straw from their bedding, leaving them vulnerable during the winter months. More important still, a large cottage industry was operated in country districts by women and children who made woolen gloves and straw hats to sell. In most cases their very livelihood depended on this extra income, and this was recognized by the magistrates who could be relied upon to issue forbidden notices where necessary.

Illicit dealings of another kind took place in the market square under the noses of the authorities. Some clever Frenchmen who were expert forgers used their expertise to manufacture coins and banknotes to such perfection that local banks were compelled to send officials to the depots to examine and initial their firm's notes before exchange. Eventually things got so bad the death penalty was introduced for any British person caught participating in this offense. At Dartmoor a militiaman who got involved in an escape attempt and was paid in forged notes was condemned to death after attempting to spend the money at the market. Yet these transgressions continued to be committed. In February 1812 Captain Cotgrave closed the market to drive home the point that forgery would not be tolerated and was supported by the Transport Office, which later issued this statement: "The market is now to be opened but you are to apprize [the prisoners] and not to put notices in writing, that if any forged notes or counterfeit coin should be again discovered to be issued in the prison, the market will be shut and not again opened on any account whatsoever."

Again it made no difference, and the threat was never carried out. As late as January 1814, when the French war was all but won, Captain Shortland received a letter from the Transport Office advising him that "prisoner D'Orangi who is confined in the cachot for having uttered forged notes must remain where he is until further orders as the Board do not consider 2 months confinement a sufficient punishment for a crime which in a British subject would have been punished with Death."

With the spread of commerce and regular money coming in from wage earners, the scene was set for trade to evolve among the prisoners themselves. Enterprising men set up coffee stalls within the prisons using ingredients bought at market and doubtless a few secret additives of their own; others used their ingenuity selling popular snacks manufactured from market produce; there were shoe repairers and tailors at work and one man had a stall selling second-hand clothes acquired from the officers.

There gradually developed a busy township within the prison walls where every level of society, culture, and trade was represented. Within this milling mass of toilers were many who possessed no ability whatsoever, and of these the lucky ones found paid jobs doing the menial work in the prison, sweeping and cleaning for example, but there were not vacancies for them all. Many of the unemployed men sat about all day in utter despair, finally sinking into a stupor. Then there were scoundrels who were determined not to work at all and battened on to those who did, begging or stealing from them. There were quarrels, an inevitable consequence of keeping sturdy young men in close confinement, which often ended in fights and the occasional murder. Among the hierarchy, the officers and gentlemen who lived in the *Petit Cautionnement*, such matters were settled in the approved manner — by dueling. Their weapons were homemade swords fashioned from wooden staves with knives, razors, or compass points attached to them. In skilled hands they could inflict terrible injuries and there were several fatalities. There were quarrels up to the end of their captivity: as late as May 1814, by which time the French war was over and the prisoners were about to be repatriated, a duel took place between Jean Vigneaux and Michael Frappin in which the latter was killed. In August, by which time all his comrades had left for home, Vigneaux still languished in Exeter jail awaiting trial for murder. The lower ranks settled their differences with improvised knives made of glass or nails embedded in wooden handles, with equally serious consequences. In 1810 the Plymouth coroner complained that in four months of that year he had conducted more inquests than in the previous ten years, some indication perhaps of the peacefulness of rural Devon before the Frenchmen came (although not all fatalities were the result of dueling, of course, because every death at the depot, from whatever cause, was investigated). The coroner spoke on behalf of the farmers and trades people who were called upon to act as jurors, with the result they were granted an extra four pence a day for expenses.

6. Life Inside the War Depot

The most common cause of dissent among the prisoners was the gambling. With so little to do and so much spare time on their hands, even for those who worked, gambling provided the main diversion, and to some it became an obsession to the point where they gambled and lost everything they had, including their clothes and bedding. This was to court death in the winter months, yet it spread like an epidemic, robbing men of their senses as well as their belongings. They played a form of "Pitch and Toss," and "Vingt-et-un," literally translated as "Twenty-one" (known today as "Pontoon").

There were races too, with rats as runners when morsels of food were strategically placed to entice them into the open, at which time someone would shout or whistle loudly to startle them and send them scampering to their hidey holes. The speed with which they achieved this decided the winners and bets were made on these creatures, some of whom came to be well-known and affectionately named. Confirmed gambling addicts were said to have bet on ridiculous events such as the number of turns a sentry might make in a given time, or on the lengths of straw plucked at random from someone's bedding. When possessions, clothes and bedding were lost some poor wretches staked their rations, the losers handing over perhaps several days' rations, a gamble with death when they sacrificed their subsistence to unscrupulous comrades. It is a terrible fact that some men did die as a result. Those in charge of the Depot did what they could to stop this vile practice but to no avail. The maximum punishment agents were empowered to mete out under the regulations was 10 days in the Black Hole on two-thirds rations, and they did not hesitate in awarding it to evil men, some of whom even traded on their winnings by setting up shop selling rations. The Transport Office gave the agent its full support at all times. A letter to Captain Cotgrave in April 1812 directed him "to keep the prisoners who have been detected in purchasing clothing and provisions of their fellow prisoners in the Cachot, on short allowance, until further orders."

He later threatened to close the market and the prisoners' stalls as well, which had the effect of terminating the practice for a short while, but there were always men who could not resist the lure of the gambling tables and were prepared to put themselves at the mercy of the operators to indulge their whims.

Looking back from the relative comfort of our modern world we can scarcely conceive the way of life the prisoners had to endure. The war dragged on and they were marooned on a stone island in a wild part of the English countryside exposed to storms that often buffeted around the depot in winter such that a man could hardly stand. Showers of rain and sleet battered them at times, penetrating their clothing in an instant should they venture outside their prison blocks, and there was no way of drying their clothes or getting warm. Shipboard life was hard but it was also active and kept the men fit and able to shrug off hardships; in the depot there was little or no physical activity and consequently they fell easy prey to disease.

We should remember the majority of the French (and many Americans too) came from homes in milder sunny climates, consequently they suffered a miserable existence on the moor. The often delightful summer interludes served only to extend their misery, trapped as they were inside the high stone walls year on year. Our wildest imaginings therefore would not conjure up an accurate vision of the life the "Romans" lived. They represented the lowest extremes of life within the prison. These horrible creatures are forever cursed by the name accorded to them in grim jest because their antisocial habits caused them to be banished to the Cockloft of No. 4 block (which they called *Le Capitole*, hence their title "Romans"). Other prisoners labeled them "Kaiserlics" because their leader regarded himself as "Emperor," a self-appointed general who ruled them with the help of a few picked henchmen. Their status was that of men who had lost or gambled away everything they had, including their self-respect. As a result they went about naked as the day they were born all the year round, starving curs who spent their days fighting and scrabbling over scraps of offal and filth often plucked from the drains. They sold their rations as they sold everything else that came into their possession and roamed the yards scavenging or stealing, always on the prowl for castoffs or leavings. So repulsive and dangerous were they the authorities forcibly moved them to No. 4 block, around which a wall was built to separate them from the other men.

Riddled with vermin, filthy in mind and body, practicing every conceivable form of vice, they somehow survived the way of life they had chosen. They survived the epidemics too (the weaker ones probably died quickly), leaving the survivors to form what was probably the most reviled community in any prison anywhere in the world. On more than one occasion they were forcibly scrubbed and clothed in an effort to get them to accept decent standards, but in vain. Everything they were given was soon lost and they resumed their revolting style of living, unwanted and shunned. It is recorded their only form of covering when they ventured out was a kind of poncho made from old blankets with a hole in the middle for their heads, and even this attire was shared. Finally their guardians came to the conclusion they were beyond redemption or help.

On October 16, 1813, following a nasty incident when they fought the American prisoners who had been interned with them, the four hundred and more "Romans" were marched to Plymouth under heavy guard and confined aboard the hulks until the war ended. It is amazing to learn that some of the very worst of men found fame and fortune at home after the war. Francis Abell (*Prisoners of War in Britain 1756–1815*) tells us at least one entered the priesthood and others entered into government service, reaching high rank. Here surely is a wealth of material for psychiatrists to study!

7

French Freemasons at Dartmoor

A Freemasons Lodge was established in Dartmoor Prison by the first French prisoners to arrive there in 1809. It was named *De la Reunion* and was active up to 1814. Freemasonry was widespread among the French armed forces (as it was with the British) and of course many of them were captured. Their lodges operated by "ambulatory discretion," a term signifying they retained their identity and validity wherever they happened to be. The first Lodge in the French army was *La Parfait Union*, which was founded in 1759. By 1787 there were more than 70, with many more to come.

How was it possible for French prisoners at Dartmoor to operate a lodge inside the depot, record their activities and retain the privacy they required for their meetings? Determination, enthusiasm and a strong sense of brotherhood would not have sufficed — help was needed, which could only have come from the brothers among the British who guarded them. The concept of Freemasonry advocated by and practiced under United Grand Lodge of England (founded in 1717) which administers lodges in England and Wales, as well as many more overseas, allows a great deal of flexibility to its members on condition that (among other things):

1. They regard their first duty to be a good citizen and to obey the laws of the country they live and work in.
2. Membership is open to all races and creeds, providing they believe in a supreme being by whatever name that being may be called.
3. Religion and politics are not discussed in the lodge.

Within these guidelines some assistance to French prisoners everywhere was possible without breaking any civil or moral law. There are several recorded instances where French officers living on parole were welcomed into

7. French Freemasons at Dartmoor

English lodges and Englishmen were admitted to French lodges, including the one at Dartmoor Depot.[1]

The foremost authority on the French prisoners' lodges in this country, the late W. Brother John T. Thorp of Leicester, spent most of his adult life researching them both at home and in France. He died in 1932 and bequeathed his fine collection of certificates to the Leicester Lodge of Research at Freemasons' Hall, Leicester. He was assisted in his work by Bro. F. J.W. Crowe, formerly of Ashburton, who later moved to Torquay. Together they succeeded in tracing more than 50 lodges founded by French prisoners of war. Among them were *De La Reunion* (Reunited) at Dartmoor Prison and *De la Reunion* on the Plymouth hulk *Bienfaisant*.

It seems amazing that on June 24, 1809, just one month after the first batch of French prisoners were admitted to Dartmoor Depot, a meeting of Lodge *De la Reunion* was held within its walls. The explanation is a simple one, however. Among the first prisoners to be transferred to Dartmoor from the Plymouth hulks were men from the hulk *Bienfaisant* at Plymouth, where there was already a lodge called *De la Reunion*. It is no coincidence that the Dartmoor Lodge bore the same name, for they were one and the same. In *A History of Freemasonry in Normandy* by Bro. H. de Loucelles (published in 1875), the author describes the formation of the lodge on board the *Bienfaisant* on June 18, 1804. He obtained his information from the minute books of the lodge, which contained detailed accounts of their activities. The final meeting on board the hulk is mentioned. It took place May 21, 1809, when a resolution was passed that the activities of the lodge "be suspended in consequence of the removal of its members ... and that the Minutes and list of members be packed up and sealed with the seal of the Lodge; and that the W. Master (M. Le Corps) be requested to take charge of them and on his arrival in France to deposit them in the archives of his Mother Lodge, 'Amitie' of Havre."

It would seem the prisoners expected to be exchanged, but they were mistaken. Instead they were transferred to Dartmoor, and it was to be another three years (December 27, 1812, to be precise) before M. Le Corps was able to fulfil his obligation to deposit the records in his home lodge at Havre, where they were located more than 100 years later by two associates of Thorp. They told him they were "so saturated and damaged by damp as to be quite illegible and useless." Such was not the case though, because they were retrieved at a still later date (after Thorp's death) by W. Bro. Lionel Vibert, who reported the writing was faded but still legible, enabling him to read every word of it. What emerged was startling, for among the pages of the books he found a loose sheet on which were written details of a meeting on June 24, 1809. This was a month after the evacuation of the *Bienfaisant* and

Certificate issued to Captain Becot. Several certificates were presented to members of the Dartmoor Lodge either on release or when transferred. They were a form of reference from their fellow Brothers confirming his membership and rank and signed by an official of the lodge. Captain Marc Guillaume Becot's document bears the signatures of five members of the original lodge on the *Bienfaisant* hulk (author's photograph, reproduced by permission of W.W. Glover, Freemasons Hall of Research, Leicester, England).

therefore could only have been an account of the first meeting of lodge *De la Reunion* at Dartmoor Depot.

Vibert wrote: "There can be no question that this meeting, with its eighteen visitors and thirteen candidates, was in fact the inauguration of a new Lodge 'La Reunion of the Orient of Dartmoor.'" The opening words of the minutes (translated) read: "Under the auspices of the Grand Orient of France ... the members of the regular Lodge 'La Reunion' held on board the hulk Bienfaisant, floating prison at Plymouth, having reassembled at Dartmoor, have opened a Lodge in the usual manner...." The following nine listed members who signed the minutes of the inaugural meeting at Dartmoor also attended the last meeting that was held on the hulk. They were: Le Corps (F), Anquetil, Moutardier (F), Gilles, L'Amy (F), Ange Colas, Du Temple (F), Cordonnier, Mee, Lassalle and Pagalet (those marked *F* were founding members on the *Bienfaisant*).

A number of certificates issued by the prisoners' lodges have been found. Thorp said there were at least 44 and he possessed 24 of them (all of which he bequeathed to the Leicester Lodge). He also indicated they were not certificates in the true sense that Masons understand them, which are documents confirming a member's rank and Masonic origin, signed and sealed with an official seal. They were, he said, "a Clearance or Travelling Certificate, only issued by a private Lodge to which a brother belongs, and only when he is leaving the Lodge temporarily or permanently ... it is a certificate of character and letter of recommendation signed, not by an official who had never seen him, but by the Brethren among whom he had lived and worked." They were therefore a kind of passport.

One of the most beautiful of these documents was issued at Dartmoor Depot to the captain of a French merchant ship, Marc Guillaume Becot, on July 6, 1810, a year after his attendance at the inaugural meeting, and it has

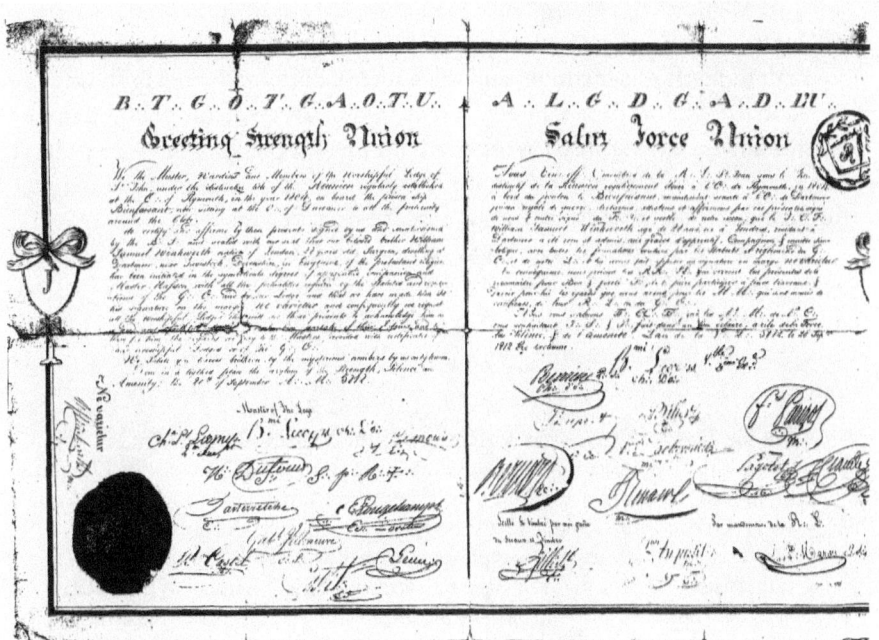

Winkworth's certificate is a rare find kindly located for the author by the Library and Museum of Freemasonry, London. There were numerous French lodges established in the parole towns where relations with the inhabitants often became so friendly Englishmen were on occasion admitted to them, but to see an English official at the war depot honored in this way is exceptional. Although he is referred to as "Surgeon," he does not appear on any official list as such, but on an old map of the depot there is a dwelling shown as "Mr. Winkworth's House," so he must have held a position of responsibility. It has been suggested he may have worked as an assistant to a surgeon and rendered some significant act of kindness to have earned such respect from a group of prisoners (courtesy Library and Museum of Freemasonry).

been the author's privilege to examine this certificate. The material is of fine linen which has ensured its wonderful state of preservation — all the more remarkable when we consider that such a document would have been kept about Captain Becot's person at the depot, on the march to the coast after being released and during his voyage home. Among the signatures on his certificate are those of five men who were together on the *Bienfaisant*.

On September 20, 1812, another certificate was issued at Dartmoor of exceptional interest because it was given to an Englishman. It is not mentioned by Thorp and we can only conclude it was one of those he predicted might one day be found. It is in the Library of United Grand Lodge, London.[2] The document relates to William Samuel Winkworth, who is referred to as "Surgeon," although there is no evidence to confirm this other than a reference to "Mr. Winkworth's House" on a map of the Depot by John Wethams dated 1812. We can be fairly sure he was on the medical staff, as he was important enough to merit this mention, and the house in question is among those allocated to the doctors. Ron Chudley, a retired journalist who directed the author to this document, surmised Winkworth may have been apprenticed to a local doctor, in which case he would not have needed formal qualifications in order to practice. This would explain his absence from the records.

How did an Englishman come to be initiated into a French prisoner of war lodge? The only inference to be drawn is he rendered some kind of service to his French patients that was above the call of duty, and this was a gesture of appreciation. The wording on the English half of his certificate is as follows:

> We the Master, Wardens and Members of the Worshipful Lodge of St. John, under the distinctive title of the Reunion regularly established at the Orient of Plymouth, in the year 1804 on board the prison ship Bienfaissant, now sitting at the Orient of Dartmoor to all the Fraternity around the globe:
> Do certify and affirm by these presents signed by us and countersigned ... and sealed with our seal that our beloved brother William Samuel Winkworth, native of London, 28 years old, Surgeon, dwelling at Dartmoor, near Tavistock, Devonshire, in England, of the Protestant religion, has been initiated in the symbolical degrees of apprentice, companion, and Master Mason, with all the formalities required ... and that we have made him set his signature on the margin ne varieteur and consequently we request all the worshipful Lodges that will see these presents to acknowledge him as a true and faithful freemason.

This transcript further affirms the connection between the *Bienfaisant* and Dartmoor lodges. Nearly three months later Le Corps was home in France, where he fulfilled his promise to deposit the minutes with his home lodge at Havre. There were three books in all with a register of members' names, including those of 24 merchant captains, 50 Navy officers, and 6 medical officers. The lodge at Dartmoor continued its activities up to at least 1814, as is proved by the certificate issued in June that year to Jean Felix Lefort, sergeant major of the 2nd Marine Artillery. This document was discovered by Mr. Crowe. Part of the transcript reads: "True testimony to the Masonic qualities, to the agreeable character, and to the social virtues of our dear Brother Jn. Felix Lefort, native of Troismereux, Dept. of Oise...." One of the signatories to this certificate was Gilles (Guardian of the Seals), who was initiated into the lodge in June 1805 and had therefore been a prisoner for nine years at least, and was probably its longest serving member.

It may be deduced that the majority of Freemasons among the prisoners everywhere were officers who would have had a degree of comfort and privacy denied their men who were herded into overcrowded depots with no parole opportunities. In the parole towns it would have been easy to set up and operate a lodge. This was certainly not the case on the hulks (in any case the officers were not kept on prison ships), but most officers had private funds on which they were allowed to draw; any lack of assistance from their guards could almost certainly have been overcome by a bribe or two. In any case their activities were often commendable; for example, it is recorded that when the charity box was passed at the end of every meeting the proceeds were used to alleviate the sufferings of their comrades, whether Masons or not.

There must have been Americans, too, who were members of the Brotherhood and who shared their activities in the depot, but to date the author has been unable to verify this. Likewise, American officers on parole would have had Freemasons among them, some of whom would most certainly have participated in the French lodge's activities. Bearing in mind what we already know concerning the records being taken to France at the end of hostilities, surely it is there somewhere that any American involvement would be found.[3]

8

Ways Out of Dartmoor and the Hulks

There were only four ways to get out of Dartmoor or any other war prison. The general entry books which were used to register the personal details of every prisoner taken into captivity also recorded the method of his departure. The particulars were arranged in columns which recorded prisoners' names, rank, unit, where captured, and the date of his departure under one of these four headings:

- E = Exchanged. There was a system of prisoner exchange whereby prisoners were repatriated in return for a corresponding number of British men of equal rank.
- D = Discharged. During hostilities this meant either being exchanged (as above), transferred to another depot or to the hulks. Troublemakers and recaptured escapees were prime candidates for transfers. When the wars ended a "Discharge" entry in the book meant repatriation, followed by the name of a port and final destination.
- R = Run (escaped). There were several escapes from Dartmoor, from the hulks, and by officers on parole.
- DD = Discharged Dead. The number of dead and their burials have already been noted for Dartmoor.

Dartmoor Depot was run by captains of the Royal Navy, and the style of the entries shown above is similar to the records kept aboard ship and by the military. Every prisoner was allocated a number, and in addition to his personal details, very precise notes were taken as to where he was captured, what ship or army unit he was serving in at the time, and relevant dates. Name and rank were supplemented by details of appearance:

- Person. This referred to a man's build, i.e., tall, short, thin, slender, heavy, stout.
- Visage. The prisoner's facial characteristics, i.e., round, long, oval, sharp.
- Complexion. Could be sallow, pale, fresh, weather-beaten, black.
- Marks. Tattoos and scars are obvious features here, but a record was also made of birth marks, genetic defects (hare lip, for example), moles and freckles, and the marks left by disease, such as pock marks.

Every man therefore had a "word picture" on record, and many of their descendants, through the Public Record Offices, have obtained a very accurate description of their ancestors, which in many cases bear a strong resemblance to themselves. This information was extremely useful in tracking down escapees and deserters. Many men "went over the wall" from Dartmoor, often in groups, having bribed the sentries to help them or simply taking a chance and running. A great number of prisoners who were captured prior to Wellington's Peninsula campaign were privateers, some of them desperate men who would not hesitate to kill anyone who got in their way, and there were occasions when murder was committed during escape bids. One cannot but admire those civilians who apprehended them and earned every penny of their reward for doing so.

Some men with escape in mind bided their time and cultivated acquaintances on the outside — the market traders, for example. It was through them that more than one prisoner managed to obtain a change of clothing, often smuggled in to them out of affection or misguided sympathy, making it possible for a prisoner to join with them on their departure and be miles away before roll call. A Dartmoor farmer called Palmer was detected giving a disguise to a Frenchman and was brought before the local magistrates, who promptly awarded him a year in jail and fined him £5. One famous incident of this kind involved a French navy officer called Louis Vanhille who was sent to Dartmoor for breaking the terms of his parole. He was supplied with civilian clothes by a market trader from Tavistock called Mary Ellis and got clean away. With the help of friends he had made while on parole in Launceston (Cornwall), he spent several months on the run before making his way to Bristol, where he embarked on a ship bound for Jamaica, hoping to make his way from there to the United States (a neutral country) and thence to France. Unfortunately for him, when the ship docked at Jamaica his identity was discovered and he was sent back to England to spend the rest of the war confined on board a Chatham hulk.

For a man on the run the wild and lonely moor itself was their most formidable guardian. There were and are few trees, and caves are a rarity, so an escapee would find no shelter either from summer sun or winter cold and the few inhabitants could get a monetary reward for turning in a fugitive. The scene before you is typical of the moorland surrounding Princetown; the road is that which was trod by French and Americans on their way to prison and the view is just as they must have seen it (photograph by James Stevenson).

There are numerous romantic stories about these escapades, but in fact escape was not easy. Severe punishments were meted out to soldiers found to have helped in an escape; nine hundred lashes was a common sentence in the British Army at that time and serious cases were concluded by a firing squad. In the depots there were roll calls every day and twice a week they took place in the presence of the agent when each man personally answered to his name. When the Americans took up work outside the prison they discovered that an escape brought retribution to the entire group and everyone forfeited their accumulated pay (they were paid three months in arrears) which in itself was a very effective deterrent. For a prisoner who did escape, there was the problem of finding his way in an alien land, obtaining food, evading capture and being brave enough to take any risk in order to get home. Even then there was a good chance of being wounded or captured again in the next engagement with the enemy.

For most prisoners the one hope that sustained them was the possibility

8. Ways Out of Dartmoor and the Hulks

of being exchanged. They dreamed about the day their turn would come. Throughout the wars with France men on both sides were exchanged at intervals on the basis of equal numbers and rank. The conditions varied from time to time, usually as a result of real or imagined breaches of the terms. During the Napoleonic wars the system allowed grade for grade and man for man. Problems then arose because Britain held by far the greater number of captives. During the Peninsula Campaign Napoleon tried (unsuccessfully) to negotiate the return of 3,000 Frenchmen for 1,000 British, the balance to be made up of Spanish and Portuguese prisoners because he was afraid once the British got all their men back they would terminate the agreement. There was so much distrust on both sides the Duke of Wellington, when fighting in the Peninsula, was instructed to negotiate exchanges man for man on the spot whenever the opportunity occurred. The British claimed it was because the French and their allies had reneged on the agreements so many times a serious imbalance often occurred, always to the advantage of the enemy. Consequently, there was uncertainty and irregularity of exchanges, even its suspension for a time.

The prisoners bore the burden of all this in two ways: the lack of exchanges meant they were in ever worsening conditions of overcrowding and their period of captivity was prolonged. Loss of their turn of exchange was one of the ways the British used to punish prisoners for misdemeanors — selling their bedding, for example — and the rules were often bent to rid the depots of sick or wounded men who were unlikely to fight again. Some men sold or gambled away their turn of exchange.

The main ports through which exchanges were made were Portsmouth, Dartmouth and Plymouth, all of which were within easy marching distance of the depots or the hulks. Morlaix was the predominant French port which was used. The whole business was fraught with danger and abuses, which compelled both sides to draw up strict regulations for the cartel ships that were hired by the two governments to convey exchanged prisoners across the channel. The main provisions, which in themselves give an idea of the sort of things that might occur, were:

1. The flag of the country of destination as well as the ship's national flag to be flown continuously.
2. Cartels to be unarmed and not to carry weapons or goods.
3. All passengers to be searched for letters or gold coins, which were forbidden articles.
4. Cartel ships were not permitted to go alongside or their crews allowed ashore.

There was a shortage of gold in France resulting in a lucrative trade in "guinea running." It was a flourishing sideline not only for smugglers but for ships' captains and agents. Articles of concealment ranged from hollow walking sticks to shoes with false heels. Probably the most profitable "trade" was in accepting bribes from escaped prisoners looking for a passage to France, a situation that got so bad the authorities arranged for embarkation to coincide with the tides, thereby enabling ships to set sail without delay once their official passengers were on board. Anyone found hanging about in dockside areas without good reason was arrested and questioned, which soon put a stop to that particular mode of escape.

The French in general are not remembered for their desperate escape attempts or the dishonor associated with those officers who broke their parole by running. They live on in British history as a brave enemy who in defeat often accepted their fate with dignity despite the hardships of prison life, the worst of which was to be condemned to the hulks or *pontons*, as the French called them. The reader will recall it was as a result of the terrible conditions on board these dreadful floating hovels that Dartmoor Prison came to be built. They were literally carcasses of redundant men o'war, many of them captured enemy ships which had for years been rotting away in half forgotten backwaters and harbors. Necessity brought them into use, firstly to hold the overwhelming numbers of prisoners and later to confine the troublesome and degraded prisoners from the depots.

To refer to the hulks as vessels or ships is to cast a slur on those normally beautiful objects. They were black, smoky, dirty, smelly and ugly — resembling burnt out wrecks. They degraded the proud names they bore and invoked heavy criticism from the British themselves (although convicts were confined on hulks for many years afterwards apparently without comment). The prison ships were usually manned by a Royal Navy lieutenant, master's mate, midshipman, and 20 ordinary sailors, many of whom were wounded veterans. The armed guards were drawn from the Marines at Portsmouth and Chatham, but at Plymouth they were mainly militiamen, each unit having an ensign, corporal, and 25 privates. At least one militiaman shared the prisoner's view that "the naval officers who commanded the hulks were totally unfit for any other kind of service," an opinion recorded in a published (anonymous) diary titled *Marches of the 1st Devon Militia*.[1] In fact many of the naval officers and veteran crews had seen active service against French and Americans and had little sympathy for them.

A prison ship held between 400 and 800 men on average. The death rate was higher than in the shore prisons and at Portsmouth in 1812 peaked at 4 percent, mainly from chest complaints as a result of breathing foul air for long periods below decks. Another contributory factor was the contaminated and evil smelling mud flats exposed at low tides. Try and imagine the orlop (lowest) deck of the *Brunswick*, which was acknowledged to be one of the better vessels. The decks measured 120 feet by 40 feet and were a mere 4 feet, 10 inches high so that few men could stand upright. Crammed into this space were 460 men, living in hideous conditions with hammocks slung so close together many of them had to make do on the deck. For security reasons only a few men were permitted on the main deck at any one time for exercise; in fact the only real exercise they got was the physical work involved in hoisting aboard fresh water and provisions from the supply boats. These were strictly monitored and only came alongside after being searched for contraband — liquor, newspapers, candles and so on.

Mental boredom was the biggest burden the prisoners on the hulks had to bear. There was so little to occupy them and with no market or social contact of any kind, gambling inevitably became the main pastime, accompanied by the attendant evils of men wagering their clothes and rations, some of them dying as a result. The naval surgeons allocated to these floating hovels were expected to live on board, but the vast majority were known to have practices ashore and lived on land with their families; consequently many of their patients on the ships were close to death before a doctor even saw them. The scrubbing of the decks and periodic airing of bedding were not always enforced. A number of surgeons were dismissed for neglect of duty and brought shame on a service universally respected and admired.

There was shame of another kind on the part of officials and contractors who provisioned the ships, namely corruption and fraud. In an advertisement in the *London Gazette* for March 17, 1814, tenders were invited "for the victualling of Prisoners of War at Mill Prison, Plymouth, and on the prison ships. Duration of contract to be six months ... each tender to be accompanied by letters from Respectable Persons engaging to become bound in the sum of £500 for the due performance of the contract."

Perhaps this last was an attempt to stamp out racketeering, it being well known that provisions for sailors on board His Majesty's ships were notorious for poor quality and short weight, resulting in (futile) letters of complaint from captains who had not had an opportunity to examine the goods until they were opened for consumption at sea.

There was little chance of an honest deal for the prisoners on the hulks. In one incident at Plymouth the French prisoners rioted and threw their provisions overboard, the surface of the sea becoming a mass of floating debris which included whole cheeses, stinking and inedible. A similar event at Chatham on board the *Samson* ended with the guards opening fire and killing

Most recaptured escapees were transferred back to the hulks at Plymouth—an effective deterrent in itself on top of spending time in the Black Hole and losing their turn of exchange. Artist Paul Deacon has captured the grim reality of prison ships in this oil painting on canvas (by permission of Paul Deacon).

fifteen Frenchmen. A prisoner afterward wrote: "I do not believe any Frenchman lives who hates this nation more than I do and all I pray for is that I may be able to revenge myself on it before I die."

Sometime after this terrible indictment, three Frenchmen on the same ship drew lots as to who should kill one of the Marine guards. The "winner" could not bring himself to kill their chosen victim, a sergeant with a family, but the debt was paid all the same by stabbing another Marine and killing him. All three prisoners involved were tried and executed.

The reputation of the hulks was well known to the enemy and many French commanders urged their men to greater effort by reminding them of the fate that awaited them on the prison ships if they lost the day. Before the Battle of Waterloo Napoleon addressed his men with these words: "Soldiers! Let those among you who have been prisoners of the English describe to you the hulks and detail the frightful miseries they have endured." Even a British General, Lord Napier, once commented: "The annals of civilised nations furnish nothing more inhuman towards captives of war than the prison ships of England."

8. Ways Out of Dartmoor and the Hulks

One brief appraisal of conditions on the hulks concludes on a lighter note[2] and concerns that very same militia unit doing guard duty at Plymouth. One of the sentries fell overboard and was rescued by a French prisoner called Masse who was afterwards promised his freedom as a reward. This led to a spate of "accidental" near drownings when soldiers were invariably saved in the nick of time by a succession of brave Frenchmen. Suspicions were aroused and Colonel Bastard, their commanding officer, ordered an enquiry with the result the first sentry was court-martialed for complicity in a plot to aid a prisoner. His fate is not recorded but Masse did not get his release and the sentries took greater care not to fall into the sea.

In the light of what we now know about confinement on the hulks, we get some idea of Dartmoor Prison's grim reputation when we read that the Americans on board two of the Plymouth hulks, on learning they might be moved there, "drew back with dread at the very mention of the name." The American prisoners played a large part in Dartmoor Prison's history and have been sadly neglected in the annals of the moor. They undoubtedly reacted more strongly than the French to the treatment they had to bear, their very natures having been nurtured on that sublime state we call freedom. What follows is a story of defiance that was the cause of much disruption and frustration for the authorities.

9

The Americans Arrive

The War of 1812 was a war that nobody won. It never developed into large scale warfare where whole armies faced each other, but there were bitter battles ferociously fought, especially at sea. The Americans emerged from the war with a feeling of pride, having won a number of land and sea fights over the armed might of Great Britain. One incident, the siege of Baltimore, which the British invasion fleet failed to accomplish, became the inspiration for the national anthem, "The Star Spangled Banner." It was composed in 1813 by the young Georgetown lawyer Francis Scott Key, although it was not officially adopted as the anthem until 1931. One of the most famous American victories was at New Orleans when battle-hardened British Redcoats were put to flight by the savage fire power of a concentrated American force. Tragically, this battle was fought on January 6, 1815, after the Treaty of Ghent was signed (the opposing forces did not yet know) and the war was over.

An account of some events that led to the war will help explain the aggravation and ill will felt by the American prisoners of war at Dartmoor.

President James Madison's government laid claim to certain Canadian territories but the British, assisted by various Indian tribes, successfully resisted the several incursions that took place. The immediate cause, however, was of a personal nature and an infringement of American sailors' rights — an expression that became a slogan when hostilities commenced. The war began as a direct result of certain British "Orders in Council" which decreed all foreign vessels trading with France during the war with Napoleon were liable to a duty to be paid according to the value of the cargo and to call at a British port to be examined for contraband. This severely restricted America's trade with the continental countries, which had slumped dramatically during the Treaty of Amiens (when British trading was resumed) and increased when the war with France recommenced in 1803.

By 1807 American trade figures had dramatically improved and it was

9. The Americans Arrive

resented by the British, who maintained that trade closed to neutral countries in time of peace should not be open to them in wartime. With what the United States rightly regarded as high-handed arrogance, the Royal Navy intercepted American ships at sea and searched them for illegal cargoes (arms, for example). The naval boarding parties had no scruples about taking advantage of the opportunity to press crew members into their service which was desperately short of men. Americans were naturally angry and resentful. "Free Trade and Sailors' Rights!" was their cry, and with some justification. Their expanding merchant fleet had led to a high demand for seamen and many British seafarers, some of them Royal Navy deserters, were happy to oblige in return for better conditions and higher rates of pay. It was the British men the naval search parties looked for but they didn't hesitate to press American crewmen who were unable to prove their national identity. On occasion the ship's captain was left with only enough seamen to get his ship safely to port.

In 1796 the American government passed the Act for the Relief and Protection of American Seamen in an effort to prevent them being pressed into British service. U.S. sailors were issued protection certificates[1] on request but there was a flaw: the documents, more often than not, were signed by a customs man or a dockside official, not by a government representative who would have asked for proof of family and birth. This meant that technically anyone who wanted such a document simply turned up and asked for one, and when British sailors took to forging them they became meaningless. It was one of the immediate causes of the War of 1812. Note the detailed description on Ignatious Parsons' certificate and the proud manner with which it is dated: "Twenty seventh day of August in the year of Our Lord 1810 and of the Independence of the United States the thirty fifth."

That great Irish playwright and philosopher Bernard Shaw once said there would never be a peaceful world so long as there was nationalism and how right he was! Here was a new nation having to endure indignities imposed upon it by the very power it had defeated in the American Revolution. It was time for the United States to assert itself, establish its independence anew and demonstrate its worth once and for all. The Republican Party, for whom things were not going too well at this time, needed a boost and saw the war as a way of arousing national fervor. This would be to their advantage because it would distract attention from domestic problems at home.

It was also an opportunity to put a long awaited ambition into effect, namely the conquest of Canada, which Americans had always regarded as their territory by right. They wanted Canada's rich farmlands to help feed a swelling population (the great expansion westward had not yet begun) and the United States government realized the war would provide some justification in pursuing that claim. As for the British, they were determined nothing would stand in the way of victory over the French, and in any case were still smarting after the humiliation of their first defeat by what they still regarded as "rebel" colonists. When both sides remained adamant over their principles, the Americans finally declared war. It was to last two years and eight months, from June 18, 1812, to February 17, 1815.

The British gained an immediate advantage in the number of prisoners taken when American sailors serving in the Royal Navy declared themselves

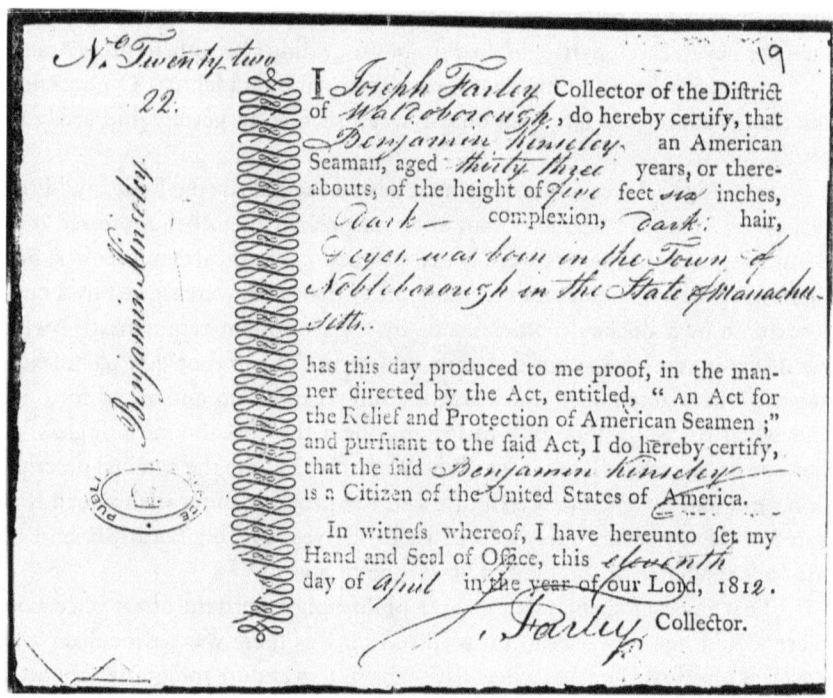

Above and Opposite: American sailors' protection certificates. When British warships stopped American merchant vessels at sea to search for contraband, they had no compunction about impressing crew members into the Royal Navy. Officially they looked for British seamen, but there was no way they could distinguish between them and their American shipmates; consequently men were indiscriminately taken, often leaving the captain just enough crew to reach the nearest port safely. Protection certificates were made available on request and were intended to certify the nationality of the holder, but they soon became meaningless when it was apparent any sailor could apply for one and any dockside official could verify them. The resulting quarrels and unjust treatment of merchant sailors was one of the immediate causes of the War of 1812.

9. The Americans Arrive

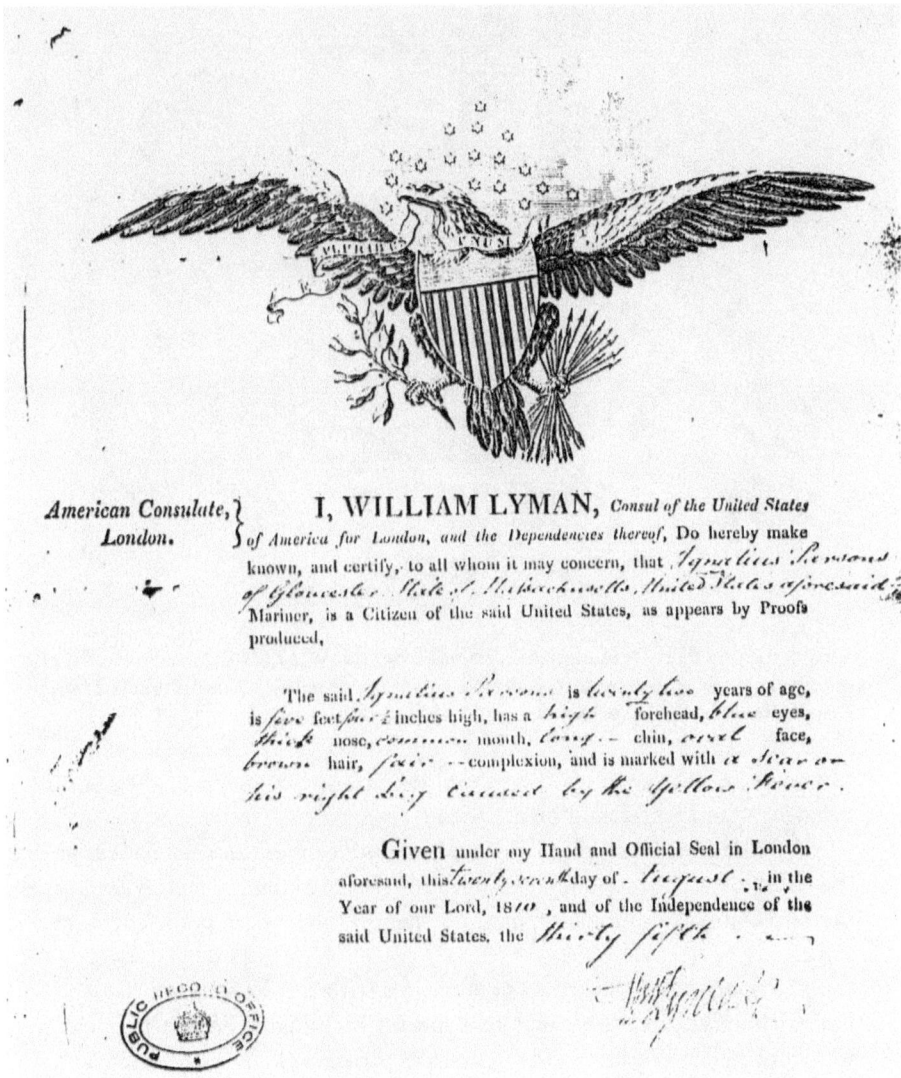

unwilling to fight against their own country and preferred imprisonment to doing so. An estimated 2,500 Americans, volunteers and pressed men were on Royal Navy ships at the time and most of them decided to "declare themselves." There was outrage in America when it became known these same men were not to be regarded as prisoners of war but as renegade sailors. This was grossly unjust when we remember many of them had served the British for years, much of their time on active service against the French. Their plight now was unusual because they were not eligible for exchange and were destined

This design by Paul Deacon depicts scenes from the War of 1812, which was fought mainly at sea by the American Navy backed by privateers, yet outnumbered by the British Royal Navy (by permission of Paul Deacon).

to remain in custody until the war ended, a cause of much of their unruly behavior — and who could blame them?

In addition, every effort was made to induce them to re-enlist either in the Army or the Royal Navy, and a number of men did so, mainly to escape the intolerable conditions imposed on them by their captors to "encourage" them.

This tactic had worked to some degree with the French, and the British Expeditionary Force later sent to America included a French prisoner of war contingent known as the *Chasseurs Brittanique* who took an active part in the conflict there. As with the French, the fact Britain held the greater number of prisoners caused consternation to the Americans when shortage of manpower developed in their armed forces. To help redress the balance and for reasons of national pride, the American government began paying a bounty of $25 per man to privateers, who as a rule preferred to land their prisoners in a neutral country at the first opportunity to save the expense of keeping them on board ship. This payment was later increased to $100 per man. In addition, the government authorized large scale privateering for Americans. Their contribution in harassing, capturing and often destroying

9. The Americans Arrive

In an area of flat undulating land, the Rock at Yelverton was and is an outstanding landmark situated roughly halfway between Plymouth and Princetown. It was here the soldiers from the depot waited for the soldiers escorting prisoners from Plymouth and took over from them. This monumental stone is over 20 feet tall and large enough for the soldiers to huddle in the lee and shelter from rain and sleet showers. The moorland hills are visible in the distance (photograph by James Stevenson).

British vessels went a long way towards redressing the balance of professional fighting men.

At the start of the war there were instances on both sides when abuse of prisoners occurred. This led to a convention being arranged to draw up rules for the proper treatment of captured men. A fixed scale of rations was established in line with those issued to the French and a strict ban on corporal punishment and forced labor was agreed to. The terms of exchange of prisoners included one rear admiral or major general for 30 private soldiers or one petty officer or noncommissioned officer for two private soldiers.

American prisoners were not the easy-going fatalistic type associated with the majority of the French. On the contrary, almost to a man they were unrelenting enemies, even the several British among them, one of the reasons being the harsh treatment they received before arriving Britain. Some of those who declared themselves, for example, were discharged from the Royal Navy with curses ringing in their ears after having fought at Trafalgar and other notable actions. Some of those who were sent to Plymouth went to Mill Prison,

This oil painting on canvas depicts the first American prisoners on the march in the snow. These men were exhausted and exasperated after the long trek from Plymouth. Although the surgeon examined them before they left to ensure their fitness, their living conditions on the hulks left them physically weak and the march was slow and painful. Consequently they were bullied and often prodded with bayonets to keep them moving; in addition the guards threated to shoot to kill if there should be an escape attempt on the way to Dartmoor. It was April 1813 when they trudged the last mile or two in the snow to the depot they had heard so much about—most of it depressing (by permission of Paul Deacon).

but most of them were put on board the hulks *Hector, Ceres,* or *Le Brave* anchored in the Hamoaze. The officers were sent on parole to the English parole towns Ashburton (Devon), Odiham (Shropshire) and Dartmouth (Devon), the most senior ones going to Reading (Berkshire).

Although life on the hulks was grim, the Americans were aware of Dartmoor Depot's evil reputation and dreaded being sent there. Unfortunately for them their fears were realized on April 2, 1813, when 250 of them were landed from the *Hector* and marched to Prince Town. On the 17 mile trek to the moor in pouring rain they passed through Mannamead, then on to Roborough (sometimes referred to as "Jump") and over the downs. At "The Rock," a well known landmark near present day Yelverton, the guards handed them over to soldiers from Dartmoor Depot for the remainder of the journey. As they tramped under heavy escort through Dousland to the wind-swept Dartmoor hills, they were reminded they would be shot to death if any of them broke ranks. The moor was under a layer of snow as they passed under the cold stone arch at the entrance to the prison and into the inner recesses to join the French already there.

The First American Prisoner

The first American prisoner was recorded as follows in the General Entry Books for Dartmoor.

Prison number	1
By what ship or how taken	Impressed
Time when	8 Jan. 1813
Place where	Grenock
Name of prize	Delivered himself up.
Whither man o'war, Privateer or merchant vessel	R.N.
Prisoner's Name	Michael Towers
Quality (rank)	Seaman
Time when received into custody (Dartmoor)	2 April 1813
From what ship and where received	Plymouth
Place of Nativity (birthplace)	Hingham
Age	37
Stature (height)	5 ft. 7 ins.
Person	Stout (muscular)
Visage and complexion	Oval/fresh
Hair	Brown
Eyes	Blue
Marks or wounds	None
Date of supply (bedding, clothing, etc.)	10 Feb. 1813
Exchanged; Run (escaped); Died; Discharged	Discharged to Dartmouth[2]
Date when (Board orders)	30 July 1813
If discharged, whither and by what order	Board Order 27 July 1813

The Americans' reception was not a happy one. All the depots were overcrowded and Dartmoor was no exception; the newcomers were resented by the French as intruders. The Americans in turn were angry and there was soon friction. The authorities responded on May 1 by sending them to No. 4 block to live among the "Romans."

Now their existence was a tough one indeed, as they found themselves cut off from the main prison by high walls and a strongly reinforced gateway. With only the stone walls to look at and the worst of the French for company, one cannot but sympathize with their predicament. They had no money, no opportunity for employment, and it was to be another ten months before Reuben Beasley, their consul and the only American representative in England, was authorized to pay them an allowance. In any case they were barred from the daily market, and desperate men resorted to selling their clothes for a little extra food and tobacco.

The Americans described the prisons as worse than horse stables, where water continually ran down the walls onto the concrete floors that were as cold as ice. They told how they ate their food huddled on the floor around wooden buckets, each containing the ration for six men, each of whom had a wooden spoon and jostled for his share. The overcrowding was so bad their hammocks were slung as many as five high, one above the other in the gloomy, drafty dormitories.

On May 28 another 250 of their countrymen joined them from Plymouth and were soon reduced to the same pitiful state with just the daily ration to sustain them. To add to their misery, they had to endure continuous harassment from the British officers, who did all they could to persuade them to enlist in their service, the Royal Navy in particular. As well as making things intolerable for them in order to encourage enlistment, the authorities offered a bounty as an added inducement. Those who did succumb were instantly segregated from their comrades for their own safety and detained in the guardroom until they could be sent to naval or army establishments. It says much for the stalwart spirit of the American prisoners that out of the 6,000 or more who passed through Dartmoor during the war, fewer than 100 took up the offer. The Americans flogged those they caught volunteering, but it is nonetheless to their credit that so few did, an indication of their resolve as well as Dartmoor's unsavory regime.

10

Yankee Ways

Despite their initial difficulties, the Yankees eventually settled down to make the best of things and in a democratic manner. They elected committees of 12 men who drew up rules to preserve order and discipline. Among the French prisoners a similar system had evolved from the beginning, and it seems the authorities were happy for the prisoners to organize themselves — a more convenient and peaceful way of keeping order. Important decisions were made by the prisoners themselves shouting "Aye!" or "No!" after "criers" circulated among them with announcements and called for their votes. The committees organized courts where offenders were tried and punished for disloyalty or acts which were judged to be against the common good. Punishments ranged from being "sent to Coventry," as we would say to a flogging, usually with hammock cords. The most common offense was stealing, which merited 24 "stripes."

Benjamin Palmer, a prisoner who witnessed these events and afterward wrote a book titled *Diary of a Privateersman*, related how one man was sentenced to 500 stripes (he does not mention the offense), of which he received 75 before his back was so severely cut he was sent to recover before having the rest administered. On another occasion the cooks were caught "skimming the pots"[1] and each of them got 25 stripes across the back. It was rough justice, but who knows what good it did in the long run at a time when brutal treatment was the order of the day. In any case these events cannot fairly be compared to modern day standards.

Here are some of the rules laid down by one of the committees, written and signed by the aforementioned Benjamin Palmer, who was a committee secretary (spelling taken directly from Palmer's book):

Regulations Established by the Committee
Appointed by the Majority of Prisoners

Article 1

Any person or persons who shall be found guilty of Gambling for money or any other thing shall pay 2 Shillings each....

Article 3

Any person or persons who shall be found guilty of Treachery, Theift, or uncleanlyness, shall receive corporal punishment — according to the Nature of the offence — & as the Jury Shall determine.

Article 4

Any person or persons who shall be found guilty of making any nuisance (except in the Necessary) shall be made to clean the same and pay one shilling.

Article 5

Any person or persons who shall be found guilty of washing in the well shall pay 1 shilling for every such offence [this must refer to their drinking water]....

Article 9

Any person who shall have cause of Complaint shall make the same Known to the Committee whose decision shall be definitive unless they shall see fit to call a jury....

Article 11

All moneys collected as fines shall be appropriated to defray the expenses of Pens Ink and Paper &c. and to pay the Constables criers for their trouble — & it shall be the duty of the Committee to appoint a person to Keep a regular account of all receipts and disbursements. It shall be the duty of the Committee to appoint 8 men out of the Sd. Committee to attend in the Cook house, and 2 to attend outside and Inspect the provision[2]....

Article 14

Any one of the Committee who shall be guilty of a breach of any of the foregoing Articles, Shall pay double.

DartmooXr Prison No. 7 p' Order of the Committee Oct. 11th. 1814.

BENJn. F. PALMER
Secty.

It was during their first months at Dartmoor — when the Americans were forced to endure the worst of conditions and subjected to humiliations heaped on them both by their captors and the French prisoners — that a famous sea battle was fought in British waters. It led to an act of chivalry seldom seen in warfare and years later a barbaric revenge taken on fellow Americans by outraged Dartmoor prisoners of war. The story illustrates the best and worst of circumstances when an early 19th century sea battle was fought, and is relevant to certain events that took place at the depot.[3]

The Saga of the Argus *and the* Pelican

This battle was fought in the Irish Channel between two naval Brigs — the American *Argus* (10 guns) and the British HBMS *Pelican* (11 guns), culminating in victory for the *Pelican* and an exceptional act of gallantry by the British when the American commander, Lieutenant William Henry Allen, who died of wounds, was given a public funeral in Plymouth with full military honors. His crew ended up at Dartmoor.

The *Argus* crossed the Atlantic in June 1813 with the American minister to France on board. After landing at L'Orient, it proceeded to raid shipping in the English Channel, sinking or burning several British merchant ships. The *Argus* then made its way into the sea lanes in St. George's Channel (between Britain and Ireland), continuing to destroy shipping and proving to be such a menace the British Admiralty determined it must be stopped.

The *Argus* ran out of luck on August 14 when it was intercepted by the *Pelican* under the command of Capt. John Fordyce Maples, Royal Navy, who had been told his quarry had been sighted in that area the previous day. Although the two vessels were fairly evenly matched the *Argus* was superior in sail and could easily have escaped, but the Captain, Lt. Allen, full of confidence after his recent successes, elected to meet his adversary and fight it out — he actually hove-to and waited for him.

The encounter was brief and bloody. After a short exchange of fire at close range the British managed to get alongside the *Argus* and board it. One of Lt. Allen's legs was shattered by cannon shot at an early stage in the fight and he was out of it five minutes after the first shots were fired. His leg was amputated shortly

This watercolor painting typifies the dashing "Jack Tar" image of early 19th century Navy men. The United States Navy was smaller than the Royal Navy and in the beginning several capital ships were unable to leave harbor because of the British blockade of U.S. ports (which is why privateering was encouraged on such a massive scale). There was a shortage of trained sailors too, which is why the *Argus* crew was given priority on government's orders and exchanged out of captivity at Dartmoor before their time (by permission of Paul Deacon).

This oil painting depicts the battle between the *Argus* and the *Pelican* on August 14, 1813. The American brig *Argus* had destroyed or captured several British merchantmen in a relatively short period and was regarded as a menace to be stopped at all costs. It was tracked down by the Royal Navy brig *Pelican* in St. Georges Channel (between Ireland and Britain). A combination of superior British gunnery, the fact the American Commander Lt. W.H. Allen and most of his officers were seriously wounded soon after the first shots were fired, and the crew was in need of rest after a recent conflict resulted in victory for the British after just 45 minutes (published by permission of Paul Deacon, courtesy M. Chamberlain).

afterwards. Most of the other officers became casualties too, including Midshipman Richard Delphey, who lost both legs by cannon fire and died three hours later. Deprived of effective leadership and weary from previous encounters, the Americans were overwhelmed in hand-to-hand fighting and were compelled to surrender 45 minutes after the battle began.

The *Argus* was taken to Plymouth by a prize crew, arriving there two days later on August 16. On August 18 the commander of the British flagship at Plymouth, Capt. Nash, sent his personal launch with a large cot to convey Lt. Allen, whose condition was fast deteriorating, to the hospital at Mill Prison. The surgeon there was Dr. George MaGrath, who afterwards transferred to Dartmoor Depot and served with distinction at a critical time (to be described later). He rendered every possible assistance and with Mr. Inderwick (the *Argus* surgeon) remained with the patient until the end. William Henry Allen died at 11 P.M.

Lt. Allen was already known to the British on account of the kindness he showed to Royal Navy prisoners taken from the *Macedonian* when it was captured by the U.S. Navy's *United States*, of which he was first lieutenant earlier in the war—hence his burial with full military honors, which took place August 21, 1813. The funeral procession included the band of the Plymouth Division of Marines, a contingent of British Marines marching with reversed arms, eight British Royal Navy captains as pallbearers, and of course the surviving officers of the *Argus*. Allen was laid to rest alongside Midshipman Delphey in a vault at St. Andrews Church in the area between the church itself and Prysten House at the rear. Thus a link with those almost forgotten times exists, but we do not know exactly where the two Americans lie. Their headstone reads as follows:

> SACRED
> To the MEMORY of
> WILLIAM HENRY ALLEN, Esq.
> Aged 27 Years
> Late Commander of the
> United States BRIG ARGUS
> Who died August 18th 1813
> In consequence of a Wound
> Received in Action
> with H.B.M. PELICAN
> August 14th 1813
> ALSO in Remembrance of
> RICHARD DELPHEY, Midshipman
> Aged 18 Years
> U.S.NAVY, Killed in the *same action*
> Whose remains are Deposited
> On the Left
>
> ———
>
> HERE SLEEP THE BRAVE
>
> ———

In his book about the *Argus* incident, Ira Dye wrote: "No detail survives about how their headstone was designed and the epitaph written." He suggests a likely explanation lies with the ship's officers, who would have wanted an American eagle to appear at the top, and when asked by the British stonemason what such an eagle would look like, one of the officers pulled a gilt brass button off his uniform jacket to use as a guide. At the top of the stone is represented an American officer's uniform button of that period: "A circle of thirteen stars, and inside the circle an eagle, its wings half open, its head turned to the right, standing on its right foot with the left talons holding up an oval shield with a foul anchor shown on it."[4]

When the *Argus* reached Plymouth as a prize on August 17, the original crew members on board were immediately transferred to the prison ship *Hector*. On August 23 the *Pelican* sailed into Plymouth with the rest of the *Argus* men, who were at once sent to join their shipmates as above, all except seventeen, who had been accused of being British Royal Navy deserters who had fought against their own country, an offense that carried the death penalty if proved. Their accuser was a fellow crewman called Robinson who confessed to being British himself and most probably was trying to save his own neck. Needless to say his life was thereby placed in great danger from his shipmates and he, together with the seventeen others, was sent to a receiving ship called *Salvador del Mundo* (a captured Spanish battleship) and held in close confinement. Robinson was confined separately for his own safety.

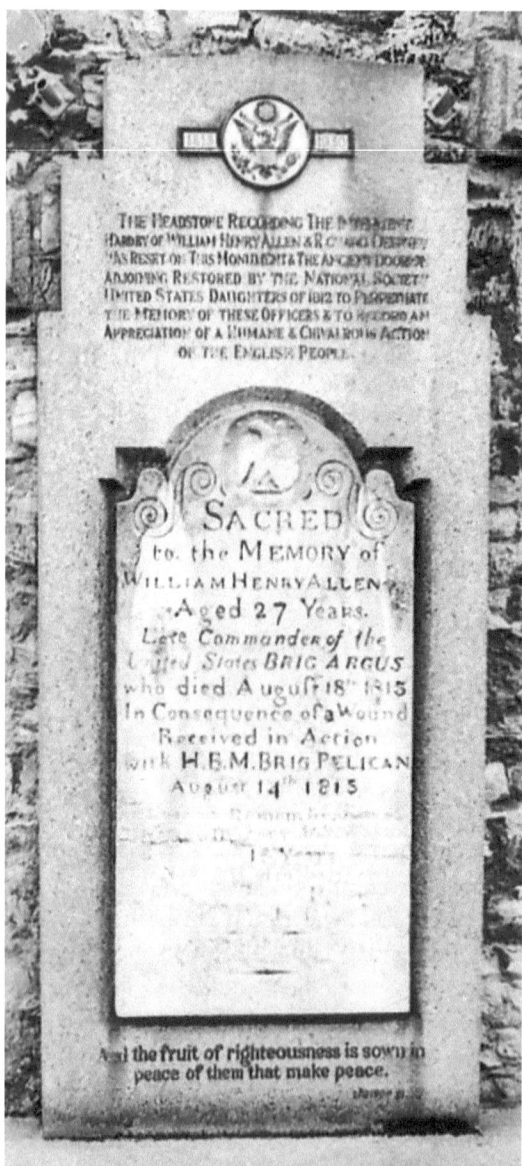

Headstone of Lt. William Henry Allen and Midshipman Richard Delphey, both fatally wounded early in the battle and buried in the churchyard of St. Andrews Church, Plymouth, England. The headstone is mounted on the wall of adjoining Prysten House, where the late Ira Dye discovered it by chance during a stroll around Plymouth. He was immediately curious and inspired to inquire further. This led to his passionate study of that event and the War of 1812. As the photo reveals, the wording has deteriorated badly and requires restoration despite having been renewed twice since first installed (author's photograph).

After an investigation on board this vessel none of the seventeen accused were proved to be British and were transferred to the *Hector*. On May 10, 1814, they and about 170 other prisoners were marched to Dartmoor Depot, where they rejoined their shipmates already there since September 8, 1813. As for Robinson, he was sent to Mill Prison, from which he later escaped and was not seen again.

The only homicide among the Americans at Dartmoor was committed by an *Argus* quartermaster called Thomas Hill, already known among his shipmates as a violent man. He and a fellow crewman, James Henry, had a serious argument and decided to settle their differences in the traditional manner — with their fists. The fight took place in the cockloft of the notorious No. 4 Block, where the Americans were confined at that time, and James Henry soon got the worst of it, Hill beating him so savagely he died on the spot. An inquest was held, as was customary with every death at the prison, and a verdict of manslaughter was recorded, resulting in Thomas Hill being sent to Exeter for trial. He was acquitted and returned to Dartmoor.

In America the *Argus* men were held in high regard because of their successes prior to the encounter with the *Pelican*. They were also the only United States Navy prisoners of war in Dartmoor at that time (the main body of captured Americans so far were privateers), and as trained sailors were badly needed for the conflict. The crewmen knew this and waited expectantly for word of their exchange. They were not disappointed. In October 1814 after being given priority over all other American prisoners in England, the officers and crew of the *Argus* were sent to Dartmouth to board a cartel for home — except one officer on parole at Ashburton.

Midshipman William Pottenger was in the lock-up by order of Ashburton magistrates. A letter dated November 9, 1814, from the Transport Office to Ashburton agent Joseph Gribble states: "No allowance can be made to Mr. Pottage while he remains in the Custody of the Civil Power, but if he should be liberated by the Magistrates before any opportunity offers for his returning to the United States, he will again be admitted to Parole."

This tells us William Pottenger had not broken the terms of his parole or committed any civil offence, because if he had he would have been sent either to Dartmoor or Mill Prison in Plymouth in the first instance, or brought before the civil courts in the second. In fact neither happened — he was married twelve days later to Frances Broom and we may safely conclude this young woman's reputation was at stake, something that was taken very seriously at the time. Under these circumstances a prisoner on parole was obliged to pay a lump sum for the support of a child should there be a birth or marry the lady in question, which is what Midshipman Pottenger did. The late Ira Dye confirmed to the author that Pottenger returned to his home in Philadelphia on August 1, 1815, and that a few months later he went back to Ashburton and brought his wife home. Consider what that journey must have entailed: first a trek (probably on horseback or by coach) to the nearest seaport; a voyage by sailing ship perhaps of several weeks' duration with all the hazards associated with trans–Atlantic travel in those days; then another land journey to Ashburton. Finally William returned home with Frances, completing his round trip in less than a year. That surely was an act of true love. Dye added that Mrs. Pottenger outlived her husband by several years and spent the rest of her life in the United States, being in receipt of a United States Navy pension. There is no record of any offspring.

In a narrative of this kind, mention should be made of another *Argus* officer on parole there who rose to high office and became an illustrious figure in the history of the United States Navy. He was Lt. Uriah P. Levy, who is best remembered for abolishing flogging in that service (it ceased in 1862, the year of his death). When in command aboard ship he preferred to punish wrongdoers by unofficial and unorthodox methods which landed him in trouble with his superiors. He himself suffered humiliation because of his Jewish origins and because he entered the navy as a lieutenant straight from the merchant service instead of the conventional route of midshipman. Altogether he survived no less than six courts-martial, being completely exonerated each time on appeal. Despite these setbacks he rose through the ranks and was promoted to commodore of the Mediterranean Fleet, the United States Navy's highest post at that time and equivalent to admiral. He is remembered now not only as an officer of outstanding ability, but as a clever investor who used much of his accumulated wealth to restore President Thomas Jefferson's home, which had fallen into a state of disrepair. He also commissioned a statue of that great man which he presented to the United States government and which was installed in the Rotunda of the United States Capitol Building, where it can be seen today. A grateful (and perhaps penitent) nation named a World War II destroyer the USS *Levy* in his honor, and the United States Navy Jewish Chapel at Norfolk, Virginia, is named Commodore Levy Chapel. Altogether an impressive record for a former prisoner of war on parole at Ashburton, England!

To return to our main story:

Just weeks after the *Argus* men went home, six American sailors who had enlisted in the Royal Navy were discharged from the service, having finally decided to "declare" themselves. They were sent to Dartmoor, where some of them were recognized by other Americans. After becoming intoxicated (drink was regularly smuggled in to the depot, as will be explained later), two who had served aboard the *Pelican* when the *Argus* was defeated began boasting about their exploits to the fury of their fellow prisoners. They paid a terrible price for their indiscretion, when their infuriated listeners vented their anger by forcibly detaining them and holding a court. The majority was for putting them to death, but their lives were spared; instead the faces of two of them were branded by tattooing in Indian ink the letters "US" (United States) on one cheek and "T" (Traitor) on the other. All six men were later transferred to Plymouth, where hospital staff tried to remove the markings by blistering but without success. One of them died after his wounds became infected.

Such was a Yankee sailor's lot at Dartmoor in 1813, cast among the worst of the French, without access to the daily market, no allowances, despised by their guards. It was an unhappy time and there was worse to come.

11

More Tribulations, Then Better Times

Love of country beat strongly in American prisoners' hearts and July 4, 1813, was celebrated by flying improvised flags, making patriotic speeches and singing national songs with musical accompaniment. These activities were actively discouraged by the guards and Independence Day that year was marred when one of the flags was confiscated in a scuffle when shots were fired, wounding two of the prisoners.

All this time their relations with the "Romans" (which were never cordial) deteriorated, culminating in a fight on July 11, 1813, when the Frenchmen emerged from their quarters early armed with homemade knives, cudgels and stones. When the Americans came out they were set upon, and during the ensuing battle at least 20 men on both sides were so badly hurt they had to be taken to the hospital. The authorities now decided to segregate the two factions by building another wall dividing the No. 4 yard in two, one for the Romans and the other for the Yankees — but not for long. In October the Romans were taken to Plymouth and confined to the hulks.

Autumn brought more tribulations when an outbreak of smallpox struck the depot, followed by the worst winter in living memory. The disease was common in those days but the burden of surviving in the subzero temperatures for weeks in the icy cold of the stone prison blocks must have been hard to bear. The prison leat froze over and water standing in buckets became solid ice overnight, forcing the men to eat snow to alleviate their thirst, never a satisfactory substitute for man's most precious need. Snow drifts were recorded as having reached the top of the boundary walls and the guards cowered inside their shelters. The danger now was of hunger and deprivation, because the supply wagons were unable to get to Prince Town. Salted emergency rations were resorted to for the military and the town's inhabitants as well as the men inside the depot (a situation which has been repeated more than once since Dartmoor became a convict prison in 1850).

The continual ill treatment the prisoners had suffered up to that time together with the harsh climate prompted one American to write home describing Dartmoor as "that accursed place [which] ... extinguished every impression we formerly entertained of the British Nation as magnanimous, pious, liberal, and honourable or brave."

These conditions and remarks indicate very clearly the hardships of depot life, but for the Yankees the turning point was at hand. Capt. Isaac Cotgrave, Royal Navy, resigned on December 22, 1813, and the new agent, Capt. Thomas Shortland, Royal Navy, took over. One of his first acts was to permit the Americans the use of the daily market — two of them were allowed to attend on behalf of them all. They were then issued proper clothing, albeit in the "King's Yellow." Each man received a jacket, waistcoat, pantaloons, and a woolen cap. The caps were "thick and coarser than rope yarn," as one man put it, and as you might expect few men got outfits that fit them. An additional stigma as far as they were concerned were the initials TO TO (Transport Office) stamped on each garment. Even so, they were far better than the worn out rags they were now able to throw away. Shirts and wooden soled shoes completed their attire.

In February 1814 came the glad news they were to be paid one and one half pence per day with which to buy soap (they could, if they wished, have bought 2 pounds of potatoes or 3 "chews" of tobacco with it). The money was paid by the American government through their London agent Reuben Beasley, who was the only official contact between that government and this country. He must have been a very busy man or a careless one, because his lack of communication with the prisoners was to cost him his integrity and good character. The American prisoners thought he was too busy lining his own pockets at their expense. This was very likely true of his subordinates, who were responsible for the clothing later issued to them from their government, because most of it was ill fitting and of poor quality. Beasley was at fault for not replying to the many letters of complaint he received and took the trouble to visit Dartmoor only once during the whole course of the war. On that occasion, rather than visit the prison blocks to see for himself the basis of their discontent, he summoned a number of men to an office he was assigned and engaged them in casual conversation concerning their homes and families. Whatever his true intentions (he wrote to his superiors after the war in very hurt tones about the injustice of the criticisms made against him), the prisoners saw him as their only hope for fair treatment; when he failed them he became in their eyes a hated figure, neglectful and uncaring.

Happily, the Americans' way of life was transformed by the money they now received. Then the gambling started. Charles Andrews, in *A Prisoner's Memoires*, tells us gambling was forbidden by the committees in February 1814, but we know from the committee rules Benjamin Palmer wrote up in October 1813 it was already banned. That gambling for money and anything else of value went on regardless is therefore certain. Palmer wrote in his account of Dartmoor life a description of a typical day: "Daylight comes with the sounds of gamblers who have been up all night—some drunk, fighting, cursing ... night comes and there is bedlam, gambling, etc. starts over again."

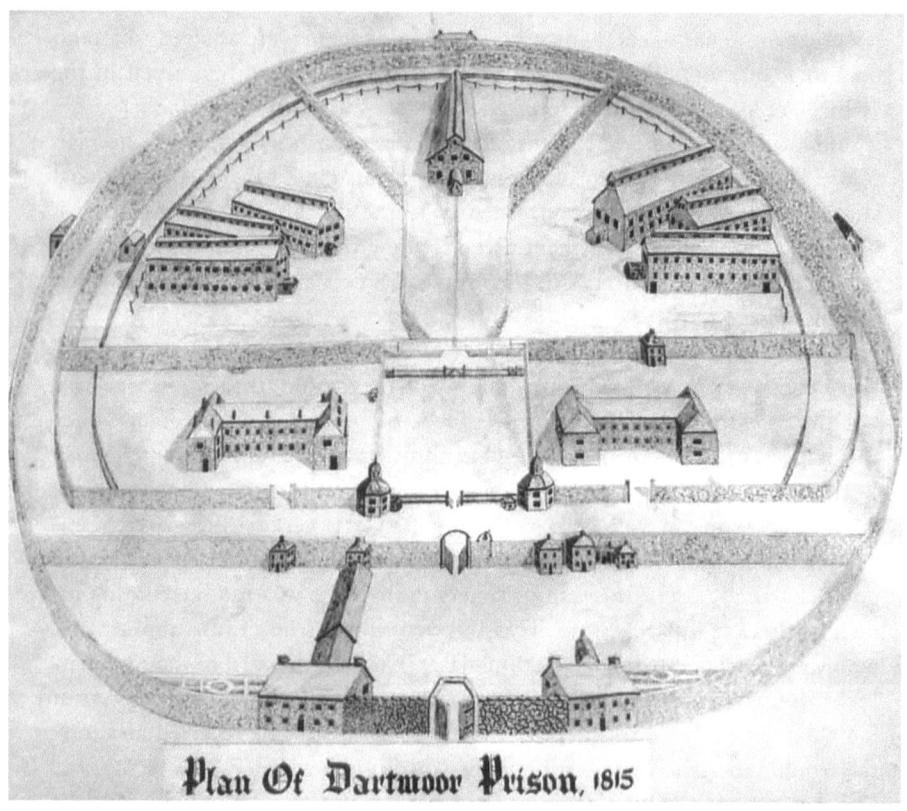

Plan Of Dartmoor Prison, 1815

This old print shows very clearly the layout of the prison as it was in 1815. Note the retaining walls around No. 4 block to separate the "Romans" from the other prisoners; also the retaining wall built down the center of the enclosed space to separate the "Romans" from the Americans. No. 6 block was lowered to just one story and converted into a kitchen for the entire prison in the early 1940s. Fifty years later a fully equipped modern kitchen was built at the lower end of what was once the market square. The old kitchen building is now derelict (courtesy Dartmoor Prison Museum).

11. More Tribulations, Then Better Times

The original No. 6 block, before it was converted to a kitchen. Apart from the three examples of the French-American blocks standing today already referred to, all the prison buildings now within that area were constructed before and after the turn of the century (1900) by convicts under the supervision of warder tradesmen (courtesy Dartmoor Prison Museum).

Card games were a favorite activity, mainly "Vingt-et-un" and "Brag." Then there was a form of roulette and backgammon which were especially popular. Palmer relates how he himself was challenged to an unusual race, for a bet of course, the "runners" being lice. His opponent kept his "steed" under his shirt collar, but when all was ready the collar was found to be empty—the beast had fled and his owner had to forfeit the bet. He also recounts how, after the French were repatriated in the summer of 1814, men employed outside the prison (more about this later) found it easy to smuggle in rum and openly distribute it. By this time they had also managed to establish an officially approved beer shop.

Meanwhile, the Americans' energies were concentrated on escape plans and aggravating the British. The latter occupation, which took the form of stone throwing, hurling insults at the guards and jeering about the several defeats the British suffered from time to time, prompted a heartfelt comment from one officer that there was more trouble from 4,000 Americans than from 40,000 Frenchmen. These distractions no doubt contributed to the continual bedlam, as Palmer called it, night after night, with the gambling tables in full swing and fights over disputed losses. In January 1815 the gambling tables were destroyed by order of the committees on the grounds some watches and other personal possessions were allegedly stolen during the proceedings. It appears therefore that the gaming went on all the time and that there were periodic crackdowns by the committees.

In March 1814 the Americans' fortunes improved still further when the gates to their compound were unlocked, leaving them free to roam the prison at will. That same month their spirits were again uplifted by a further money allowance. The news came in a letter from Beasley:

> Fellow Citizens,
>
> In addition to the three halfpence per day which has heretofore been allowed, I shall make remittance to Captain Shortland to enable you to have coffee and sugar twice a week, that is, the days on which your rations consist of fish: my intention at first was to have the articles themselves sent to be distributed, but it being suggested to me by the committees at other depots that the value in money would be more serviceable to the prisoners, I have determined to allow three pence halfpenny per man, two days in the week, being the value of those articles and I hope the committee will find the means to ensure it being applied to the purpose intended.

The letter was accompanied by the first payment of the additional allowance, which must have caused Beasley's standing with the men to reach an all time high. Every man was now entitled to the equivalent of an extra penny per day in addition to the one and a half pence per day already received. This represented a total of 6s. 8d. per man each month. In fact, it was paid every 32 days in the form of two £1 notes per six men.[1]

This large injection of money on a regular basis was more than welcome, as can be imagined. This was when the men got permission to open a shop selling beer at "twopence halfpenny a pot," but even more gratifying was the instruction to the guards that every one of the Americans was to have access to the daily market. The enterprising Americans, like the French, manufactured items with which to barter at market, exchanging carved models made of wood and bone, paintings, ornaments, and other items for tobacco or other little luxuries.

A civilized and flourishing community now evolved. For example, there were a number of boys held in the prison, mostly ship's boys, many of whom were related to members of the crew (it was British policy and a wise one not to separate them in the boys' own interests). There were among the Americans at Dartmoor seven boys under the age of 12, and 75 under 16. Most of them had been employed as waiters by the French officers; now a school was established for them where they were taught reading, writing and arithmetic for a fee of 6d. per month. The future looked brighter for the Yankees at last.

The French War Ends

Britain was engaged in fighting two wars simultaneously against France and the United States, but for Napoleon the end was near. A series of defeats found France fighting for survival on French soil. An excerpt from the *Times* of December 29, 1813, reads:

> Christmas Present for the British Nation!
> Wellington's Victories, etc.
>
> In one little year Russia, Austria, Prussia, Holland, Petty Sovereignties of the Rhine, Portugal, Spain — all freed from their tyrranic oppressors! Now must Bonaparte humbly sue for the Peace he might have Commanded! A Victorious British Army has entered his Kingdom!

In April 1814 the French emperor was in residence at Fontainbleu with the Allied armies poised to enter Paris. On April 11 he abdicated, enabling the

This is the one remaining window in the cockloft (top floor) of No. 4 block. This area had wooden flooring and was designed as a place where the prisoners could relax and exercise when the weather was bad but was used as an extra dormitory when the overcrowding became severe. There was no glass to keep out the draught and winter cold, just wooden shutters supplemented by rags and anything else the men could stuff in the cracks. The unhealthy atmosphere bred disease and killed many of the prisoners (author's photograph, reproduced by permission of Dartmoor Prison Governor T. Witton).

Treaty of Paris to be signed on April 30, 1814. The long French wars were over at last. There were tumultuous scenes all over England — church bells rang out, there were thanksgiving services, dinners, elaborate parades, and rejoicing in the streets. For the French prisoners of war, some of whom had been captive for nearly 11 years, it was a time of wild elation. On Dartmoor some of the local gentry rode over the moor to the war depot to congratulate the French on their imminent freedom.

The officers were presented with a white flag and white cockades (the emblem color of the Bourbon king who would succeed Bonaparte), but their reaction was not at all what was expected. The flag was burned in front of them in full view of the British officers. "We would remain prisoners another 11 years before we betrayed our emperor!" they declared. Loyalty such as this in the face of defeat is a rare thing and says much for the stature of the man they so faithfully served.

On May 16, 1814, the Transport Office wrote to Capt. Shortland instructing him that "your depot should be cleared of (French) prisoners with as little delay as possible" and "to acquaint you that Captain Pellowe has been directed to inform you from time to time of the numbers he may be able to receive at Mill Prison ... and that you will send off the prisoners without waiting for particular orders, reporting from time to time the numbers you may have so discharged."

They were being shipped home as soon as transport became available. Dartmoor Depot was being prepared for a specific purpose — the confinement of all American prisoners of war in Britain.

The first 500 French left the depot on May 21, the last of them departing on June 20. Among them were some Americans who had served on French vessels and others who were fluent in the French language, passing themselves off as Frenchmen after observing the British were not too particular about checking identities. Some French sailors who had been captured on American ships were also freed at this time. Preparations for their departure included their various tools and artifacts, market stalls and other belongings being eagerly purchased by the Yankees, who were now wise to prison ways and saw an opportunity to exploit their own talents in the market without competition. They were also able to take advantage of the fact they were now the sole occupants and overcrowding was ended.

At about the time the French were leaving, certain American seamen who had served in the Royal Navy received their back pay and prize money that was due to them, an indication of the *intended* fair treatment of prisoners by the British authorities (there were good and not so good agents running the depots who interpreted and applied the regulations as they saw fit, but this would have been an unequivocal directive from the Admiralty). The extra money was soon dispersed within the prison community to the benefit of the gambling fraternity and the market stallholders. As a bonus they were visited by Beasley's representative, a man called Williams, who was accompanied by a Jewish trader bearing fresh clothes for them from their own country. No clothing of any kind had been allowed them since 15 March, almost two months previous, on orders from the Transport Office directing Captain Shortland "not to issue any more clothing ... and to transmit lists of such Americans as may have been supplied with any article of clothing since January."

They had evidently been informed that the United States had assumed responsibility for furnishing their men with clothing and no doubt hoped to claim the cost of what had already been issued. Now jackets, shirts, and trousers in "pilot blue" were handed out together and with the news that from now on Americans would be supplied by their own government. The Yankees threw away the hated yellow garments and spruced themselves up with pride.

12

Dartmoor Becomes an American Depot

By the end of June 1814 all the French had gone home, Napoleon was living in exile on the Mediterranean island of Elba and the Americans had Dartmoor Depot to themselves. Roughly 15 percent of them were colored men — Negroes and mulattos (mixed race). These unfortunates suffered the most from the effects of climate and disease, accounting for nearly one-third of all American deaths at Dartmoor. This was said at the time to be related to their unclean habits and poor sanitary standards, which in turn led them to be segregated at the insistence of the whites, who also accused them of persistent stealing. On February 22, 1814, the "Black Jacks," as the Yankee sailors called them, were banished to the top floor of the infamous No. 4 block, where they established a community of their own. By September all the white men had abandoned No. 4 and it was occupied exclusively by the colored outcasts.

Yet for all the contempt in which they were held by the white Americans, their newly established community of blacks was very orderly and disciplined. This was due to the iron rule of "King Dick," a Negro six feet, three inches in height, whose real name was Richard Crafus. He was a native of Vienna (Chesapeake Bay) and only 23 years old when he was captured in March 1814 on board a privateer. This powerful individual kept a tight rein on his little kingdom and earned for it a grudging admiration on account of the orderliness he commanded. The proverbial "iron fist" was much in evidence, and he was described by one observer as a king in his own right, wielding a club and wearing a bearskin hat and accompanied everywhere by two boy attendants.

The way of life over which he presided (with the help of a few hard-case associates) commanded the respect not only of his fellow prisoners but the authorities as well. There were boxing matches and other entertainments, including plays and concerts which often attracted the other prisoners, indi-

12. Dartmoor Becomes an American Depot

Princetown Church of St. Michael and All Angels. By June 1814 the French war was over and the prisoners at Dartmoor had been repatriated. The agent received notice from the Transport Office to employ Americans in a variety of work previously carried out by the French, to include completion of the church the French had almost finished. This church therefore is unique in that it was built by two nationalities of prisoners of war (author's photograph).

cating the standards must have been high. They even had a band. Benjamin Palmer tells us about a visit to No. 4 to see a play, with tickets on sale at 6d. each. "Mob rule prevailed though and most men simply shoved their way in to a packed house where the performance rendered by the players received no less genuine applause from them than if they'd paid full price for admission!"

Sunday was always a special day and was observed by all the Americans as a day of quiet leisure. In No. 4 block church services were held. The style was evangelical and conducted by Preacher Simon, an apparently very ugly black man who nonetheless attracted good audiences, supported by an all black choir. There came a time, however, when the black men were forced to accept other prisoners in their midst. For example, in April 1815 three men were severely flogged after being discovered committing homosexual acts and

"The Old Chapel," formerly No. 4 block. This building is no longer a place of worship; alternative premises have been made available and the place awaits a new role. It has a somber air, as might be expected considering it was here the outcast "Romans" lived, and, at a later date, the "Rough Allies," all sentenced to banishment for their unruly and often disgusting ways. In this building arguments were settled in a traditional manner, with improvised swords for the French officers, homemade daggers for the rank and file of both nationalities, and in one case an American sailor was killed in a ferocious bare knuckle fight with a crewmate. There were happier times when concerts and occasional plays were performed to such high standards there was often a full house audience of fellow prisoners from the rest of the depot (courtesy M. Chamberlain).

were banished to No. 4 block. They were later joined by the "Rough Allies," the name the Yankees bestowed on troublemakers and undesirables. It says much for King Dick and the colored men generally that they were not involved to any great extent in the unruly behavior and turmoil that often occurred at Dartmoor.

On June 24, 1814, Captain Shortland announced he was empowered to employ masons, carpenters and laborers for work on the church (now Princetown's Parish Church of St. Michaels and All Angels) and the neighboring parsonage, which the French had left unfinished. Men were also needed as road menders, blacksmiths, coopers, painters, nurses, and for other jobs. There

12. Dartmoor Becomes an American Depot

was no shortage of volunteers, and more than 150 men were taken on. Charles Andrews recorded the rate of pay per day for those lucky enough to be employed, including the following:

1 Sweeper per 1,000 men	3d.
1 Cook per 200 men	4½ d.
Barbers	3d.
Nurses	6d.
Carpenters	3d.
Hospital helps (1 to every 10)	6d.

Those who worked outside the depot are said to have made up to five shillings a day extra by smuggling *out* forbidden items (straw hats for example), and smuggling *in* items such as candles, oil and rum. The prisoners in work took to wearing tin badges in their caps denoting their trade or occupation. Their fellow prisoners, who were not lacking in industry, took up the manufacture of articles to barter with at the market.

Trewman's Exeter Flying Post in London reported on April 16, 1814, "200 American prisoners passed through Exeter from Stapleton en route to Dartmoor War prison." The Transport Office, probably for reasons of security and economy, had decided to confine all American prisoners of war in Britain in one place. Stapleton near Bristol had been the first choice but for reasons not entirely clear (perhaps Sir Thomas Tyrwhitt had a hand in the matter), the depot at Dartmoor was chosen instead. As well as Stapleton, American prisoners were moved to Dartmoor from Norman Cross (near Peterborough), Mill Prison (Plymouth) and the hulks at Chatham, Portsmouth and Plymouth. The prisoners who came from Stapleton were mainly ex–Royal Navy sailors who had seen active service and naturally were resentful of the treatment they'd endured. At the end of January 1814 there were about 1,000 Americans on the moor, rising to 3,000 by August and 5,500 by December. All the same, with the departure of the French and the overcrowding at an end, life in the depot started to improve.

All was not sweetness and honey though. Much ill feeling was generated by malcontents among the lower classes of seamen prisoners, some of them British, who had found employment on American vessels where they were later captured. The bulk of these men were ruffians, toughs, and sullen rascals of the worst kind whose activities closely resembled those of the notorious "Romans." After being recognized for what they were by the decent men, they were sent, like all the other undesirables, to No. 4 block to live with the black men. There they became known as the "Rough Allies," a title they reveled in and tried to live up to at every opportunity; they were not as vile as the Romans, but were certainly incurable troublemakers.

Into this mixture of resentful humanity were added a number of bitter ingredients. When the French capitulated a number of British officers swaggered into the depot, taunting the Americans with exaggerated tales of British valor and the fearful consequences that would befall their folk at home now that the full might of British arms could be employed against them. Another cause of friction and injustice among the Yankees was the fate of 24 of their countrymen who had been captured with the French in 1810. They were ignored by the French and British alike, being recognized as neither French nor American, and during all those years had been forced to live by begging from their fellow captives. When the Frenchmen were repatriated they were detained and were not acknowledged by their own government until early 1815 after hostilities had ceased.

Ira Dye supplies the details concerning the cruel fate of four American sailors in *A Green Hand's First Cruise* (Baltimore, 1841). I give a summary of the contents:

The most inhuman punishment inflicted on prisoners at Dartmoor Depot was endured by four seamen captured under unusual circumstances. They had shipped aboard the armed schooner *Surprise* of Baltimore, a privateer which went cruising in the Pacific Ocean looking for enemy merchantmen to capture and loot. There they met up with a fleet of likely prizes and determined to attack and take them one at a time. Their first and only capture was a schooner of little value, but it was decided to put four seamen on board as a prize crew with the intention of transferring to this ship captured crewmen from other vessels they hoped to take, who would eventually be left to make their way to a port of their choice. When a Royal Navy man o'war guarding the merchant ships appeared and pursued the *Surprise* over the horizon, they were left stranded with very little food or water.

Several days later a brig was sighted, whereupon it was decided to fly a distress signal to lure the stranger close enough to engage and hopefully capture it. However, the brig became suspicious and hove-to at a distance but within range of the schooner's six pounder guns, which opened fire. The intended prey made off and easily out-sailed its attacker. In their haste the four privateer crew members had carelessly flung aside the burnt matches used to fire the guns, some of which fell into the hold. This was crucial to their later sufferings, when later on they were captured by another Royal Navy ship and taken off as prisoners, their place having been taken by navy "tars." The burnt matches were discovered in the hold close to the powder kegs and it was at once assumed the intention had been to blow up the captured ship. This action would have been against all naval etiquette in time of war, when the victorious officers and crew had the undisputed right to claim a portion of the prize value for distribution among themselves. In fact many officers in the Royal Navy (and other navies too) relied on this to supplement their pay.

Consequently, the four alleged saboteurs, despite their protestations, spent the 42 day voyage back to England in irons and were sent to Dartmoor in August 1814, having been sentenced by the Transport Office to spend their entire captivity in the dreaded Black Hole. There they would have died but for the merciful attention of their jailor, who smuggled items of food to them in addition to the two-thirds rations allowed to prisoners under punishment. Their American comrades voted to donate a halfpenny per man per month to help with this (and to bribe the jailor?) after their petition to the Transport Office for clemency was rejected. The men who suffered the worst punishment ever inflicted at Dartmoor were Elisha Whitten of Massachussets, Simeon Hayes of Baltimore, John Miller, an Englishman, and James Ricker of unknown origin. For nearly eight months they were confined in the stone coffin that was the cachot, in semi-darkness and (officially) on short rations. The sequel to this unhappy episode will be related in the next chapter.

At about the same time (August 1814) a large number of ex–Royal Navy men were shipped by sea from Chatham, where they had been detained on the hulks ever since the war began, to Plymouth and marched up to the depot. Most of them had chosen to go to prison when war was declared rather than fight against their homeland. They had fought for Britain in the war against France, something that not only embarrassed the guards but was another cause of the resentment that was carried to the depots by men who were true to the highest of principles — loyalty to one's country.

13

Escapes

No prison was or ever will be escape proof, and Dartmoor Depot was no exception. As previously noted most of the prisoners were privateers, some of them vicious desperadoes who would stop at nothing in an effort to escape. Under cover of darkness, mist, or heavy rain, many a man, sometimes groups of men, found a way of scaling the boundary walls undetected. This was an achievement in itself, because there were wires strung around the walls with bells suspended from them. If the wire was disturbed, the jangling of the bells was the signal for drummers to beat "To arms!" Then every guard, on or off duty, armed himself and rushed to apprehend the escapees. The ruthlessness with which this was done is illustrated in the following incident.

We have learned already how in 1810 the Nottinghamshire Militia arrived at Dartmoor and how several French prisoners, seeking to take advantage of the new arrival's supposed lack of vigilance on their first night on guard duty, attempted a mass escape, but were detected milling about in the area between the two walls known as the Military Walk. When the alarm was given, every militiaman, some half-clothed, ran to the scene, and in the confusion one of their own men, who hadn't had time to put on his uniform and was mistaken for a prisoner, was stabbed to death by bayonet thrusts.

A Dartmoor prisoner of war attempting to escape not only had the stone walls, alarm bells, and armed sentries to contend with. There was the moor to cross, without signposts, and a population against him, either for fear of punishment if they helped him or the possibility of a guinea reward if they turned him in. The tors and bogs made travel difficult and there was little shelter; besides, a man needed rest, food, and the means of crossing the English Channel.

Torbay was usually their objective, where there was a chance of stealing a boat, or maybe persuading a fisherman to take them to France (fishermen on both sides were, by mutual agreement, immune from hostilities during the

French wars). Occasionally boats and their occupants were hijacked and forced to sail to France under threat of death. Eventually things got so bad the Admiralty ordered all unattended vessels on the south coast to have their oars and sails removed as a precaution against theft by escaping war prisoners.

Smugglers were involved in the escape trade, and "trade" is precisely what developed when professional "escape agents" began to appear. These men were unscrupulous scallywags who would arrange everything for an escapee — for a price. Lucky customers were whisked away to somewhere safe, perhaps an isolated house or a quiet inn with an understanding (and equally expensive) landlord who would arrange transportation to France. Sometimes things could go tragically wrong, though.

On January 26, 1811, five French officers living on parole at Moretonhampstead stole away from their lodgings after dark and met a local carrier called Richard Tapper who had horses waiting to take them to Topsham on the River Exe near Exeter. There they were joined by two well-known smugglers from Cheriton Bishop, brothers Thomas and William Vinnicombe, who, for a down payment of £25 and the promise of another £250, took them on board their boat and set sail for France. At the mouth of the river their luck ran out when the vessel ran aground off Exmouth and they were caught. The French officers, three of whom were ship's captains, were sent to Plymouth, probably to Mill Prison. Tapper and the Vinnicombes were tried at the Devon Assizes in the summer of 1812 and sentenced to a penal colony for life.

The winter of 1813–1814 was the worst for more than 50 years on Dartmoor. The snow began falling in November interspersed with hail and rain. By the end of the month the ground was white.

At this time the Americans were kept separate from the main body of prisoners and denied access to the market, where they could have purchased tobacco, coffee, fresh vegetables, poultry, and other items that would help make life tolerable. Instead they traded their few pitiful belongings — shoes, blankets, clothing and ultimately their rations to unscrupulous Frenchmen all too eager to take advantage of them in return for a chew of "baccy" or some soap, among other comforts. Another burden they had to bear was the early morning turnout, when they were paraded in the yards for a roll call that sometimes took hours to complete. Many of them were without shoes or stockings and some had cut up their blankets to cover their bodies and their feet. Several men each day collapsed from the cold and had to be carried to the hospital in a state of hypothermia, but the routine continued relentlessly. All protests were answered with the reply it was a requirement of the Transport Board, which administered the custody of prisoners of war.

It was against this background that eight Americans determined to make their escape at any cost. In December 1813 the cold worsened to the extent nearly all the prisoners stayed in their hammocks which, being packed closely side by side and in tiers often five high, ensured the men's body heat literally kept them alive in the stone dormitories they occupied. Toward the end of the month it snowed every day and the cold was intense.

On New Year's Day the temperature plummeted further and in just four hours buckets of water froze solid, as did the drinking water. The men again kept to their beds for warmth while outside the snow was getting higher daily until the drifts reached almost to the top of the boundary walls. The sentries who manned the walls were permitted to stand down, such was the severity of the cold, and they retired to their guardrooms. At midnight on January 14, 1814, eight stalwart Americans decided to take advantage of this to make their escape, an indictment if ever there was one of the severity of the treatment which prompted them to take such a formidable risk.

With the aid of a makeshift ladder they got over the inner wall, taking advantage of the high snowdrifts, and descended to the Military Walk, where they prepared to scale the outside boundary wall to freedom. Sadly for them, they had entered this area adjacent to one of the guardrooms and the soldier guards were alerted. The guards apprehended seven of them but the eighth man got over the wall and disappeared into the frozen wastes of the moor.

The recaptured men were placed in the cachot without heating and on two-thirds rations. It was the normal punishment for attempting to escape, but with the weather so severely cold it was a terrible thing to endure. Meanwhile their comrade had survived the frightful conditions on the moor for a day and a night, an outstanding feat of endurance. On his second day at large without food or shelter he stumbled on a remote cottage and was taken in by the inhabitants. They of course guessed who he was and at the first opportunity returned him to the depot where he joined his friends in the cachot. He had been given up for dead by prisoners and guards alike and on his return the guards were so impressed by his fortitude and resilience they openly stated if they had their way he would be set free.

Captain Shortland, the agent in charge of the depot, took pity on them and ordered them to be taken back to their respective prison blocks. And so the eight men survived. Not only that, but the morning roll call was abolished.

A number of prisoners were employed outside the prison on road making and various building projects that included the church and parsonage. They were paid a daily wage but, as reported by the Americans who took over when the French war ended, payment was made every three months and not at all if there was an escape during that period. That didn't stop one bold Frenchman achieving a unique escape when colleagues encased him in a recess in the chimney they were constructing in the parsonage and walled him in, leaving air holes in loose mortar and successfully concealing his absence at roll call. The prisoner waited until they departed at the end of the day, forced his way out (the mortar not having had time to set) and made his getaway. The question might be asked: what motivated his companions, knowing they faced certain punishment when he was found to be missing?

As already mentioned, heavy penalties were inflicted on sentries who aided escapees. A barrier of iron railings inside the inner wall prevented prisoners from approaching the guards and fraternizing with them, and maybe bribing them for help in escaping. Despite this several instances of bribery came to light as well as an unknown number that didn't. In 1812 three French prisoners paid a Roscommons (an Irish unit) Militiaman £2, the going rate at the time, to help them "over the wall." Paddy wasn't the only one among the rank and file who had no scruples about supplementing his pay in this manner. Militia soldiers were poorly paid and conscripted from the lowest classes, drunkards almost to a man, so it was no surprise to find so many of them willing to risk a flogging, or perhaps their lives, for the price of a drink. There was a sting in the tail though; the Irishman was detected trying to pass forged notes, the price of his treachery, at the daily market that was held within the prison. Forgery was a big problem in every prisoner of war depot and the death penalty had been introduced to try and stop it. The forger, a prisoner called Lustique, was later identified, and both he and the soldier were tried and hanged.

On a lighter note, the best known story is that of *Le Capitaine Calonne et sa Dame*, the title of a play performed by the French prisoners. Theatricals were a prominent feature of prison life and on this occasion a British officer and his wife generously offered to help by lending the leading actors a uniform and female clothing. The offer was gladly accepted and the performance was a huge success until, toward the end, an announcement was made: "Messieurs, the captain and his wife have left the prison." The implication was clear and only too true — the French "captain and his wife" in their costumes had passed unchallenged out of the main prison entrance to freedom, leaving an embarrassed officer and his lady having to endure hoots and whistles of derision from a delighted prisoner audience!

When the war with Napoleon ended in April 1814, the French were repatriated and all American prisoners in England were transferred to Dartmoor, except the officers who were on parole. They lost no time in planning an escape, and in August 1814 they formulated a master escape plan to tunnel their way out under the prison walls. This was to be the most ambitious attempt at a mass breakout ever devised by prisoners on the moor. They had the place to themselves now that the French had gone. They had previously been confined to the north side of the compound; now they were permitted to make use of No. 6 block to ease the congestion, and as more prisoners arrived, they too went to No. 6. This is where the digging began.

Secrecy was vital, of course. Bibles were procured and every man involved swore on oath not to reveal by word or sign what was going on; the penalty for treachery was to be death by hanging, a sentence they themselves would carry out. The overcrowding in No. 4 block, which was inside a separate walled-off area, was to be eased by moving men to No. 6, so it was decided to extend the plan to include tunneling from No. 4 as well. Then the unoccupied No. 5 block was included in the plan. With prisoners passing the entrance all day it was easy for some to slip inside and start work there; thus there were three tunnels being excavated at once, and their feeling was that should any one tunnel be discovered the chances were at least one would remain undetected.

According to Charles Andrews (*A Prisoner's Memoires*), they sank shafts

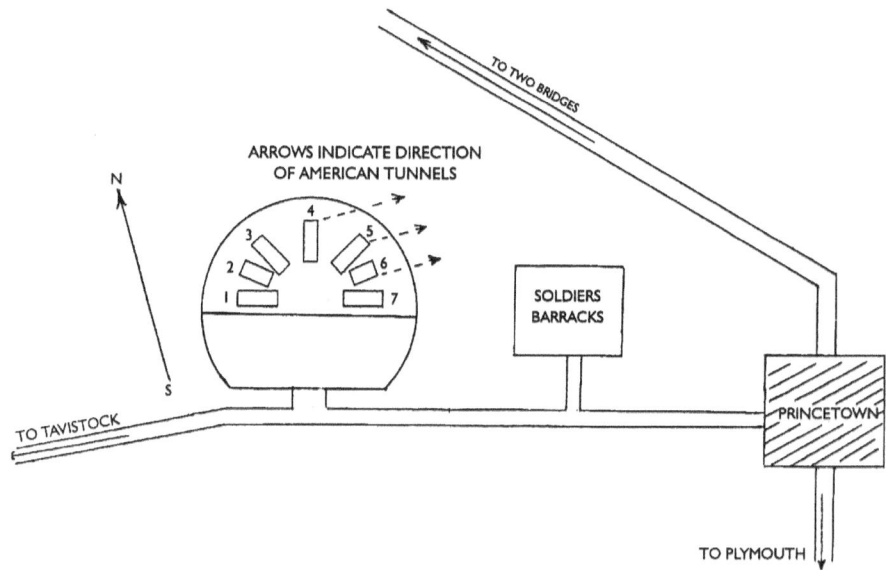

The Americans conceived a mass escape plan that entailed three tunnels being dug outwards under the boundary walls by which means hundreds of prisoners would make their getaway on a certain night when conditions were favorable. It was cleverly planned and executed but ended in failure when the participants were betrayed by one of their own (author's drawing).

20 feet deep before digging horizontally in an easterly direction. They found the subterranean soil to be light and relatively free of stones, so progress was good. The entrances were very narrow but underground the holes were wide enough for four men to work abreast, and they rigged lamps in a way that induced a circulation of air, stale air being expelled as fresh air entered. The biggest problem was disposing of the excavated material. At first pocketfuls of earth were scattered over the yards, but a more effective way had to be found if progress was to be maintained. The bulk of the dirt was thrown into the fast flowing foul water outlets, and an ingenious method was devised for getting rid of the remainder. As we know, the prisons were built of roughly dressed moor stone, which left large crevices in the walls. The Americans mixed the sandy soil they brought up into a rough mortar and filled in the cracks with it, disguising their work by whitewashing over it. The prison officials afterwards expressed amazement at the amount of material that must have been dug out and never understood how it was disposed of.

By the end of August they had progressed over 60 feet in each tunnel. Then disaster struck when, on September 2, the authorities began a search of No. 5 and 6 blocks. They found one of the entrances, but only after tapping the floors with crowbars, so cleverly was it concealed. All of the prisoners were sent back to occupy No. 1, 2, and 3 blocks and the tunnel was sealed off with stones. (In 1881, during excavations to lay the foundations for a new convict prison, the tunnel was uncovered and found to be 14 feet deep, not 20 feet as the Americans had claimed. An enterprising convict who later occupied a cell directly over the tunnel tried to escape by digging down into it, only to find it was still full of stones.)

Had they been betrayed? An inquiry was held among themselves and several prisoners were interrogated on suspicion of turning traitor, but the evidence was inconclusive. It was supposed that careless talk had alerted the authorities. The (segregated) No. 4 prison not having been searched, work there recommenced at once. In September more prisoners began arriving and No. 5, 6, and 7 blocks had to be made available again to accommodate them. Excavations were immediately resumed and No. 6 tunnel was reopened by men digging around the blockages to reach the old workings. The task was again coordinated with the intention of completing all three tunnels simultaneously, when hundreds of men would pass through them and make their way to the coast. The mass escape was planned for 10 P.M. one stormy night, which would allow time for them to reach the Torbay area before daylight.

Then there was a betrayal when one of their number approached the guards and went off with them, never to be seen again. Almost certainly he had betrayed his comrades, and it was thought he had been repatriated as a reward for his treachery. Once more every man was sent back to the north side of the prison, regardless of overcrowding, while repairs were made and the tunnels blocked up. All Americans were placed on two-thirds rations for 10 days, the remainder being retained to cover the cost of the work.

It was a devastating blow for them, and Andrews wrote, "If the villain had been caught, they should scarcely have tried him, but would have torn him to atoms before the life could have time to leave his traitorous body."

Until the very day of their release the Yankees were bitter enemies, causing unrest and exasperating their captors. Had their tunnels gone undetected many hundreds of them would have been at large and the prison officials would have had to face a problem of unprecedented magnitude — with a headache to match! There were still individual escapes of course, but this would have been a notable episode in the annals of prison escapes and typical of Britain's American cousins, who do not do things by halves.

14

Frustration and a New Regime

There now occurred a series of events that culminated in a ghastly tragedy. From the *Sherbourne and Yeovil Mercury* of Monday, November 7, 1814:

> The 1st Somerset Regt. of Militia which lately returned into Taunton from Ireland for the purpose of being disembodied, marched in two Divisions on Monday and Tuesday last for the Royal Prison, Dartmoor, to do duty over the American prisoners. The first division passed through Exeter on Wednesday morning. This fine body of soldiers who have ever been distinguished for the excellence of their Discipline and Good Conduct, marched on this service in the highest spirits.

No doubt there was a lot of truth in the description of the "fine body of soldiers" marching to Dartmoor. However, many militia regiments were being disbanded at this time, including the Devons, and the Somerset men must have felt they were also entitled to go home, having previously served in Ireland and Mill Prison in Plymouth. They were no strangers to prison duty and must have resented the fact their latest assignment meant being posted miles from any town, probably in poor accommodation with very little social life. Nearly all the war depots were situated in just such locations for security reasons, but the soldiers must have known Dartmoor had the reputation of being the worst of them. Furthermore, the task allotted to them would be vastly different from guarding the French. Another newspaper had stated: "The Americans are unruly, and refuse to settle down to manufacturing pastimes."

The Somerset militiamen did not yet know it, but there was the pent up passion of desperate men to contend with on the moor, men who felt they had endured more than their fair share of injustices and were ready to rebel. *The Times* of November 13, 1814, reported, "The American prisoners of war there [Dartmoor] are far from orderly and quiet — they are constantly trying plans of escape, not occupying themselves as their predecessors the French did in different works to while away the time, and it had been found necessary to have an efficient Militia force there." The impression given is that the Somerset militia was selected for the role they were to play at Dartmoor on account of their efficiency.

Meanwhile, the war with the United States was being fought to a standstill. Both sides were financially drained and ready to seek a compromise. For prisoners of war everywhere, the long awaited peace came at an appropriate time — Christmas Eve 1814 — when the Treaty of Ghent was signed, effectively ending hostilities. There was a delay, however, because the treaty had to be ratified by the United States government. A fast Royal Navy sloop, the *Favourite*, was dispatched across the Atlantic bearing the precious document, while at Dartmoor Depot where the news was received on December 29 after several false rumors, the Americans sang with glee. Their elation was still high when they flew their homemade flags, boldly painted with the slogan "Free Trade and Sailors' Rights," a defiant gesture dating from the first day of the war. It was repeated on New Year's Day 1815, with the prisoners' band playing "Yankee Doodle." This was trying Captain Shortland's patience too far and the celebrations were terminated on his orders, with the comment that hostilities had not yet officially ceased. All the same, the excitement and hopes for the future must have dominated the thoughts of every man — but there was to be more suffering before those happier days arrived.

In January 1815 there was an outbreak of smallpox of exceptional virulence that killed more than 200 Americans. It was referred to as the African Pox and soon reached epidemic proportions, overwhelming the hospital staff who struggled valiantly to contain the disease. Ultimately extra medical assistance was called for and the chief surgeon of England was summoned to Dartmoor. He attributed the rapid spread of the disease to the impure air in the dormitories. The very conditions that had for so many years prevented deaths from winter cold were now proving fatal, his opinion being partly confirmed when he took temperature readings both inside and outside the prison blocks on a cold February morning. With the outside temperature standing at 38 degrees F at 7:30 A.M., the readings inside one of the prisons registered 56 degrees F on the first two floors, rising to a maximum of 66 degrees F on the top level. The prisoners had evidently acquired stoves for heating because the authorities at once ordered them to be doused and more adequate ventilation provided. We can be certain the inmates blocked up the apertures around the windows to help keep the heat in, and this of course led to a shortage of fresh air with all the accompanying bad results.

Charles Andrews has left a vivid description of how bodies were removed to the Dead House after being stripped of their clothing and cut open to

14. Frustration and a New Regime

determine the cause of death. They were then placed naked in rough coffins, after which, when a sufficient number had accumulated, they were buried in communal graves on the moor. The number of dead from the dreaded pox was no reflection on the abilities of the resident surgeon, Dr. George MaGrath, who labored incessantly despite his own ill health at the time. It was he who summoned the extra help to alleviate the suffering, which was all that could be done in the early stages. The outbreak was finally brought under control by vaccination (still a relatively new remedy) which the noble doctor initiated. Many Americans rejected this form of treatment and had to be persuaded by their government, which threatened to stop their allowances if they refused.

In February there occurred the first serious confrontation between the Americans and Agent Shortland. He had granted a concession to the four men who had been locked in the Black Hole for so long and were due to be confined there for the whole of their imprisonment. He allowed them to exercise for half an hour every day on the grassy area between the inner wall and the iron railings. When they emerged from the Black Hole the entire prison community was shocked at their appearance, an emotion not easily aroused among tough seafarers in the days of sail. Plans were made, and on February 13, Simeon Hayes, actively encouraged by the onlookers, managed to evade the guard and scale the railings, where he was seized by the other prisoners and borne triumphantly away. It only took a few moments to transform Hayes into a "black jack" sailor using smuts from the cookeries, enabling him to mingle undetected among his comrades, with frequent changes of clothing. When extra roll calls were made and the prison blocks examined by search parties, Hayes was hustled from one block to another among a crowd of men or concealed in a hollow space beneath a stone. In the end Captain Shortland personally led a search for him, only to be confronted by a jubilant mob egged on by the Rough Allies, taunting and jeering.

When he found no trace of the wanted man, Shortland, in a moment of impotent anger, told them if Hayes was not surrendered he would close the market and if necessary stop the water supply too. This was the spark that turned rough banter to ugly rage, and soon stones were flying amid the insults, one of which passed very close to Captain Shortland's cheek. This was too much. Confronted with an angry mob and outraged by their aggressive behavior, he halted the soldiers and ordered them to open fire, but the captain of the guard averted sudden death by striking up the muskets with his sword, upon which both sides retreated in sullen silence, it being clear a tragedy had only just been prevented.

Captain Shortland did not stop the water supply — such a course would have had disastrous consequences, but he was determined to stamp his author-

The prison leat, which conducted water from the River Walkham four miles away, terminated at a reservoir opposite the depot main entrance from whence sluice gates in the round stone tower controlled the amount of water that flowed by gravity to all parts of the prison (the ground slopes from front to rear). The photograph was taken in 1993 when the so-called "bog water" was still in use (for sanitary purposes only); the drinking water was from the mains supply. Today the system is obsolete and the reservoir has been filled in and landscaped (author's photograph, reproduced by permission of Dartmoor Prison Governor T. Witton).

ity on the depot by stopping the market. As expected, American pride and the goading of the Rough Allies united them in a fierce resistance. They decided the market would be boycotted for as many days as Shortland kept it closed and anyone caught trading would be liable to corporal punishment. One American stallholder who suggested Hayes should be given up for the common good had his stall smashed up and all his goods confiscated. Another man who was caught selling tobacco at inflated prices, taking advantage of the shortage that resulted from the market being closed, suffered the same fate.

One prisoner had no regrets about the market and wrote: "No longer shall Yankee tars support innumerable shoals of farmers, market women, and Jews ... they have fattened on the hard earnings of American prisoners, charging what prices they liked, knowing they had no competition in the market and that prisoners could not be supplied elsewhere." If what he said were true, it bears out the assertion that the authorities paid only lip service to the regulations and permitted traders a free hand to extract what they could from their captive customers.

It took almost a week for tempers to cool sufficiently for a compromise to be reached: it was agreed the market would reopen provided a promise was given that "no Englishman in Captain Shortland's employ would be molested." This was a strange and weak response by the agent, and we can only surmise he must have had the peace agreement in mind and the thought that he would soon be able to lay down the burden of being responsible for more than 5,000 prisoners impatient for their release. It so happened that Simeon Hayes was recaptured shortly afterwards, but he and the others who shared his fate were released from the cachot when the peace was confirmed.

A New York newspaper made the announcement this way:

> New York, Saturday Evening, 9 o'clock, February 11, 1815.
> PEACE!
>
> The great and joyful news of PEACE between the United States and Great Britain reached this city this evening by the British sloop of war Favorite, the Hon. J. U. Mowatt, Esq., commander, in forty-two days from Plymouth. Henry Carroll, Esq., Secretary of the American Legation at Ghent, is the welcome bearer of the treaty, which was signed at Ghent on the 24th December by the respective commissioners, and ratified by the British government on the 28th December. Mr. Baker, late Secretary to the British Legation at Washington, has also arrived in the sloop of war with a copy of the treaty ratified by the British government.

Napoleon Returns from Elba

Suddenly other events took place which shook all of Europe, sending tremors to every corner of Britain and all the way to Dartmoor Depot. On the evening of March 26, 1815, Napoleon sailed from Elba and returned to France. Even this news was overshadowed when it became known many thousands of French soldiers were abandoning the Bourbon king and joining their emperor (he had retained his rank by agreement at the Treaty of Paris) on his march from the south of France to Paris amid an ecstatic welcome from the people. It was the beginning of what came to be called the "Hundred Days" (more accurately 136 days), during which time he set about restoring to France the form of government he had abdicated less than twelve months previously. The charisma of the man who once made Europe tremble was undiminished as countless numbers of old comrades hastened to swell the ranks of his re-established army, cheered by the hope they might win back the power and the lost territories of once mighty France.

Napoleon returns from exile and the French war resumes. After the Treaty of Paris in 1814 the Emperor Napoleon agreed to live in exile on the Mediterranean island of Elba. In March 1815 he returned to France amid tumultuous scenes of joy; soldiers came running to join his re-established army. Britain and its allies determined to bring about his downfall and restore the Bourbon King. It took 136 days, culminating in the Battle of Waterloo and the emperor being exiled again, this time to the remote Atlantic island of St. Helena, where he died in 1821 (courtesy artist Paul Deacon).

At Dartmoor Depot there was gloom on the part of the militiamen, who envisaged more years of service than they'd bargained for, most of them having enlisted to serve until the end of hostilities. The Americans backed "Old Boney" and taunted their guards to distraction. Beneath it all the ferment of dissatisfaction and enmity was still simmering, fuelled by rumors that varied almost daily — an inevitable result in a situation where thousands of war weary captives were waiting to be returned to their homeland.

Yet there were moments when these hardened veterans displayed compassion of a rare quality. On March 4 an insane hospital patient ran amok and stabbed a prisoner nurse who later died. The dead man, Jonathan Paul, had an English wife living nearby in poor circumstances and this aroused the sympathy of the Yankees, every one of whom voted to go without his fish ration for one day. A contractor bought the lot (25 barrels of pickled herrings) for the equivalent of $100, all of which was given to the woman who had lost

14. Frustration and a New Regime

her man. Truly there is hope for the world when prisoners living in great hardship voluntarily go without their precious dinner to help alleviate personal distress.

On March 14, 1815, the *Favourite* returned to England with the now ratified peace treaty and the American war was officially over. Three days later the news reached Dartmoor Depot where, after the initial rejoicing, there was anger as the men were told their allowances were to cease. No authority having been given to pay it in peacetime. Then the market stopped, the flow of money having ceased, all commerce was stifled. Conditions rapidly deteriorated to practically the same level as when the Americans first arrived on the moor and things were going from bad to worse at a time when they should have got better. The only beneficiaries were the 24 Yankee sailors who had been captured with the French and were neglected for so long: four days later (and nine years too late) the American government at last sent clothes for them and formally recognized them as their own.

The depot seethed with discontent, the brunt of which was borne by the sentries who were subjected to endless insults and the occasional missile from their charges. There was an increase in the number of escapes, many of them successful with the guards actively assisting the escapees over the walls, no doubt for bribes. Those who got away were not pursued, their only fear being the Royal Navy press gangs that were still active — in fact the menace they presented effectively deterred the faint hearted from even attempting to abscond. The rumors, the uncertainty, the delay in procuring their release, was proving an intolerable strain on prisoners and guards alike.

On the last day of March 1815 Charles Andrews personally counted all the prisoners at Dartmoor and found there were:

Those discharged from the Royal Navy, etc.	2,200
From privateers and merchant ships	2,243
United States soldiers and navy men	250
Coloured men (various)	1,000
Total:	5,693

Of these 130 were in the hospital.

That same day they were told their cartels were held up by adverse winds. This could have been a ploy to try and calm a situation which was understandably getting out of hand. It so happened Beasley was doing his best to obtain ships to take the men home, but ship owners generally preferred to wait for more lucrative cargoes which were bound to come their way now the war was over. To their shame the British and American governments were bickering over who should bear the cost of repatriating prisoners. The American view was that each nation should charter the number of vessels needed to repatriate the prisoners they held. The British, who held twice as many captives, insisted each country should organize transport for its own men. The fact of the matter was both countries were impoverished by the cost of warfare and while British prisoners waited patiently for release from America's shores, the Americans fretted at Dartmoor.

15

The Princetown Massacre

With an explosive atmosphere at the depot and men dying of disease, two blunders were made which precipitated the Princetown Massacre, an event that marred the reputation of the militia and brought death to several Americans, all of whom who were fired upon at a time when they were no longer prisoners of war but free men waiting to go home.

On April 4, 1815, Captain Shortland left the depot to attend to some business in Plymouth. It was widely known that the prisoners at Dartmoor were not only restive but threatening to break out if they were not released soon. A prudent agent would surely have remained at his post. In his absence, a worse error of judgment was made when it became known the bread ration for that day was to be stopped (allegedly on orders from the Transport Office) and "hard bread" or biscuit normally kept in store for emergencies was to be issued instead. This would have been the notorious ship's biscuit, baked in small rectangles and hard as iron. Moreover, the amount was to be reduced from 1½ pounds per man to 1 pound, which in itself would arouse the prisoners' anger. With hostilities at an end, perhaps it was decided to use up the emergency supplies, but more than one prison riot has been triggered by a dispute over the food and this was to be such a case.

The American "criers" received a roar of approval when it was put to them the substitute biscuit should be rejected. Loud and uncompromising demands were made for their rightful ration of soft bread, and by nightfall the position was critical. The contractor responsible maintained fresh bread could not be obtained until the next day, but the Americans, who knew the storehouses contained their proper rations, were in no mood for feeble excuses. By evening hunger and frustration drove them to a dramatic course of action: it was resolved to force the gates leading to the market square and the storehouses, disarm the soldiers and help themselves to their rightful bread allowance, whatever the consequences might be.

At dusk when they were summoned to their respective prisons for the night everyone congregated at the gates instead, ignoring the order. At a pre-arranged signal the gates were forced open and there was a rush for the storehouses. The few sentries on duty together with the turnkeys hurriedly retreated to the guardhouse. Within minutes the drummers were beating 'To arms!' and the alarm bell was rung. A party of soldiers soon came on the scene with bayonets fixed and advanced to within yards of the prisoners.

Bloodshed seemed inevitable. The Americans declared to the officers in charge that unless their bread was issued they would level the storehouses to the ground and every man would march out of the depot. Furthermore, if the troops charged them or opened fire, they must take the consequences. At this point the contractor intervened, saying that provided they withdrew to the main prison yard, their proper issue of bread would be given out. The men agreed but only on condition they took one of the clerks with them as a hostage until they were satisfied he meant what he said. This was done and at midnight the soft bread they were entitled to was issued.

The noise and shouts had alerted the neighborhood, and (according to Charles Andrews), at the sound of the alarm some of the women living nearby fled in terror, afraid the prisoners would wreak revenge upon them should there be a mass break out. For weeks it had been expected that sooner or later the discontent at Dartmoor would erupt into open revolt. Families in Prince Town thought that moment had come. The haste with which the guard had turned out was evident by their disheveled appearance — some were in shirtsleeves, others without their breeches, all of which induced much hilarity and aggressive banter from the Rough Allies. Fortunately the officers managed to maintain discipline. No one wanted a head-on confrontation, yet this was the very thing the rowdier elements among the prisoners regarded as a weakness, making their feelings known with yells of contempt.

The decision solved an immediate problem, but a deep feeling of resentment was planted in the soldiers' minds. Not only that, but the incident prompted Major Jolliffe, the military commander at Dartmoor, to write to Major General Browne, officer commanding the Plymouth Garrison, "for instructions as to ordering the troops to fire in case of necessity" and received very proper directions. The author has been unable to ascertain what those directions were, but the fact that guidance was sought and given indicates very strongly the scale of agitation brewing among the prisoners and the growing alarm in the minds of those responsible for the security of the depot.

Captain Shortland got news of the affair from a messenger who had been dispatched to Plymouth at the first sign of trouble. He lost no time in obtaining reinforcements from the Plymouth Citadel (a military fortress on Plymouth

15. The Princetown Massacre

Hoe) and arrived back at Dartmoor Depot early the next morning with 200 extra soldiers only to find everything quiet and peaceful. A nasty incident had only just been avoided and the agent realized this, for he lost no time in summoning the prisoners to apologize personally to them for what had happened, according to Charles Andrews.

While the garrison and civilian population of Prince Town got the fright of their lives (perhaps Captain Shortland too had been unnerved) the Rough Allies considered they had won a victory and felt a glow of satisfaction at having gotten the better of their captors. It was an error of judgment for which a high price would be paid.

Thursday, April 6, 1815, will forever be a black day in the history of the 1st Somerset Militia and the Derbyshire Militia, the two units guarding the depot at that time. The everlasting shame for what took place lies in the fact the victims were prisoners in name only, peace having been declared several weeks earlier. Accounts of what exactly happened in the market square and the vicinity that day are shrouded in confusion, inaccuracy, and the contradictory evidence of those who were present, depending on which side they were on. Every account admits to a misunderstanding on one vital point: who gave the order to shoot. An on the spot inquiry failed to get at the truth of the matter, and a further international inquiry, under the direction of one British and one American representative, was unable to resolve the question as to why and how British troops shot and killed unarmed Americans.

It had been a warm, sunny day. The Americans were in cheerful mood, reveling in the evening sunshine, with games being played and a lot of "skylarking" (horseplay) going on. The turnkeys, who were responsible for the men being locked up each night, had signaled by the sounding of a horn (other accounts say the turnkeys always hallooed "Turn in! Turn in!") it was time for the men to retire to their respective prison blocks. Most of them were already inside and all but one door to each block had been locked in anticipation of a normal conclusion to the day. Only some stragglers lingering outside were still to be accounted for. It was six o'clock.

A few minutes later Captain Shortland was informed a hole had been made by the prisoners in one of the retaining walls near the Petty Officers' Prison, which, it will be remembered, had been commandeered and converted to a barracks for the troops. The hole was near where the muskets were stored, but a great deal of the evidence given at the subsequent inquiries indicated a small hole was already there (something the soldiers must have been aware of) and had merely been enlarged. Nevertheless, the aperture was now large enough for a man to pass through and a number of Americans were congregating there, which probably gave the impression an escape attempt was about to take place. The Americans later argued, why should they attempt a break out when deliverance was close at hand? Their assertion that the hole had been made by some of the boy prisoners for the sole purpose of retrieving a ball they'd been playing football with seems a plausible explanation. From the soldiers' point of view, bearing in mind the events of the previous day during the bread dispute, it is understandable the agent ordered the alarm bell to be rung for the second time in three days. Some accounts accuse Captain Shortland of panic, but the orders he gave merit a kinder judgment. He was a seasoned officer of the Royal Navy who had seen active service. Hot blooded he may have been, but his actions so far were fully justified and as so often happens, the officers on the spot have but a minute or two to assess a situation before acting on the information they receive, while the critics more often than not reach their conclusions after long deliberation over written reports.

Unfortunately it was the sounding of the alarm bell that proved to be the critical factor that led to what followed. It aroused the curiosity of the men already in the prisons who came tumbling out in hundreds to find out what was going on and who assembled around the entrance to the market square. Whether by force or because of the sheer weight of numbers straining to see what was happening, the gates gave way and a confused jostling crowd spilled into the lower end of the square just as Captain Shortland appeared at the upper part at the head of about 100 soldiers. He was accompanied by two of the guard commanders, Lt. Fortyne and Lt. Aveline, while another officer, Ensign White, had taken his men to the breach in the wall to prevent any prisoners breaking out through it.

These events coincided with dinner time. The militia officers were dining in their mess in Prince Town, so those present were the only ones on duty when the alarm was raised. The Americans claim Captain Shortland took full charge and that the officers relinquished their commands, an assertion confirmed by the officers themselves at the subsequent inquiry. Certainly he was very quick in sizing up the situation, and noting a large body of Americans in the forbidden area of the market square, gave the order for the soldiers to form an extended line across the square to contain them. It is equally certain he and Dr. MaGrath, the highly respected surgeon, remonstrated with the Americans, as the doctor afterward testified. He related how they had both tried to reason with the men, but because of the heaving mass of bodies it was impossible for those in front to go back owing to the pressure of those behind them pushing to see what was going on. The Rough Allies were shouting insults and taunting the guards, openly daring them to take action. After winning a showdown two days previously, they probably felt they could get away with anything short of actual revolt.

15. The Princetown Massacre

"There was some scuffling...." The confrontation that triggered the Princetown Massacre began when hundreds of Americans broke into the market square, a forbidden area, to be faced by armed soldiers with fixed bayonets. The boldest among the Yankees engaged the soldiers and some of them tried to snatch their muskets. They were so close, the soldiers could not obey the order to "present" (level their weapons and bayonets at their adversaries). Then, above the turmoil and shouting one word was heard above all else: "Fire!" This drawing by Paul Deacon is about 18 by 12 inches (courtesy Paul Deacon).

This time, though, the authorities were determined not to back down. Captain Shortland and his men faced a potentially dangerous situation with hundreds of hostile men advancing towards them in a menacing manner in a forbidden area with the gates open for others to follow. At the same time the bread wagon was being unloaded, and if the contractor were to leave and the upper gates to the square opened to enable him to do so, there would be just a line of soldiers between the unruly crowd and the outside world.

When the now angry mob showed no sign of retreating, the soldiers were ordered to the charge (i.e., to level their muskets and advance at the point of the bayonet), but it was impossible for all of them to do so because of the close proximity of the foremost prisoners, who were still under pressure from those behind. There was then some scuffling and throwing of stones. Some of the soldiers later said there were attempts to snatch their muskets

It was firmly established at the subsequent inquiries that Captain Shortland and Surgeon MaGrath had pleaded with the men to return to their blocks peacefully. American evidence was to the contrary, alleging the incident was planned by Captain Shortland and that he gave the fatal order. We will probably never know the true series of events, but there can be no doubt once the shooting began the agent realized things had gone too far and did all he could to stop the firing, to no avail. This vivid oil painting on canvas depicts Captain Shortland waving his sword in a futile effort to end the affair. Nine unarmed Americans were killed. The war was at an end and the casualties were prisoners no longer (by permission of Paul Deacon).

while other prisoners defied them to fire, all of which was denied by the Yankees, who maintained they were all by this time "hurrying and flying in terrible flight." By their own account, however, they had stood firm in the bread crisis, and it is difficult to believe they ran away so soon on this occasion. What is undisputed is that someone shouted *"Fire!"* The response was an erratic burst of fire, mainly over the prisoners' heads, the soldiers finding it almost impossible to take aim in the melee.

The prisoners maintained it was Captain Shortland who gave this order; all other evidence is to the contrary and that someone else gave it. Furthermore, Captain Shortland, in his written statement to the inquiry that followed, said it was Major Jolliffe who gave the order to open fire. The major vigorously denied this, and with justification, for he was at dinner a quarter of a mile away in Prince Town when the alarm was raised, and by the time he arrived on the scene with a body of grenadiers the shooting had already started. One of the conclusions reached by the inquiry was that if all the officers had been present, the shooting and bayoneting would most likely have been stopped sooner and the soldiers prevented from pursuing the prisoners to the doors of their prison blocks.

The Americans finally realized the serious intent of the military and there was a general retreat to the prison yards. A few defiant men, noting there were no casualties, yelled "blank cartridges!" upon which a large number of them halted their flight. It should be borne in mind most of these men were no strangers to a fight—they were captured on active service and did not scare easily. All the same, it is an undisputed fact they were all inside the prison yards when the shooting resumed. Dead and wounded men fell, causing panic on the part of those who had not regained their prison blocks. The turnkeys had already locked some of the doors, consequently access to the blocks was restricted as crowds of struggling men were trying to gain entry. The musket fire, although sporadic, was now continuous.

The tension at Dartmoor had finally snapped and the soldiers' tempers with it. For months they had endured insults, taunts, and stone throwing; now the time had come when once the first shots were fired, the troops were out for bloody revenge. One brave American, a U.S. Navy warrant officer named James Greenlaw, ignored the whizzing musket balls and actually advanced toward them, pleading with the soldiery to desist. He was ignored (the Americans claimed Captain Shortland called him "a damned rascal" and said he "would listen to nothing"). The more credible evidence is that seeing matters had gotten out of hand, the agent was at this time trying to stop the shooting, but it was to no avail. The soldiers in the market square were joined by the sentries on the walls in executing a terrible cross fire on the mass of men below. Other soldiers broke ranks and pursued the prisoners to the very doors of their prisons, shooting and bayoneting as they went, firing into doorways at close quarters. This was later verified by an examination of the pockmarked interior walls.

The entire episode was over in minutes. Captain Shortland and the militiamen finally left the scene, leaving the indomitable Dr. MaGrath and his helpers to collect the dead and succor the living. The doctor realized at once the serious condition of the wounded and sent to the nearest town (almost certainly Tavistock) for help. It says a great deal about his integrity and the respect he commanded among the Americans that he was allowed into the prison blocks to see if there were further casualties who might need treatment.

A frightful price had been paid for what was most likely a misunderstanding on both sides.

Accounts vary as to the exact number of casualties, but Whiteford, the coroner for the district, held inquests on five men who were killed on the spot and four of the badly wounded who died later, bringing the total number of dead to nine. The Americans at first said there were 63 dead and injured, claiming there had been victims who were buried secretly so as to minimize the official number killed. This was refuted by Charles Andrews, who checked the victims' names against the hospital records. The true casualty figure will never be known, because apart from the 30 seriously hurt, a large number of wounded men retired to their dormitories and stayed there, too frightened to come out even to receive medical attention. Several others had holes in their hats and clothing from bayonet thrusts or musket balls. The condition of the casualties can scarcely be imagined — the bone crushing musket shot inflicted injuries of a horrifying nature — and looking back from our modern world we can hardly begin to conceive the agonies of undergoing surgery without anesthetics or pain killing drugs.

Most significant of all was the prisoners' knowledge they had been attacked at a time when they were in fact free men by troops of a now "friendly" nation. One individual alone was singled out for blame: Captain Shortland. The militia officers who took part in the affair, perhaps unnerved by events, were quick to deny responsibility. Lt. Aveline, for example, later testified, "The soldiers did not fire by my order. I considered myself under Captain Shortland's orders." But he also said if he had been in command he would have ordered the troops to fire sooner than they did. Lt. Fortyne said, "My guard took up the firing from the others without my orders." The Americans branded the agent "a Nero and an inhuman monster." One has to sympathize with them, but as their individual testimony afterward revealed, and as any police officer would tell you today, events are seen and interpreted quite differently by different observers. One incident that occurred is to the everlasting credit of the Americans. When the shooting began and the prisoners ran for safety, a lamplighter from the very regiment engaged in killing their comrades was caught in the rush and carried bodily inside one of the prisons. There the Americans could have taken their revenge, but good sense prevailed: after some consultation the man was freed "that the whole world might distinguish the difference between unprovoked British soldiers and the injured and provoked American seamen."

At 9 A.M. the next day the American flag was hoisted and flown at half mast from every prison block. Colonel Ayre arrived from Plymouth with a body of troops and assumed command of the depot. He met and talked with prisoners, informing them an inquest would be held the next day and that "a strict investigation would be held." This was confirmed later in the day by Rear Admiral J. Rowley, who also met and talked to them. The admiral was sympathetic and conciliatory in his manner, which encouraged the Americans to believe their account of the affair would be accepted.

Meanwhile some of the prisoners, including Charles Andrews, visited the hospital and were appalled at what they saw. The tables were still littered with amputated limbs and the groans of the wounded men; this with the sight of their injuries, Andrews wrote, "was enough to freeze the blood of the most hardened parricide." The horrors of the wards revealed all the dead had been killed by musket shot and every one of the wounded suffered from musket shot or bayonet wounds, in some cases both. Several men had been wounded up to five times. When account is taken of those who declined to seek medical attention and the number of near misses, the savagery of the attack is convincingly apparent.

A jury of twelve Dartmoor farmers under Coroner Joseph Whiteford spent nearly two days taking evidence from all concerned. On the evening of the second day, April 9, they returned a verdict of "justifiable homicide." Now the dead could be buried and this was done in the usual manner without any ceremony. No one was permitted to attend the burials, something which only served to deepen the bitter feelings of their fellow prisoners.

Details of Casualties

Dr. MaGrath, the prison surgeon, made the following reports concerning the dead and injured.

John Haywood, a black man from Virginia.
The ball entered a little posterior to the acromien of the left shoulder, and, passing upwards, made its egress about the middle of the right side of the neck.
Prison No............................3134
Quality ....Seaman
From what ship..................Gave himself up from HMS *Scipion*

Thomas Jackson, from New York, a boy of fourteen.
The ball entered the left side of the belly, nearly in a line with the navel, and made its egress a little below the false ribs in the opposite side; a large portion of the intestinal canal protruded through the wound made by the ingress of the ball. He languished until 8 o'clock on the morning of the 7th, when he died.
Prison No............................6520
Quality ....Boy
From what ship..................Gave himself up from HMS *Prontes*

John Washington from Maryland.
The ball entered at the squamose process of the left temporal bone, and, passing through the head, made its exit a little below the crucial ridge of the occipital bone.
Prison No............................3936
Quality ....Seaman
From what ship...................*Rolla* (Merchant vessel)

James Mann from Boston.
The ball entered at the inferior angle of the left scapula and lodged under the integument of the right pectoral muscle. In its course it passed through the inferior margin of the right and left lobes of the lungs.
Prison No............................970
Quality ....Seaman
From what ship...................*Siroc* (Letter of Marque)

Joseph Toker Johnson from Connecticut.
The ball entered at the inferior angle of the left scapula, penetrated the heart, and passing through both lobes of the lungs, made its egress at the right axilla.
Prison No............................1347
Quality ....Seaman
From what ship...................Privateer

William Laverage (Leveridge in the report) from New York.
The ball entered about the middle of the left arm, through which it passed, and, penetrating the corresponding side, betwixt the second and third ribs, passing through the left lobe of the lungs, the mediastinum, and over the right lobe, lodged between the fifth and sixth ribs.
Prison No............................4884
Quality ....Seaman
From what ship...................*Enterprise*, prize to *Saratoga*

James Campbell from New York.
The ball entered at the outer angle of the right eye, and in its course it fractured and depressed the greater part of the frontal bone, fractured the nasal bones, and made its egress above the orbital ridge of the left eye. He languished until the morning of the 8th, when he died.
Prison No............................2647
Quality ....Seaman
From what ship...................*Volontaire* (Merchant vessel)

Five men were shot dead on April 6; 14-year-old Thomas Jackson died on the 7th and James Campbell died on the 8th. The coroner's verdict described John Haywood as "an American prisoner who was killed by the military in attempting to break prison." The others were referred to individually as "another American prisoner also killed by the military." This was not the end of this unsavory incident, for among the wounded were two men who died several days afterward and for whom the Coroner Whiteford was obliged to arrange further inquests. They were:

John Roberts, died April 12.
Wounded in the thigh. Killed by musket shot.
Prison No...........................486
Quality ....Seaman
From what ship..................*Two Brothers*. Impressed at Cork.
Verdict: An American killed by the military firing to prevent the escape of prisoners.

John Grey, died April 26.
Wounded in the left arm which had to be amputated. Killed by musket shot.
Prison No...........................94
Quality ....Seaman
From what ship..................*St. Martin's Planter* (Merchant vessel)
Verdict: Killed by the military firing on the prisoners to prevent their escape.

All the spellings of the dead men's names (except Grey and Roberts) are taken from Charles Andrews' account. To this day the opinion held by the British is that either a mutiny or a mass escape attempt was the cause of the massacre.

Hatred and revulsion festered among the Americans: "Your whole nation is involved as a black accomplice to your monstrous guilt," wrote Charles Andrews, "the blood of my unfortunate countrymen, shed by your base hand, must ever remain a stain on the character of your nation." Benjamin Palmer's reaction was more blunt: "We cry for vengeance!" American outrage and anger lasted for more than a generation.

The Americans' sentiments were expressed by an anonymous poet who penned a graphic account in rhyme titled the "Horrid Massacre at Dartmoor Prison, England," too long to be included in full but which concludes:

> Give us redress, let Shortland swing, or meet our swords again.
> Old George beware! If you again the contest shall renew
> We'll show you that the Yankee lads have better pluck than you!
> Revenge is sweet, and on the Book of Heav'n now stands enrolled
> Your hellish deeds, your murd'rous acts, your bribery with your gold,
> Look to Yourself, for should again the veng'ful sword be drawn
> The setting sun of England's pride should hail Columbia's dawn.

> The Stripes and Stars should proudly wave, that Neptune from his car
> Would yield to us his Tridents up to hurl the bolts of war!
> Your haughty Ensign by our own tars from your tall masts be torn,
> Your red Coats dread to see True Blue, on swiftest pinions borne.
> So for the present, fare ye well, your long lost fame regain
> And when we settle up accounts — we'll call on you again.

16

The Inquiries into the "Melancholy Occurrence"

Captain Shortland reported the tragedy to the Royal Navy commander in chief at Plymouth, Admiral Sir John Duckworth, who received the news in writing from the captain late at night on the day it happened. He at once ordered an inquiry, and in a letter dated April 7, 1815, he instructed Rear Admiral Sir J. Rowley to proceed immediately to the prison at Dartmoor, taking with him Capt. A. W. Schomberg of HMS *York*, the senior captain at Plymouth. After indicating what form the questioning should take, his letter goes on:

> You will then address the prisoners and will use every argument that may suggest itself to you to conciliate them, to tranquilize their minds, and to prevail upon them cheerfully to look forward to their speedy return to their own country. You will explain to them ... they ought not to feel as prisoners but as passengers waiting for conveyance.

This was the speech previously referred to which caused the Americans to think their version of events would be believed. The army held a separate military court of inquiry on the orders of Major General Browne, officer commanding the Plymouth Garrison. The details of this inquiry were not made known at the time, having been forwarded to the Horse Guards (London), but were made available for the consideration of those who conducted the second, international, inquiry later. The naval inquiry was prompt but brief and was completed in a day. It did not take account of the soldiers' statements because, they said, they were "not feeling ourselves authorised to carry our investigation into the transactions of the military."

Four of the statements taken were:

1. Captain Shortland. After describing the events leading up to the shooting, he mentions the efforts made by Dr. MaGrath and himself to

"induce them [the Americans] not to go on in their attempt, which I looked upon to be to surround the guard and disarm them. Upon them still advancing close to the military they [the soldiers] charged and fired, but not before the prisoners attempted to wrest the muskets out of some of their hands. My advanced situation ... at the time of firing would have made it an imprudent act of mine to have directed the military to fire.... The reason of the present riot I have not been able to ascertain further than that general dissatisfaction prevails at being detained in England."

2. Lt. Aveline, 1st Somerset Militia. Described Captain Shortland's unsuccessful attempt to remonstrate with the prisoners who were advancing when "a shot was fired from a soldier, when the guard fired ... it is my opinion that if the guard had not acted in that manner they would have been endangered ... the prisoners had hold of the musket of the soldier who fired so that he was obliged to fire in his own defence. I understand that some of the military thought that Captain Shortland had given the order to fire, but this morning contradicted it."
3. Surgeon George MaGrath. Described his and Captain Shortland's exhortations to the prisoners: "I heard some person say Charge and I was then driven at the point of the bayonet towards the lower part of the square, and when I was endeavouring to get in the rear a discharge of musketry took place. I then immediately left the place to make preparation for the expected wounded."
4. Lt. (Ensign) White, 1st Somerset Militia. Told how he went with the West Guard to the breach in the wall, which was "a considerable hole.... I repeatedly desired the prisoners to desist but they continued throwing stones and behaved in a most insulting manner." He and his men stayed there until half past eight, so were unable to help further in the inquiry.

In the report submitted to Admiral Duckworth dated April 7, Rear Admiral Rowley and Captain Schomberg affirmed they had assembled all the American prisoners at Dartmoor and asked them whether they had any complaint as to their treatment in the prison. "They answered they had none whatsoever. They had complained a few days ago of the alteration of their allowance of biscuit in lieu of soft bread ... but this had been remedied. They repeatedly and unanimously declared that they did not attribute their protracted confinement to any fault of the British government but from their own not having sent conveyance for their removal."

The Americans were asked to give an explanation. "They denied everything relative to any riot and said the hole had been made by some of their boys at play." The report concluded: "But as a powerful force of men was found at the breach at the time of the riot, ready to force their way through it, it is clear that the breach was intended as a part of the attack upon the depot. We are of the opinion that there had been no ostensible cause for the riot ... and can only attribute it to a strong desire on their part to escape from confinement at any risk notwithstanding their assurance to us of the contrary."[1]

The Americans were stunned. They had thought their evidence to be irrefutable, and their anger was further inflamed by a newspaper report which referred to their actions on that fateful day as a "mutiny." There was a glowing account of how the valiant Captain Shortland faced the mob alone and unarmed; the same report said 12 men were shot to death, thereby refueling rumors about secret burials.

By this time several prisoners were leaving the depot ahead of the rest, having volunteered in response to requests by American agents to man a number of vessels in European ports under American command. Most of these men passed through London and made it their business to deposit sworn statements with the authorities there which contradicted the outcome of the inquiry and the inquest verdicts.

A letter from the Transport Office to Captain Shortland of April 18, 1815, stated in part:

The Market Square today is instantly recognizable, but now all is peaceful (author's photograph).

16. The Inquiries into the "Melancholy Occurrence"

A dramatic representation of the "Melancholy Occurrence" is painted in oil on canvas by Paul Deacon. The uniforms are those of the 1st Somerset Militia, but there was one other unit involved, the Derbyshire Militia, which took part in the proceedings and gave evidence at the subsequent inquiries (published with permission of Paul Deacon).

Sir,

It having been represented to His Majesty's government that the cause of the late riot among the prisoners at Dartmoor was very different from what has been reported to us, and it being expedient that in an affair of such importance there should be no misapprehension, we acquaint you that Mr. King has been appointed on the part of the American government and Mr. Larpent by His Majesty's government to proceed to Dartmoor for the purpose of investigating the causes of the melancholy occurrence, and we desire that the greatest attention be paid to these gentlemen.

Francis Seymour Larpent was an ideal choice for this delicate task, having had wide experience as judge advocate to the Duke of Wellington in the Peninsula from 1812 to 1814. In 1813 he was taken prisoner by the French but was quickly released on exchange. All the same, the experience must have enabled him to play his part with some sympathy, and he was probably the most fair-minded person available on the British side. Charles King was an eminent businessman from the State of New York, merchant, editor, and 9th president of Columbia University. He had also served as captain of an American militia regiment, despite the fact he was privately opposed to the war. He happened to be in England on business when he was asked to participate in the inquiry. Charming, handsome, dignified, and with a reputation for impartiality, he was considered an ideal choice, but when the findings were made known, his summing up was thought by the Americans to be far too magnanimous. King and his father were afterward ostracized at home by politicians and businessmen alike. This second inquiry was to be the final and most exhaustive one, with evidence taken from Americans in Plymouth who had been released and were on the point of sailing for home. Some of them were from the cartel ships, among them the *Maria Christiana*, on which Charles Andrews was one of the passengers.

The Transport Office sent the following letter to the lord mayor of Plymouth:

Whitehall 18th April 1815

Sir,

I have Lord Sidmouth's directions to acquaint you that Mr. Seymour Larpent and Mr. Charles King have been appointed on behalf of the British and American governments respectively to proceed forthwith to Dartmoor for the purpose of investigating the late unfortunate event in the prison at that place. For the purpose of executing their commission it will be necessary that these gentlemen should have the assistance of the civil authorities of that district for the purpose of calling witnesses and administering oaths. I am therefore to request that you would take the trouble of attending the inquiry above alluded to, and of rendering such assistance to the gentlemen above mentioned as may be necessary in the course of their investigation, and that you would solicit some other magistrate to accompany you on this important occasion for the same purpose.

I have the honour to be, Sir,
Your Most Obedient and Humble Servant,
J. Becket.

The proceedings were conducted in the City Hall at Plymouth, and as the mayor was unable to attend, city magistrate Woolcombe officiated, assisted by Hawker, a county magistrate and former American consul. Several members of the American Committee at Dartmoor[2] who had been released and were in Plymouth at the time were invited to inquire around the city and on the cartels for any of their countrymen who were prepared to give evidence. A number of soldiers of the 1st Somerset Militia who had been present in the market square were selected to appear, and the depositions made at the Military Court of Inquiry were made available by Major General Browne.

The investigation then removed to the depot for three days; there the other members of the American committee who had not yet been released and any other prisoners willing to attend were questioned. This was followed

16. The Inquiries into the "Melancholy Occurrence"

by an examination of the prison blocks. It was a very thorough inquiry where statements from a total of 72 witnesses were scrutinized.

The American committee report said there was no intention on the Americans' part to attempt an escape. They refuted claims that they had thrown stones or harassed the soldiers. They intimated the whole episode had been planned by Captain Shortland to punish them for not being compliant captives and in revenge for what happened two days previously when they demanded (and got) their bread ration instead of biscuits. They claimed he was heard to say, "I'll teach the damned rascals directly!" before sending soldiers to man the walls in readiness for what followed and that he was intoxicated. This assertion was refuted by Surgeon MaGrath, who said in evidence "that there was not the least pretence for this accusation as he was most perfectly sober ... and that in his mode of living and domestic habits [he] was in every respect particularly abstemious." They said a soldier had warned them they "would be charged upon directly."

The most serious and controversial allegation they made, after admitting a number of prisoners had invaded the market square, was that "Captain Shortland ordered the soldiers to charge upon them; which orders the soldiers were reluctant in obeying, as the prisoners used no violence; but on the order being repeated, they made a charge, and the prisoners retreated out of the square into their respective yards and shut the gates after them. Captain Shortland himself opened the gates, and ordered the soldiers to fire in among the prisoners who were retreating in different directions towards their respective prisons.... There was some hesitation in the minds of the officers whether or not it was proper to fire upon the prisoners.... Shortland seized a musket out of the hands of a soldier, which he fired."

Prisoner witnesses who gave evidence before Larpent and King swore two prisoners were cornered by soldiers outside their prisons and were shot to death while pleading for mercy. The rest of the evidence given by the prisoners was just as biased, either glossing over the stone throwing and abuse hurled at the military by their comrades or simply leaving out anything that might incriminate them.

The soldiers' testimony was equally one-sided. Nearly every one of them who was called said there were stones thrown at them (one was hit in the head and had his cap knocked off by another missile); that the Americans persisted in trying to push past them; that some of them tried to get hold of their muskets and that they were (most of them) unsure about how the firing commenced, only that someone had given the order to do so. A turnkey, William Wakeline, described how a prisoner called Reeves "was very violent and opened his breast and challenged them to fire saying 'fire you bastards—fire!'" giving credence to a suggestion by the investigators that it could have been one of the prisoners shouting that caused the shooting to begin.

Lt. Aveline confirmed Captain Shortland had pleaded with the prisoners to return to their prisons and that in ignoring his pleas "they were pressing on the left where the line did not go close to the walls [this would have been the wall of the hospital] ... the men fell back that the prisoners might not get too near them." This was noted by Captain Shortland, who cried, "for God's sake soldiers, keep your ground!" It was also noted "that his men finally charged, and he was with them ... it was not by his order or he would have charged before or indeed have fired before, judging that this was necessary from the threatening manner of the prisoners ... who could have surrounded his guard."

Captain Shortland himself made a statement later judged to be a confused one. He described being told about the breach in the wall and going to examine it. After arguing with prisoners who were attempting to enlarge it, he heard someone call out that the lower gates to the market square were being forced and saw prisoners in the square. He ordered the alarm bell to be sounded and led one of the guards under Lt. Aveline to the market square, where he estimated there were between four hundred and five hundred prisoners. He described the soldiers forming a line across the square and how he was trying to reason with the prisoners when the shooting started — a musket ball actually grazed his temple, he said. He then claimed Major Jolliffe must have given an order to fire, having just seen him appear at the scene (in fact the major arrived after the firing began and all the evidence confirmed that his first act was to order it to stop). Shortland's evidence concluded with: "I did not hear any orders to fire. It must be understood that I was with the prisoners who were making a great noise, hurrahing and rioting at the time ... taking into consideration the apparent temper and resolution of the prisoners, and my remonstrances having no effect, I do not think they could have been driven back without firing."

Here are some of the more important findings of the inquiry:

1. Since the ratification of the Treaty of Ghent, the prisoners' impatience for release did lead to a threat to break out of the depot.
2. The "bread riot" was resolved without the use of force.
3. The breach in the wall was large enough for a man to pass through. At the time of day when the men should be returning to their prisons a large body of men had congregated adjacent to the hole (in the area between the wall and the railings) which in itself was against the regulations as well as giving cause for alarm.

16. The Inquiries into the "Melancholy Occurrence"

4. Arms were kept in an armory adjacent to the hole in the wall. There was no evidence to suggest this was the motive for making the hole, but it was further cause for suspicion and alarm.
5. Captain Shortland did have sufficient grounds for sounding the alarm.
6. It was confirmed the gates were forced. There was no evidence that a planned escape was about to take place, but the only inference to be drawn from the number of prisoners in the market square was that it might be attempted. It was confirmed the bread wagon was due and that the outer gates might be opened at about this time, giving the prisoners an escape opportunity if they got past the line of soldiers drawn up across the square [the bread wagon had already arrived and was being unloaded].
7. When firing commenced there was an unruly group still in the gateway. As to who gave the order to shoot, Captain Shortland was an unlikely suspect because, as was pointed out, he was standing in front of the soldiers at the time.
8. The stone throwing, the pushing of large numbers of men against those in front and the remonstrances of the agent and Dr. MaGrath were all confirmed in the evidence given.

As for Captain Shortland and the question of who gave the order to fire, the conclusion drawn by the inquiry was concisely expressed by Larpent in the final remarks he made in a separate report to Viscount Castlereagh:

> Captain Shortland had been most judicious and humane and until very lately he had always been on very good terms with the prisoners under his charge. It is but justice also to mention that whether the firing did or did not commence by his order ... he was one of the first to endeavour to make it cease, and that in my opinion (though not a decided one) no regular order to fire was ever given by anyone. On the contrary I rather conceive the firing to have commenced from the accidental discharge of one musquet, or from someone without authority calling fire, perhaps even the prisoners themselves who appear from the evidence to have done so, little expecting to be taken at their word.

The inquiry also noted:

> This firing was to an extent justifiable in a military point of view in order to intimidate the prisoners and compel them to thereby desist from all acts of violence and to retire as they were ordered from a situation in which the responsibility of the agent and the military could not permit them with safety to remain.

Concerning the shots fired after the prisoners had fled to their prison yards, they had this to say: "The firing continued evidently as a result of individual irritation." With the troops getting out of hand, there were too few officers to restrain them (most of the officers were at dinner) and it was branded as "quite indefensible."

It was a penetrating effort to establish exactly what happened, but once again Captain Shortland was cleared of blame and it was the inquiry's belief he had acted with justifiable intent in every respect. King had a private opinion, however, which he confided to John Quincy Adams, the American ambassador to Britain, to whom he wrote: "Whether the order to fire came from Captain Shortland, I yet confess myself unable to form any satisfactory opinion, though the balance of my mind is that he did give such an order."

He then goes on to praise the agent in glowing terms: "His anxiety and exertions to stop it after it had continued for some little time are fully proved, and his general conduct as far as we could with propriety enter into such details, appears to have been characterised with great fairness and even kindness in the light in which he stood towards the prisoners." Of the prisoners themselves, he said: "They made no complaint whatsoever as to their provisions and general mode of living and treatment in the prison."

This last aspect of the affair seems to have been overlooked in some accounts — after all, it was Captain Shortland who admitted Americans to the market immediately after he took office and showed some compassion (probably against instructions) to Simeon Hayes and his companions in the Black Hole. As for King, his final comments to Adams were: "I cannot conclude, Sir, without expressing my high sense of the impartiality and manly firmness with which this enquiry has been conducted on the part of Mr. Larpent, nor without mentioning that every facility was afforded to us in its prosecution as well as by the military officers here at the prison, and by the magistrates in the vicinity."[3]

The inquiry report concluded with the following words: "We used every endeavour to ascertain, if there was the least prospect of identifying any of the soldiers who had been guilty of the particular outrages ... or of tracing any particular death ... to the firing of any particular individual, but without success, and all hopes of bringing the offenders to punishment seem to be at an end."

In conclusion: "We the undersigned, have only to add, that while we lament, as we do most deeply, the unfortunate transaction which has been the subject if this inquiry, we find ourselves totally unable to suggest any steps to be taken as to those parts of it which seem most to call for redress and punishment." This was signed by Francis Seymour Larpent at Plymouth, April 26, 1815.[4]

No one was to be punished.

It was suggested that repatriation was afterwards speeded up by the British

16. The Inquiries into the "Melancholy Occurrence" 149

in order to get important witnesses home to disperse and probably be untraceable should yet another investigation be made. After two inquiries (three, including the military one) it is difficult to believe this, yet it is a fact that only six days after the tragedy Captain Shortland was ordered to prepare 200 men for release. It had been agreed the British should pay for the cartels and would negotiate recovery of the cost from any post-war settlement.

Questions Yet Unanswered

Was it a mutiny? Surely not when at the start thousands of prisoners had already returned to their prisons and only some stragglers remained to be accounted for.

Was it an escape attempt? Again unlikely and for the same reasons. It was the ringing of the alarm bell that brought the men back out to see what was going on.

Was it a riot? This is a more accurate description of what took place.

Was Captain Shortland the black-hearted villain the Americans viewed him as? He was a complicated character who showed the prisoners sympathetic consideration to begin with but whose temper often got the better of him.

Who really shouted "fire!" Captain Shortland? A frightened soldier? Or maybe a defiant American?

These questions remain unresolved to this day — it all depends on whose side you are on and how you view the evidence. It was summed up rather neatly in a BBC television documentary about the incident some years ago in which the commentator remarked: "The Americans blamed Captain Shortland, the British blamed no one — it just happened."

The families of the men who were killed or wounded were offered compensation by the prince regent on behalf of the British government, but the Americans politely declined the offer.

In August, James Monroe, secretary of state (later 5th U.S. president) wrote to Anthony James Baker, British charge d'affairs and resident in the U.S.[5]:

Philadelphia
August 3, 1815

Sir,
In a communication made by Viscount Castlereagh, His Majesty's secretary of state for foreign affairs, to Messrs. Clay and Gallatin on the 20th of last May, relative to the unfortunate occurrence at Dartmoor prison, His Lordship expressed to those gentlemen, by the command of H.R.H. the Prince Regent, how deeply His Royal Highness lamented the consequences of that unhappy affair, and that if anything could have alleviated the distress which His Royal

Highness felt on that occasion, it was the consideration that the conduct of the soldiers had not been actuated by any spirit of animosity towards the prisoners, and that the inactivity of the officers was to be attributed rather to the inexperience of a militia force, than to any want of zeal or inclination to afford that liberal protection which is ever due to prisoners of war.

His Lordship likewise informed them that although the firing appeared to have been justified at its commencement by the turbulent behaviour of the prisoners, yet that as the extent of the calamity was to be ascribed to a want of steadiness in the troops and of exertion in the officers, calling for the most severe animadversion, His Royal Highness had been pleased to direct the Commander in Chief to address to the Commanding Officer of the Somerset Militia, his disapprobation of the conduct of the troops, so that a due impression might be made on the minds of the officers and men engaged in that unfortunate transaction.

As an additional proof of the sentiments which animated the Prince Regent on this painful occasion, His Lordship was also further commanded to impress to Messrs. Clay and Gallatin[6] His Royal Highness' desire to make a compensation to the widows and families of the sufferers.

In re-iterating these sentiments on the part of His Majesty's government for the information of the President of the United States, I have the honour to acquaint you that I have been directed to concert with the American Government the most efficient means of carrying into execution these benevolent intentions of His Royal Highness the Prince Regent; and shall be ready, with a view of expediting the arrangements to be made, to proceed to Washington without delay for the purpose of communicating with you personally on the subject, should it suit your convenience to meet me there. I beg leave at the same time to suggest as a necessary preliminary to any measures which may be adopted, that information should be procured from the different states with respect to the families of the sufferers, and any other circumstances which may facilitate the completion of the arrangements alluded to.

I have the honour to be etc.

Anthony St. John Baker

The American response was made from Secretary of State James Monroe to Anthony St. John Baker, British charge d'affairs, on December 11, 1815.[7]

Sir,

I have had the honour to receive your letter of the 3rd of August, communicating a proposition of your government to make provision for the widows and families of the sufferers in the much to be lamented occurrence at Dartmoor.

It is painful to touch on this unfortunate event, from the deep distress it has caused to the whole American people. This repugnance is increased by the consideration that our governments, though penetrated with regret, do not agree in sentiment respecting the conduct of the parties engaged in it.

While the President [James Madison] declines accepting the provision contem-

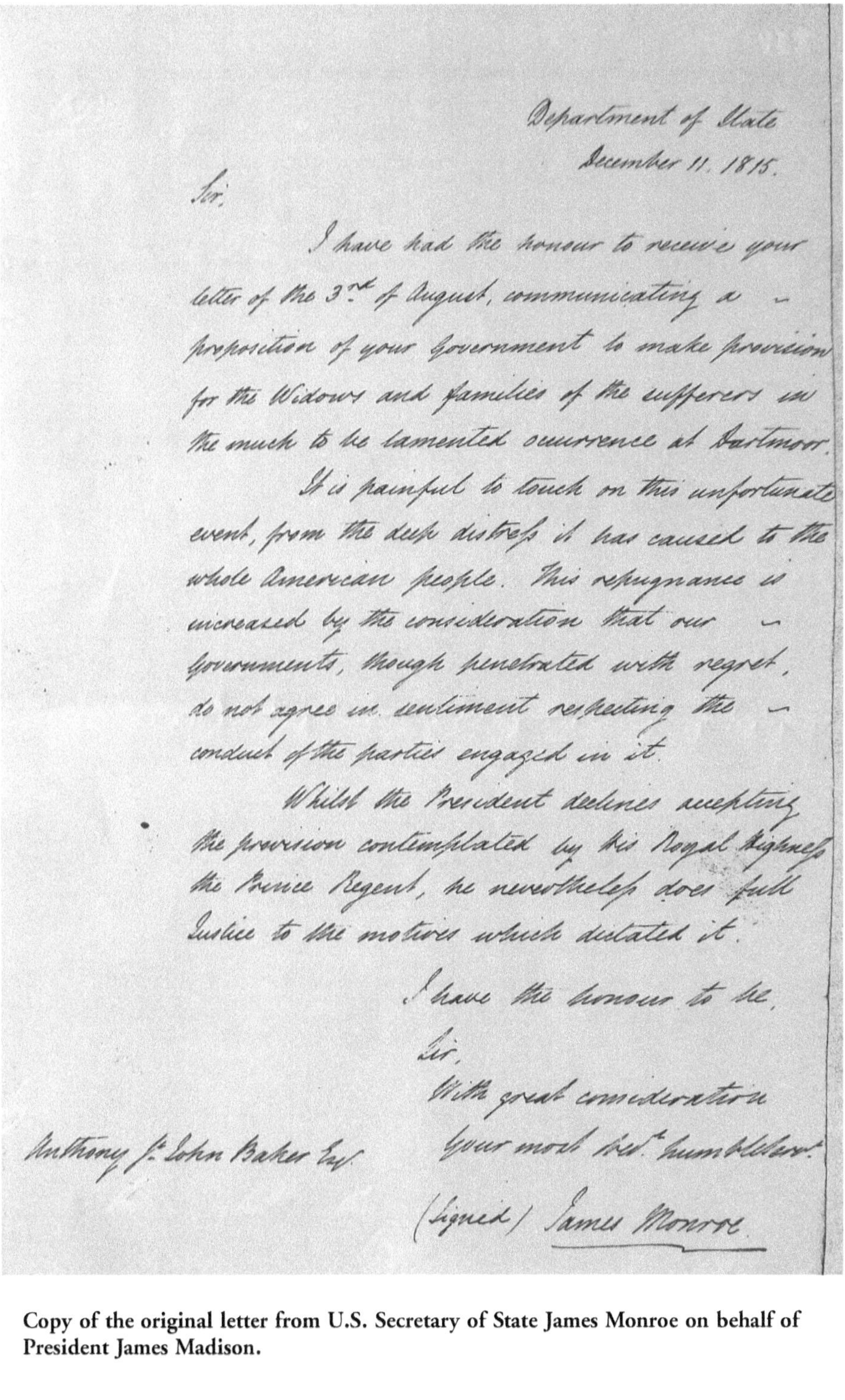

Department of State
December 11, 1815.

Sir,

I have had the honour to receive your letter of the 3rd of August, communicating a proposition of your government to make provision for the Widows and families of the sufferers in the much to be lamented occurrence at Dartmoor.

It is painful to touch on this unfortunate event, from the deep distress it has caused to the whole American people. This repugnance is increased by the consideration that our Governments, though penetrated with regret, do not agree in sentiment respecting the conduct of the parties engaged in it.

Whilst the President declines accepting the provision contemplated by his Royal Highness the Prince Regent, he nevertheless does full justice to the motives which dictated it.

I have the honour to be,
Sir,
With great consideration
Your most obedt. humble Servt.
(Signed) James Monroe

Anthony St. John Baker Esq.

Copy of the original letter from U.S. Secretary of State James Monroe on behalf of President James Madison.

plated by His Royal Highness the Prince Regent, he nevertheless does full justice to the motive which dictated it.

> I have the honour to be, Sir,
> With great consideration,
> Your most humble servt.
> [Signed] James Monroe.

So it remains to this day, an embarrassment to the British; an outrage to the Americans.

17

Privateers

What was a privateer? The dictionary tells us they were "armed ships owned and officered by private individuals holding a government commission and authorised for use in war, especially in the capture of merchant shipping." An alternative term for "government commission" was "letter of marque," a document also issued by the government, or the president, or in days gone by, the sovereign. Queen Elizabeth I granted one such letter to Sir Francis Drake, whose exploits against Spanish ships were so successful he brought home to the queen enormous riches in gold, silver and coinage. It also made him a wealthy man because a percentage of the loot was awarded him and his crew. Authorized or not, there was a stigma on such men, who were often classed as pirates,[1] which they were not.

One subtle difference was the restriction placed on such vessels concerning where they could ply their trade. Privateers were told where to cruise and which country's ships to intercept and if possible capture. Letter of marque ships were armed merchantmen that plied the normal trade routes but were authorized to attack and capture certain other ships. In both cases the instructions applied only in time of war and referred to vessels flying the enemy flag.

During the American Revolution, the Napoleonic Wars, and later still the War of 1812, privateering was big business and was encouraged on all sides. In the course of the latter war the American government actively supported this type of warfare, its Navy being unequal in size to Britain's Royal Navy. Furthermore, the Americans found it difficult to muster enough trained men for naval service. The British maintained an effective blockade of the American ports, thus preventing its capital ships from putting to sea. American privateers did invaluable service; apart from the often huge rewards to be had, they disrupted British shipping[2] and very essential trade to the extent a convoy system had to be adopted with Royal Navy escorts.

The damage was extensive and worldwide; for example even the British whaling ships in the Pacific Ocean were not safe from attack and several losses were sustained in home waters under the very noses of the Royal Navy warships. In return for all the daring and risks they took, the privateersmen were rewarded with a share of the proceeds, i.e., the value of the cargoes and the captured ship itself (if not too badly damaged in the capturing of it). A "prize captain" was appointed from the privateer crew and sufficient seamen allocated to sail their prize to designated ports, where the owners would auction the cargo from which the crew would claim their rewards. An example of such a privateering voyage will make the position clear.

In December 1812 the private armed ship *John* of Salem, Massachusetts, was fitted out and a captain and crew appointed in preparation for a cruise off the coast of South America and the West Indies. The captain was James M. Fairfield, recently appointed after serving as first lieutenant in the same ship. The following excerpts are taken from his letter of appointment.

> Dear Sir,
> You are appointed captain of the private armed ship "John" of Salem and duly commissioned by the government of the U.S.A. to capture and bring into the ports the ships and vessels of the gov't of Great Britain and her colonies and of any of her subjects. We have armed, manned and well appointed the above ship and entrusted her command to you, trusting that you will do honour to yourself and your country; for which purpose you must be steady and cool, and preserve good order.

A detailed order is included directing Captain Fairfield where he may roam and where to send the prizes he may take, and concludes:

> Always send home the captain or mate of any vessel you take, together with all her papers in charge with the prize master and tell him to take care of the captain's arms etc.
> We know not what more to say only take as many prizes as you can and send them home. Relying on your good conduct we are your friends — the owners. Dec. 12th 1812. I acknowledge the foregoing to be a true copy of my Instructions & will follow them.
>
> Witness Bruce L.
Signed James M. Fairfield

His crew numbered 89 and included a surgeon, seven prize masters,[3] gunner, armorer, a captain of Marines and four Marines, as well as the usual complement of mates, seamen, and others needed. There were seven boys. Altogether it was a typical crew for an armed vessel of this kind.

Despite the charge that a large percentage of privateers were ruffians, there was a strict code of conduct laid down by the owners. Dartmoor prisoner of war George Little (see Chapter 18) wrote: "Many were gathered from the vilest haunts of dissipation and vice from perhaps all the seaports of the United States." He was referring to the Rough Allies at Dartmoor, where the vast majority of prisoners were privateers. Maybe the owners recognized the dubious quality of some seafarers they employed and made provision for a certain code of behavior to be observed aboard their ships. The rules laid down were generally much the same and included:

- That for preserving due decorum on board the said Vessel, no man is to quit or go out of her, or board any other vessel or go on shore without leave of the commanding officer.
- That the cruise shall be where the owners direct.
- If any person shall steal or convert for his own use any part of a prize, he shall be punished and forfeit his share.
- That whosoever first discovers a prize that proves worth one hundred dollars per share shall receive twenty dollars from the gross sum, and if orders are given for boarding the first man on the deck of the enemy shall receive one half of a share.
- That of any one of the said company shall die or be killed ... his share shall be paid to his legal representative.
- That of any of the company strike or assault any male prisoner or rudely treat any female prisoner, he shall be punished.
- That whoever shall desert the said vessel shall forfeit his prize money.
- That if any one of the ship's company shall lose an eye or a joint he shall receive fifty dollars; and if he lose a leg or an arm he shall receive three hundred dollars.

The terms seem fair and the rewards for a successful cruise could be generous. As you might expect, the captain was due the greatest reward in the number of shares he received at the end of a successful voyage. A brief sample of crew shares reads:

Captain	10	Shares
1st Lieutenant	7½	"
Surgeon	5	"
Gunner	2	"
Mates	1½	"
Seamen	1	"
Boys	¾	"

On a previous voyage (September 1812) the *John* (Captain B.W. Crowninshield) brought back three prize ships captured which are worthy of note. The Brig *Ceres* yielded 247 tons of timber and hundreds of feet of plank and eight cords of wood. The Schooner *Union*'s contents included 141 casks of rum, eight barrels of sugar and 264 pounds of lead. The brig *Elizabeth* only had ship's stores, including beef, pork, bread, muskets, flour and brooms.

The total sum raised at sale realized $28,423.56. The captain himself bought several quantities of goods and the crew must have been well pleased with their shares. Some captains became wealthy men and Crowninshield was one of them, enabling him to rise to ownership and his first lieutenant James Fairfield to captaincy.

Captain Fairfield's luck ran out in November 1814 when his ship was captured and he ended up a prisoner at Dartmoor. His official record is given below.

Prison number	5678
By what ship or how taken	*Bacchante*
Time when	1 Nov. 1814.
Place where	Lat. 42 Long. 67
Name of prize	McDonough
Whither man o' war, privateer or merchant vessel	*Privateer*
Prisoner's Name	James Fairfield
Quality (rank)	Prize Master
Time when received into custody (Dartmoor)	24 Dec. 1814
From what ship and where received	HMS *Penelope*
Place of Nativity (birthplace)	Arundle
Age	31
Stature (height)	5 ft. 5½ ins.
Person	Stout
Visage and complexion	Oval/Dark
Hair	Brown
Eyes	Brown
Marks or wounds	None
Date of supply (bedding, clothing, etc.)	24 Dec. 1814
Exchanged; Run (escaped); Died; Discharged	Discharged
Date when (Board Orders)	28 April 1815
If discharged, whither and by what order	Boards Order 16 March 1815

Most vessels then and now will number a few men of dubious character among the crew, but in the main privateers employed a mixture of professional merchant seamen, ex–Navy men, some British Royal Navy deserters, and a sprinkling of sailors from every maritime nation. Some were indeed the sweepings of the American eastern seaboard. All of them, however, were in it for just one thing: prize money. It was that which molded them into a fighting force when attacking their prey. A few actually invested in the venture they undertook. All of them fought and died as comrades and suffered the same hardships at depots like Dartmoor should they be captured. For the United States the government considered their contribution to the war effort — harassing, capturing and sinking British merchantmen — invaluable at a time when regular U.S. Navy ships were either blockaded or outnumbered by the Royal Navy.

18

Voices from Dartmoor Prison

A surprising number of American sailor prisoners were not only literate but were able to express their thoughts and write about their experiences with a very high degree of accuracy and articulation. As privateers, many of them had contributed to the purchase and fitting out of the vessels they sailed in (for a share of the prize takings) and therefore were a cut above the ordinary sailor men of that time. Among them were Charles Andrews, Benjamin Palmer, George Little, Benjamin Brown, Perez Drinkwater and others who are well known to researchers. However, the list is far from complete, as new written recollections are continually being discovered and some of those are referred to here.

All the introductory passages about the journals that follow (except Drinkwater's) were provided by the late Ira Dye, formerly of the University of Virginia and a foremost authority on the War of 1812. The narratives that follow give the official recorded details of the four Americans mentioned above and excerpts from their journals. Brief details of another four Americans follow with Ira Dye's summaries for the records.[1]

Benjamin Brown

Papers of an Old Dartmoor Prisoner
Edited by Nathaniel Hawthorne
Published in the *U.S. Democratic Review*, New York, in seven parts, January to September 1846
A copy is in the Alderman Library of the University of Virginia
This is the journal of Benjamin Brown, which was raised into literature by Nathaniel Hawthorne. Brown was a pharmacist in Salem who went to sea on the *Frolic* privateer as a captain's clerk. Captured in the West Indies by HMS *Heron*, the *Frolic* crew were taken to Barbados, and after a brief stay, to England. Brown arrived at Dartmoor on September 30th, 1814, and was released on May 1st, 1815. He went home to Salem, where he remained for the rest of a long life. He wrote down the narrative of his experiences shortly after the war. He was a neighbour of Nathaniel Hawthorne, who edited the narrative and arranged for its publication.

Brown's narrative closely matches official records, and is consistent with the other journals. It is good reading and in addition contains some details not found in other journals.

— Ira Dye

As recorded in the General Entry Books for Dartmoor Prison.

Prison number	3598
By what ship or how taken	*Heron*
Time when	25 January 1814
Place where	West Indies
Name of prize	*Frolic*
Whither man o' war, Privateer or merchant vessel	Privateer
Prisoner's Name	Benjamin Brown
Quality (rank)	Clerk
Time when received into custody (Dartmoor)	30 Sept. 1814
From what ship and where received	HMS *Sybille*
Place of Nativity (birthplace)	Salem
Age	21
Stature (height)	5 ft. 5½ ins.
Person	Slender
Visage and complexion	Oval/pale
Hair	Black
Eyes	Hazle
Marks or wounds	None
Date of supply (bedding, clothing, etc.)	30 Sept. 1814
Exchanged; Run (escaped); Died; Discharged	Discharged
Date when (Board orders)	1 May 1815
If discharged, whither and by what order	Board's Order 16 March 1815

On arrival at Portsmouth, Brown and his companions were put on board HMS *Sybille* to be transported to Plymouth and Dartmoor. Conditions were grim on this vessel.

"Seventy of us were herded into an area parted from the main hold, six feet long and twenty feet wide.... It was not possible for me, who was one of the smallest of the company, to stand upright." This place was where the water casks were stored and on top of them was a layer of soft mud six or eight inches thick on which another layer of water casks had been embedded. A number of casks of this upper tier had been taken away and it was into this vacant space the prisoners were herded.

"We had nothing to sit or lay down on but the mud.... we were not permitted to go up except one at a time for any purpose ... the hold very shortly became redolent of all manner of effluvia" (page 202).

After describing the excessive number of armed guards assigned to watch over them, he relates how one night "the sentinel at the hatchway fell asleep and dropped his musket down among us. We took it away; but when the poor fellow discovered his loss he cried so piteously in view of the punishment that awaited him, that we gave it back to him again" (page 202).

At Plymouth the prisoners were put on board an unnamed prison hulk for the night with nothing to eat. The next morning they were taken on shore and mustered for the march to Dartmoor. "At last," wrote Brown, "the soldiers shouldered arms, the music struck up a lively tune, and away we trudged, as weather-beaten, dirty-looking a crew as ever paraded ... we may have shaken the dust of the 'Sybille' from our feet but it could not dislodge the mud from our tattered habiliments and tangled locks; it was too firmly embedded and required many days purification in the bathing pool at Dartmoor before we got rid of it. Before we started, we were surrounded by men, women, and children offering cakes, and fruit and ale for sale; and those of our company who had any money had thus an opportunity of breaking their fast" (page 203).

Next a revealing comment describes passing ale houses where sailors already were carousing and the crowds watched them go by. "The people were civil enough; they did not insult us, either by language or gesture; and some I thought, seemed to eye us with an air of compassion" (page 203).

Contrast this with the attitude of a number of market women they passed going to and from Plymouth: "We were objects of great curiosity to them, and they upbraided us for being renegade Englishmen and traitors and predicted they should shortly have the pleasure of seeing us all hung. It was in vain to protest we were Americans; they would not believe it; they could not conceive how, being Yankees, we had white skins and talked the language 'almost as good as we do ... there is but one Yankee among ye all' said one ... pointing to a black man from the West Indies" (page 204).

Finally they arrived at the depot, as it was called then. "The baggage carts had not yet come up; so we were all huddled into an empty prison, without any change of raiment, and without any bedding. Presently we had some pickled fish, and some bread and water sent in. Never, never, to my dying day shall I forget it; for it was the sweetest repast I ever partook of. Having thus broken, what to many of us was a thirty hour fast, we laid ourselves down in our wet and muddy clothes, on the cold stone floor and soon forgot our weariness and wretchedness in sleep" (page 204).

Next day the new arrivals were interrogated and their physical details recorded. Then "each man received a hammock, bed, blanket, pillow, a bunch of rope yarns to sling his hammock, with a wooden spoon, a tin pot, and, to every six men, a three gallon bucket." Here is part of Brown's description of the prison he was assigned to: "The interior was very gloomy ... very damp, very dirty. There were stanchions, or upright posts, some of wood and some of iron, running through each prison and forming an alley on each side to pass from one end to the other. These stanchions were one foot and a half apart and were used for suspending our hammocks. Three of these, comprising a space of four and a half feet were allowed to six men to live in — being nine inches for each man in width, and about eight feet in length. The hammocks were hung one above the other — sometimes in three tiers. It was necessary therefore that we should have a pretty good understanding, each with his neighbour about turning in, as one wishing to get into the upper one would have to tread on the tenant of the lower" (page 207).

The notorious No. 4 prison attracted some comment from Brown with regard to the self-appointed rulers, one of which was "Big Dick Crafus"[2] already mentioned. Also mentioned was Preacher Simon, and here is what Brown had to say: "The Pontifex Maximus of the diocese of Dartmoor was an ugly, thick lipped black man named Simon; I believe, notwithstanding his professions of piety, that he was a consummate rascal. Simon, King Dick, and a civil and inoffensive black man who had previously been a servant to the Duke of Kent who was known as 'The Duke.' Simon preached, the Duke responded with the amens ... while Dick stood by with his big club like a Roman lector" (page 361).

> There were market stalls manned by prisoners who had a little money to invest. There were cook-shops and stalls of every kind ... from taverns down to the humble vendors of coffee and plum-gudgeons. At these taverns might be found meats, roast and boiled, and stewed and fried; pastry cakes, fruits, wine and liqors. The cries of "hot plum-gudgeons! Hot freco! Lobscouse, nice and hot! Hot coffee! Burgoo!" were continually resounding through the prisons. Some of these dainties I dare say have never before been heard of by my readers. I will explain. A plum-gudgeon was a compound of fish and potatoes ... formed into pointed cones about the size of a tea saucer, fried in a little butter and sold for a penny. It made a very decent mess for breakfast. Freco was a stew made of the marrow and fat of bones, boiled with a few pieces of meat and some potatoes, and thickened with barley. A pint might be bought for two pence. Lobscouse was a thicker stew made with a larger proportion of meat and sold for double the price of freco. Burgoo is, I believe, better known; it is a hasty pudding made out of oatmeal, and eaten with butter or molasses, called in Dartmoor "trickles" which is a corruption of treacle. Coffee was made from burnt peas or burnt crusts of bread. As it required little capital besides a kettle and a tin pot to set up a coffee merchant, and as the beverage was much in demand, it was a thriving occupation of a great many of the prisoners. One might see the fires of the coffee makers all round the yards as soon as the doors were opened in the morning; but some of them whose customers expected an earlier supply, had little furnaces within the prisons with pipes to convey the smoke through the windows [page 365].

A daring but not unusual escape occurred during Brown's captivity. He describes what happened:

The most common mode of escape was to bribe a soldier [this is confirmed by other prisoners who wrote about their experiences]. The guard was relieved every night and the relieved soldiers marched out to their quarters in Princetown.... A prisoner therefore who had made up his mind to escape would procure a grey overcoat like those worn by the soldiers; he would place some article in the back to resemble a knapsack, a pasteboard front (peak?) to his hat, and the rim of his hat cut off all but in front, would bear a resemblance in the night to a soldier's cap; a stick carried under his arm was a substitute for a gun. I had an acquaintance who escaped in this way, got to the coast, stole a boat and went across the channel to France. There he joined a privateer, sailed in her, was captured and came back to his old quarters at Dartmoor just two weeks from the day he made his escape! [page 462].

Benjamin Brown witnessed the "Massacre" first hand and gives a lengthy description. It is a straightforward and balanced account well worth reading in full. He also sums up the character of Captain Shortland in a very fair manner, notwithstanding his alleged part in the shooting.

Benjamin Palmer

The Diary of Benjamin F. Palmer, Privateersman
Printed for the Acorn Club by the Tuttle, Morehouse and Taylor Press 1914. 274 pages.
There is a copy in the Library of Congress.
Benjamin Palmer, 21, was captured in the *Rolla* privateer by HMS *Loire* on December 10, 1813. He was taken to Bermuda and put in a prison ship until August 1814, then transferred to England, arriving at Dartmoor on October 5, 1814. He was released on April 27, 1815, having bought the name of another man.
This journal is especially valuable for its description of the daily life of the American prisoners at Bermuda, and is the best of two accounts of this. For the seven months that Palmer spent at Dartmoor his diary is consistent with official records and the other journals. He also describes in detail the trip home in a hired ship after the war, with the taking over of the ship by the ex-POWs [prisoners of war] in order to divert her into New York rather than the planned destination of Norfolk.

— Ira Dye

As recorded in the General Entry Books for Dartmoor Prison

Prison number..3944
By what ship or how taken ....HMS *Loire*
Time when ....10 Dec. 1813
Place where ....Off Bulo Island (?)
Name of prize ....*Rolla*
Whither man o' war, Privateer or merchant vessel ......Privateer
Prisoner's Name ....Benjamin Palmer
Quality (rank)..Seaman
Time when received into custody (Dartmoor) ....5 Oct. 1814

18. Voices from Dartmoor Prison

From what ship and where received ....HMS *President* from Halifax
Place of Nativity (birthplace) ....Connecticut (faint)
Age 21
Stature (height) ....5 ft. 7 ins.
Person ....Slender
Visage and complexion ....Oval/fresh
Hair..Black
Eyes ....Hazel
Marks or wounds ....?
Date of supply (bedding, clothing, etc.) ....5 Oct. 1814
Exchanged; Run (escaped); Died; Discharged ....Discharged
Date when (Board orders)...9 June 1815
If discharged, whither and by what order...................Boards Order 6 March 1815

Palmer was an educated man and an observant one. He meticulously recorded the daily events he experienced at Dartmoor, much of which gives us an illuminating glimpse of life there as it really was. Here is his account of a visit to No. 4 prison for entertainment (all spellings as he wrote them):

> Yesterday evening I went over to No. 4 Prison among the blacks to see a play. Tickets 6d. each ... but as mob rule prevailed among the prisoners they made a rush in and there being no seats, some stood up and some sit on the deck (these activities took place in the cockloft which had timber flooring) and such crowding you never saw ... the scenery was very good and so was the performance. After the play we had a grand dance and kept it up till daylight [page 108].[2]

Palmer was a teacher paid a monthly sum for every pupil. In December 1814 their numbers were falling and he made this revealing comment about the food: "I find my money is at its lowest ebb; we have formerly purchased our potatoes and cooked our own meals as the soup from the coppers is not fit to eat; and likewise made our own coffee out of Barley finding that much cheaper and equally as good, but I fear we shall not be able to purchase Molasses or coffee for the ensuing month. Alas Poverty, thou hideous monster" (page 116).

On Dec. 16, 1814, he wrote: "There is said to be an expedition fitting at Bermuda and Jamaica destined for New Orleans; this does not look like peace (there were rumors of peace within the prison) no! no! far from it. If the English government thought that peace was likely — would they still keep fitting out expeditions ... I think not"[3] (page 120).

> On December 29 came the momentous news every man had been waiting for:
> PEACE! We have official accounts from Gent that the preliminaries of peace were signed on the 24th Inst. The Cabinet Counsil has acceded to them ... they are now writing the ratification of the Prince Regent and Mr. Madison to become a permanent treaty. Happy happy news and still hapyer are we when we consider on what terms the treaty is made — honourable to us but disgraceful to

the pride of old England ... and we in fact remain the sole conquerors of the field.[4] This news has so agitated my mind I have not been able to compose myself sufficient to write or hardly set down ... they are now brought to where they long since ought to have been. PEACE. PEACE. I cannot write any more at present [page 125].

"I WISH YOU A HAPPY NEW YEAR," he wrote to his family on January 1, 1815. "I am certain t'is the happy'st I ever experienced although my liberty is yet denied me.... I will this day have a ½ gall. of rum and some porter and with my friends sit down and drink a health to my Friends at HOME. Dont be downhearted my friends you will soon see your long lost Frank[5] home again. Although poor raged and lousey.... his past sufferings shall then be talkd over and buried in the happiness of the present." He continued:

> Today the prisoners of No. 1 5 7 and 3 assembled in the yard of No. 3 and fired A Grand Salute of 17 guns — composed of rope yarns and paper with powder inside. A signal gun was fired at the time the flag was hoisted with Free Trade and Sailors Rights displayed in large capital letters when 9 hearty cheers were given and in answer to every gun we gave 3 cheers, some drunk, some groggy and some tipsy, we passed the day rejoicing. Sun down my rum has just come — and I shall now turn to and have a clear blowout [page 125–126].

Much has been said concerning the many attributes of French prisoners and their talents in manufacturing and other crafts. The American sailors were equally able, as observed by Palmer: "Today I took a walk round the prison and view'd the different avocations which were going on; some I found making bone ships, some making fiddles, some making straw boxes, some shoemaking, and some of every other different employment; in fact one only can judge how time passes away unless he has visited State prison" (page 141).

Benjamin Palmer now takes the trouble to relate the events of a whole day in a prisoner's life:

> In the morning we are awakened by the sound of the horn — which announces the bread is to be served; every prisoner starts at the sound and gets his bread, and those that has money gets some tea for breakfast, those that has not takes a little bread and water. Now everyone (except the gambles) turns to something useful — some writing, some reading, some shoe making, some making tin ware and some straw boxes, some bone ships, and some fabricating and circulating news....
>
> Next you hear the trading men called Jews sing out, "who'll buy some fine cloathes, trowses, shoes and boots buy or sell ... here is fine tobacco, here is nice seegars. Buy apples, here is candy — who'll buy Murphys all hot!' A battle is faught with some shop keepers who apply to their debtors to get their debts and if the shop keeper is the stoutest they will pay him; if not you loos and get flogged in the bargain...

Next comes dinner which uniformly consists of poor soup..., At length night comes and then you hear the gambling tribe singing out — this noise passes away the evening till 10 o'clock and so to bed [page 161].

As well as concerts and plays the occupants of No. 4 prison organized boxing (or should that read fighting?) matches for the entertainment of their comrades. They were ferocious bouts, as the following makes clear:

> Pugilism at this time is all the rage in the different prisons. Two matches were decided this morning [March 7, 1815]. The first battle was fought for a pound note — the combatants exhibited great scientific skill. After several rounds of very hard fighting the gunner of the Paul Jones [name of a privateer] gave in to his antagonist. He was most shockingly cut to pieces. The second battle was very severe, both the pugilists contended with the utmost desperation for victory but I did not stay to see it decided, being very sick of the sport [page 163].

An entry for March 17, 1815, is a scathing summing up of the treatment Palmer and his comrades were compelled to endure from all and sundry at Dartmoor Depot:

> At length — the most pleasing intelligence of the ratification of the treaty has come to hand and in such a shape as to have no doubt as to its authenticity. The most pleasing anticipation fills the breast of each joyous prisoner — we can hardly contain ourselves — no more shall British soldiers, sailors, turnkeys, or agents, domineer over the unfortunate captive. No more shall Yankee tars support innumerable shoals of farmers, market women and Jews — who has subsisted during the war entirely on the outgoings of these prisons, charging what prices they chose for their produce and goods, knowing they had no competitors in the market and that the prisoners could not be supply'd elsewhere. They have fattened on the hard earnings of American prisoners, but their race is run and they may now return like the bear to their homes and suck heir claws and pay their taxes as they can [page 168].

All the pent up feelings of captivity under a merciless regime is reflected here, and again after seeing his fellow prisoners fired upon and killed in the "Massacre" incident. His comments are in common with every other written account and more intense than most:

> Never (so help me God) will I make peace with the English until I revenge the blood of my countrymen.... O you damned infernal villains; where shall you meet with punishment such a crime deserves — I fear not in this world and in Hell. You are so leagued with the Devil that you will be favored. Enough cannot be said on the subject — for men to chase their brothers about like the hunting of foxes. Brothers did I say? Let me race [erase] out that name.... Never are they worthy of such a name — inhuman, savage, blood thursty, monsters in what history will you find ... guilty of so many acts of inhuman barbarity as the English [page 183].

Soon after the "Massacre," cartel ships were found and Americans began leaving the prison as the ships became available. Palmer was officially released on March 6, 1815, with an estimated actual discharge date for July, but there was a thriving trade in purchasing men's releases and he took advantage of it. On April 26 he wrote:

> Another draft was called out this afternoon — and I have for once in my life had fortune favour me. It was very difficult to procure a turn as they were in great demand, but after some length of time I found a Black man by the name of Charles Carrol who sold me his name for £2 which was deposited in the hands of one of the turnkeys to be delivered should I get off. If not I should have it again.... At 2 P.M. we were called to give in our bedding and put into an empty prison for the night. Those who had spare beds turned in but I having none paced the prison in silent agitation with the gloomy retrospection of the past and the pleasing anticipation of the future [page 199].

"Happy go lucky has at length received the smile of fortune," he wrote in an entry dated April 27:

> The cleark musters us over and the baggage waggons takes our belongings. As we passed through the outer gate each one who really stood in need had shoes served them. At about 8 o'clock we set sail from Dartmoor Prison giving three cheers which was answered by the prisoners on top of the prisons — my feelings at this moment can be better judged than described. Once more to set our face towards the land of liberty.

Soon afterwards an incident took place worthy of note:

> We marched on quick step without any halt till 10 o'clock when arriving halfway we were met by the relief guard of soldiers from Plymouth. A stage coach here overtook us — which the prisoners had hired. I with a number of others took passage on top by paying 2/- each[6]; those who were lame and had no money the English Commanding Officer paid their fare — Capt. Cradoc cannot be spoken of in terms so high as his character deserves. Although an Englishman, he is really deserving the praise of every one who has the honour to be acquainted with his humanity [page 201].

And so Benjamin Palmer reached Plymouth and at last boarded his cartel for home. And as with thousands of other prisoners from both sides, his feelings then can be imagined. Sadly, he only lived another ten years and died April 28, 1816, aged 31.

Charles Andrews

The Prisoner's Memoires
Dartmoor Prison, containing a complete and impartial history of the Americans in England, from the commencement of the late war between the United States and Great Britain, until all prisoners were released by the Treaty of Ghent.

Printed for the author New York 1815 (283 pages).
There is a copy in the Library of Congress.

Charles Andrews was the second mate of the merchant vessel *Virginia Planter*. Born in Newport, R.I., he was 36 years old at the time of the capture of his ship off Nantes, France, by HMS *Pyramus*. Although he asserts in his journal he was one of the first prisoners captured, the General Entry Book of the prison ship *Hector* shows him to have been captured on March 18, 1813. Along with other prisoners of war from the *Hector*, he was sent to Dartmoor on July 1, 1813 (he says April 3, 1813, in his journal). He states, and the Dartmoor General Entry Book agrees, that he was discharged from Dartmoor on April 20, 1815.

Andrews' journal has a stronger anti–British tone than any of the other journals. It agrees with the other journals and with the official records on most important details, except for dates in the early part of the journal. Perhaps he started it after he had been in Dartmoor for some time and was relying on memory for the earlier dates. It is apparently the only journal that was kept with the purpose of providing a log of the prisoner experience, as contrasted with a personal diary. He gives a list of American deaths at Dartmoor.

— Ira Dye

As recorded in the General Entry Books for Dartmoor Prison

Prison number..381 (first) 678 (second)
By what ship or how taken ....*Pyramus*
Time when ....18 March 1813
Place where ....Off Nantes
Name of prize ....*Virginia Planter*
Whither man o' war, privateer or merchant vessel ......Merchant vessel
Prisoner's Name ....Charles Andrews
Quality (rank)..Seaman
Time when received into custody (Dartmoor) ....1 July 1813
From what ship and where received ....*Hector* (hulk, Plymouth)
Place of Nativity (birthplace) ....Newport
Age 36
Stature (height) ....5ft 7½ ins.
Person ....Stout
Visage and complexion ....Long/sallow
Hair..Black
Eyes ....Hazle
Marks or wounds ....None
Date of supply (bedding, clothing, etc.) ....22 April 1813
Exchanged; Run (escaped); Died; Discharged ....Discharged to Mill Prison, Plymouth.[7]
Date when (Board Orders) ....22 July 1813
If discharged, whither and by what order...................Boards Order
Sent back to Dartmoor 18 Sept. 1813.
Finally discharged from Dartmoor (board's order) 20 April 1815

What Charles Andrews described is vouched for by an impressive list of signatures of his fellow prisoners, including several ships' captains, and therefore is relied upon more than any other recollections of that kind at Dartmoor. More than one commentator has said his book is very anti–British.[8]

Andrews' arrival in England was at Plymouth, referred to by him as Hamoze, the landlocked estuary of the River Tamar before that river exits into Plymouth Sound. This was where the infamous hulks were moored, and it was to the *Hector* he was sent. Some of his remarks about the hulks follow:

> After (reception) there was delivered to each man a very coarse and worthless hammock, with a thin coarse bed-sack, with at most not more than three or four pounds of flops or chopped rags, one coarse and sleazy blanket; this furniture of the bed-chamber was to last for a year and a half before we could draw others [page 6]....
>
> We were then informed that the Transport Board had most graciously and humanely, for the health and happiness of the prisoners, imposed on them the following duty; to keep clean the ship's decks and hold; to hoist in water, provisions, coal, and every other article expended or used within the ship; and also to permit the prisoners to cook their own victuals [the weekly rations per man are then listed].... The confinement, and the scanty and meager diet for men who were brought up in the land of liberty, and ever used to feast on the luscious fruits of plenty, soon brought on a pale and sickly countenance, a feeble and dejected spirit, and a lean, half animate body [page 7].

Andrews had this to say of his transfer to Dartmoor:

> The Transport Board issued an order for removing all the prisoners on board the Hector prison-ship at Plymouth to the depot at Dartmoor.... On the morning of the third of April[9] they were ordered on deck with their hammocks, baggage etc. in readiness to march to the prison, the very name of which made the mind of every prisoner "shrink back with dread and startle at the thought" for fame had made them well acquainted with the horrors of that infernal abode which was by far the most dreadful prison in all England.
>
> Two hundred and fifty dejected and unhappy sufferers, already too wretched, were called each of whom received a pair of shoes, and his allowance of bread and salt fish.... We were landed at New Passage, near Plymouth, and were placed under the guard of a company of soldiers equal in number to the prisoners! Orders were then given to march at half past ten in the morning, with a positive injunction that no prisoner should step out of, or leave the ranks on pain of instant death.
>
> Thus we marched surrounded by a strong guard, through a heavy rain, over a bad road, with only our usual scanty allowance of bread and fish. We were allowed to stop only once during the march of seventeen miles. We arrived at Dartmoor late on the after part of the day and found the ground covered with snow. Nothing could form a more dreary prospect than that which now presented itself to our hopeless view. Death itself ... seemed less terrible than this gloomy prison.
>
> "The prison at Dartmoor ... is surrounded on all sides as far as the eye can

see by the gloomy features of a black moor, uncultivated and uninhabited, except for one or two miserable cottages," he wrote. It was Charles Andrews who coined the phrase "horse stables" when describing the prison block he was assigned to: "We entered the prisons; but here the heart of every American was appalled ... he saw water constantly dropping from the cold stone walls on every side, which kept the floor (made of stone) constantly wet and cold as ice ... the prison floors were all of stone or cement and each storey contained but one apartment and resembled long vacant horse stables." He sums up: "The place is deprived of everything that is pleasant or agreeable, and is productive of nothing but human woe and misery" (page 10).

The prisoners made their woes known to Reuben Beasley, agent for the American prisoners of war, but to no avail.

> We informed him that our allowance was too scant, that the whole day's allowance was scarcely enough for one meal, that the greater part of the prisoners were in a state of nakedness; and also that great numbers had enlisted into the king's service.... We informed him also of the distinction that was made between the French and American prisoners. The former were allowed many privileges and advantages which were denied the latter; that we were hurried into the prisons before dark and locked up, to remain without any light or fire till seven or eight o'clock in the morning. If a prisoner had to leave his hammock, per necessitatem, he was obliged to grope from one end of the room to the other, and often could not regain it during the night. To all these petitions, complaints and remonstrances, Mr. Beaseley returned no answer nor took any notice of them whatsoever [page 15].

Of daily rations per man, he writes:

> On beef days the whole (every man's ration) is thrown into a large copper; when it is sufficiently boiled the bone is taken out, and each mess, consisting of six, receives twenty seven ounces of beef, and one gallon and one pint of soup. On the fish days, every mess boiled their potatoes and fish in a net made of rope-yarn, that they might have it separately to themselves; after it was boiled it was taken up in wooden buckets, with which each mess was provided; and each prisoner, being furnished with a wooden spoon, sets round the bucket, on the wet floor, and makes a fierce attack.

Andrews describes the scale of rations allocated to each man "to be served out daily by the contractors. We watched the contractor and found he weighed all the articles at once, neat weight; and saw him scrimp the weight to fill his pocket out of the prisoners' bellies." He then criticizes the American agent, Reuben Beasley: "These contractors would have been as honest as many other men, with sharp looking after. Was it not then the duty of Mr. Beasley to see that the prisoners had what the Government of England allowed them?" (page 22).

A description of the clothing they were issued follows: The cap was woolen, about an inch thick, but much coarser then common rope yarn. The jacket was not large enough to meet around the smallest of us, although reduced to mere skeletons by continued fasting; the sleeves came half way down the arm and the hand stuck out like a spade; the waistcoat was short, it would not meet before, nor down to the pantaloons, thus leaving a space of between three or four inches; the pantaloons, which were as tight as our skins, came down to the middle of the shin. The shoes, made of list,[10] were interwoven and fastened to pieces of wood an inch and a half thick…. My friends, could you keep from laughing when you see us … skeletons as we were?

By 25 March 25, 1815, the prisoners were understandably becoming impatient with the delay in obtaining ships to take them home. With all their previous complaints and mistreatment ignored (as they saw it) by their agent, their patience was at an end and Beasley was tried and executed in effigy. As the following description makes clear, it was a serious affair:

They were determined to punish him as much as it was in their power; they therefore caused an effigy to be hanged on top of one of the prisons, after which it was taken down and burned in the presence of all the officers and soldiers. At his trial it was stated, "You, Reuben G. Beasley in effigy are found guilty by an impartial and judicious jury … of depriving many hundreds of your countrymen of their lives … by nakedness, starvation, and exposure to pestilence…. You this day must be hanged by the neck on the top of the prison no. 7…. Your body is then to be taken down and fastened to a stake, and burned to ashes which are to be distributed to the winds [page 86].

Charles Andrews was finally released with a draft of 249 men who were the first to be admitted to Dartmoor. One baggage wagon was allowed for every hundred men to convey their belongings to Plymouth, where a cartel ship was waiting to take them home. He tells us:

The prisoners being the greater part barefooted made enquiry whether any arrangements had been made for providing them with shoes and clothes, as they were much in want of them, but were much surprised and disappointed when they found no provision had been made. The next morning we took our departure for Plymouth and with joy in our hearts bid farewell to that pale of misery, and at four in the afternoon arrived at Plymouth having travelled all the way under the direction of a strong guard.

His narrative concludes with lists of captive Americans who died, those who enlisted in the "king's service," and those who escaped (page 117).

This brief appraisal concludes with the declaration that was made by his 62 fellow prisoners and which lent so much authority to his account of prison life at Dartmoor. Those who signed it included 14 ships' captains, two lieutenants and a doctor. I include the declaration with the names of the captains, lieutenant and doctor cited in Andrews' list because at least some of them will be known by name today in the seaports they came from:

> We, the undersigned, late prisoners of war, having been confined the greater part of the last war between the United States of America and Great Britain, and having carefully perused and examined the following manuscript journal, kept by Charles Andrews, our fellow prisoner at Dartmoor, in the County of Devon, in the kingdom of Great Britain, do solemnly declare, that all matter and occurrences herein contained, are just and true, to the best of our knowledge and belief; and that this is the only journal kept at Dartmoor.

Capt. Joshua Wait	New York
Capt. Samuel. H. Ginnodo	Newport, R.I.
Capt. Frederick H. Coffin	Hudson, N.Y.
Capt. Benjamin F. Cheseborough	Conn.
Capt. Richard Longly	Portland, D.M.
Capt. Charles Bennet	Hudson, N.Y.
Capt. John C. Rowles	Baltimore, Md.
Capt. James S. Smith	Stonington, Conn.
Capt. Matthew. S. Steel	Philadelphia, Penn.
Lieut. Homer Hull	Conn.
Capt. James McQuilter	Baltimore, Md.
Capt. Thomas Hussey	Hudson, N.Y.
Capt. James Boggs	Philadelphia, Penn.
Capt. James Gays	Virginia
Capt. Thomas Mumford	Newport, R.I.
Lieut. Homer Hull	Conn.
Lieut. S. S. Fitch	Connecticut
Doc. Benjamin Mercer	New York

George Little

Life on the Ocean or Twenty Years at Sea
Baltimore, Armstrong and Berry, 1843
This book has, in addition to the above, an account of a prisoner's life at Stapleton and Dartmoor under the title *The American Cruiser — A Tale of the Last War.* Boston; W.M.J. Reynolds and Company, and Waite, Peirce, and Co., 1847
There is a copy in the Maryland Room, University of Maryland Library. Captain Little was a prizemaster when he was captured in January 1813 and landed at Plymouth, where he spent a month on one of the hulks before being transferred to Stapleton. When the war with France ended in 1814, Stapleton Depot closed and he was among those who were sent to Dartmoor Prison, which had been nominated an American depot. This is one of the best accounts of privateering, prison life and details of prisoners and their habits.
— Ira Dye

In the General Entry Book (below) the "Place where captured" is recorded as "Channel." This could only have been the Irish Channel because Captain Little describes rounding Lands End en route to Plymouth.

As recorded in the General Entry Books for Dartmoor Prison.

Prison number...1367
By what ship or how taken ....*Leonidas*
Time when ....23 May 1813
Place where ....Channel
Name of prize ....*Paul Jones*
Whither man o' war, Privateer or merchant vessel......*Privateer*
Prisoner's Name ....George Little
Quality (rank)...Prizemaster
Time when received into custody (Dartmoor) ....19 June 1814.
From what ship and where received ....*Stapleton*
Place of Nativity (birthplace) ....Massachusetts
Age 25
Stature (height) ....5 ft. 6½ Ins.
Person ....Stout
Visage and complexion ....Round/fair
Hair..Light brown
Eyes ....Hazle
Marks or wounds ....Scar right eye
Date of supply (bedding, clothing, etc.) ....19 June 1814
Exchanged; Run (escaped); Died; Discharged ....Discharged
Date when (board orders) ....25 March 1815
If discharged, whither and by what order...................board's order 21 March 1815

Captain Little's early comments on being taken prisoner reflect much of what others experienced and wrote about. Their reception on board HMS *Leonidas* "was not of the most agreeable and delicate nature," he wrote. "Whether this was owing to the loss of the prize we may leave the reader to judge (his ship, the *Paul Jones*, was badly damaged in the fight to capture it and sank) ... as they [the crew] came over the gangway they were strictly searched and examined, after which a genteel epithet was bestowed such as 'piratical villain' etc. and then they were driven down into the cable tier.... Nor did the officers meet with a much better reception — they stowed them against the wardroom bulkhead and their sleeping place was the soft side of a plank" (page 818).

Captain Little and his crew were taken to Plymouth and spent three weeks on one of the hulks before being transferred to the prisoner of war depot at Stapleton, near Bristol. The Americans were dispatched in drafts of a hundred, each guarded by an equal number of soldiers, a mixture of infantry and mounted dragoons. It took seven days to reach their destination. Those who are interested will find a detailed description of Stapleton Depot and the way of life for the prisoners there which generally resembled that which prevailed at Dartmoor.

As already noted, the war with France ended in April 1814 and the French prisoners were repatriated. All American prisoners in Britain were then moved to Dartmoor and at Stapleton preparations were made for the first draft to leave. Captain Little described their departure:

> They were transferred in the same order — the draft which arrived first was the first to be sent to Dartmoor, which brought together the seamen and officers of the cruiser [the *Paul Jones*]. The commander of the escort was a full-blooded Englishman in all his notions, feelings, and prejudices; and as a matter of course was not well disposed towards the 'Yankees' ... there were no distinctions, for the officers and sailors fared equally alike ... the march was attended with great hardship and suffering, for every privilege was cut off, even the purchasing of food; the allowance was not at all sufficient to sustain men on a fatiguing march. The thoughts of going to a prison could not be agreeable under any circumstances, yet such were the sufferings and misery this draft had to endure under their inhuman and despotic leaders, even Dartmoor with all its horrors was preferable to such treatment; it was with no little joy and satisfaction that these wretched beings came in sight of the depot. It was early in the afternoon of the eighth day since leaving Stapleton [page 847].

After being processed and issued with hammock, blanket, and other necessities, the new arrivals entered the prison yard "and came to a sudden halt, being struck with amazement and wonder at what they now saw and heard. Here was a group of human beings fantastically dressed and at a short distance was another engaged in every species of gambling, while another party were amusing themselves in the polite accomplishment of pugilism." A further revelation greeted them when they entered one of the prison blocks, the sight of which was graphically described by Captain Little: "Upon entering the first floor they stood at the upper end of the building ... each part thickly peopled with human beings of every possible shape, dress and occupation. Some were cooking, some were reading, some were walking, dancing, singing, fiddling, and fifing; more were gambling or clustering around tables on which were piled heaps of all colours and value." Someone directed them to another, uninhabited prison where they serried in with room to spare (page 849).

> At eight o'clock next morning the prisoners were notified to be in readiness to count out in messes. They passed out by a door left open for the purpose and to every sixth man was given a numbered ticket, indicative of the number of his mess. Directly after the they received their tickets the cook's horn gave notice the bread was in readiness to be served out; when the one from each mess who received the ticket, being dubbed cook for the day, proceeded to the cook house and there waited until his number was called .

He surrendered his ticket and was issued with the bread for his mess. "At the next serving out the cook of themes received his ticket with the provisions for the day and each member of the mess took his turn as cook" (page 851).

Little's description of the Rough Allies is more vivid and detailed than most other accounts; speaking of his fellow prisoners he describes their listlessness and addiction to gambling, in which most of them lost all they had — clothing and even their food:

> A large majority of them have been gathered from the vilest haunts of dissipation and vice from perhaps all the seaports of the United States ... indeed it is a melancholy sight to behold these men gathering from the piles of offal and dirt, cabbage stumps, potato and turnip skins, which they devour with the greediness of a vulture to satisfy their craving appetites and to prevent starvation. The result was many of them did die of starvation or died by gorging themselves with unwholesome food.
>
> The worst consequences were when a large body of these miserable men banded together and if they had a pique against any of the more orderly, it was their custom to drag them up to the whipping post and scourge their backs unmercifully; this was invariably done to officers who had been good disciplinarians on their vessels. The captain of the depot had frequently to send a guard of soldiers to rescue the unfortunate victims [page 853].

On a lighter note, he mentions an uncommon form of entertainment they enjoyed: "The smooth surface of rising ground a short distance to the left of Princetown was used as the parade ground for the troops doing duty at the depot. It was not unfrequent for a couple of regiments to close their two hours drill with a sham fight, when as many of the prisoners as could clamber to the roofs of the buildings, enjoyed a fair sight of this harmless but highly picturesque battle, often raging fiercely between the red coated soldiery whose gaudy trappings glittered in the sun's rays as seen when half enveloped in the smoke of battalion fire" (page 861).

Every American who recorded his experiences at Dartmoor Depot complained about the miserable weather. In his inimitable descriptive style Captain Little, who as a seaman must have endured many a fierce storm at sea, takes pains to describe a typical Dartmoor storm that occurred during March 1815:

> It was the season of the year, of all others the most gloomy in this district; the barren heath as well as the spot on which the prisons stood, was shrouded in an almost impenetrable mist; the falling rain splashed heavily on the tops of the prisons and the prison yard, and the wild wind blew in fitful gusts with a sound so melancholy ... the atmosphere was dense and cold ... now and then a loud peal of thunder would seem to shake the massive walls of the prison, while ever and anon a livid flash of lightning shot through the iron grates of the windows which for a moment made the stoutest hearts to quail; the pelting storm raged for nearly an hour with unabating violence [page 863].

18. Voices from Dartmoor Prison

For many weeks there had been unconfirmed reports of a peace treaty having been signed. The news had been received with adulation but could not be official until ratification by President James Madison. Now we go back to the dreary prisons where the storm has finally

> ceased its fury and the minds of the prisoners had become somewhat tranquilised. Two men were sitting composedly in one of the mean berths, deeply interested in a book which the younger of the two was reading aloud; they were so much absorbed that for some moments they took no notice of the loud and extravagant expressions of joy which rang throughout the prisons ... nor were they entirely aroused until a loud peal resounded through the air like rolling thunder, in three cheers from more than three thousand human beings, after which one of the prisoners entered with a newspaper and read with stentorian lungs the overwhelming and joyous intelligence 'that peace was proclaimed between America and England.' Nothing could now exceed the manifestations of joy exhibited among the prisoners; it is in vain to attempt an expression of the deep and powerful feelings of men, some of whom had been incarcerated in a British prison for more than two years. Some danced, while others sung; many of them broke out into extravagant bursts of laughter while others actually wept for joy ... and there were not a few that night that drained the intoxicating bowl of its very dregs [page 864].

The Princetown Massacre is of course included in his appraisal of Dartmoor prison life, but as it differs only slightly from all the other accounts and as they all are similar in their condemnation of Agent Shortland, it is felt nothing can be materially added to the full description previously given. Nevertheless, Captain Little's final comment expresses most concisely the opinion held by the Americans who were there: "Thus ended one of the most disgraceful and inhuman massacres that was ever perpetrated by a civilized nation and will forever remain an eternal blot on the escutcheon of British history."

Perez Drinkwater

> This man's letters to his wife and family from within Dartmoor prison are widely quoted and mentioned in several books. I discovered the late Bruce Felknor's website with an introduction to Perez Drinkwater and copies of his letters. More interesting was the revelation that a direct American lady descendant was a literary editor by the name of Kimberley VanDerveer. I have not been able to contact this lady and, as Mr. Felknor is deceased, I take the liberty of reproducing the letters in the interest of my readers and ask her pardon for so doing.
>
> Perez Drinkwater was a lieutenant aboard a privateer when he was captured in the last days of 1813. After a brief confinement on the *Brave* hulk at Plymouth he was transferred to Dartmoor where he spent fourteen months before his release. During that time he observed and retained the worst aspects of the treatment he and his fellow prisoners received. His description of their miserable existence makes compelling reading.
> — Ira Dye

There are some differences between the official Dartmoor Entry Book details (below) and the information provided on Felknor's Web site. These are inserted in italics alongside the relevant items for the reader's consideration, but it should be noted Drinkwater mentions a fellow crewman (James Mann) who was killed in the massacre and is recorded as having been captured on the Siroc, a letter of marque vessel.

As recorded in the General Entry Books for Dartmoor Prison

Prison number..937
By what ship or how taken ....*Pelican* (HMS *Billerikin*)
Time when ....13 Jan. 1813
Place where ....At sea
Name of prize ....*Siroc* (*Lucy*)
Whither man o' war, privateer or merchant vessel ......*Letter of Marque* (*Privateer*)
Prisoner's Name ....Perez Drinkwater
Quality (rank)...3rd Lieutenant (Lieutenant)
Time when received into custody (Dartmoor) ....31 Jan. 1814
From what ship and where received ....Plymouth hulk
Place of Nativity (birthplace) ....Port ? (North Yarmouth) Maine
Age 25
Stature (height) ....5ft. 9 ins.
Person ....Stout
Visage and complexion ....Long-haired (possibly bearded)
Hair..Brown
Eyes ....Hazel
Marks or wounds ....None
Date of supply (bedding, clothing, etc.) ....20 Feb. 1814
Exchanged; Run (escaped); Died; Discharged ....Discharged
Date when (Board Orders) ....10 April 1815
If discharged, whither and by what order..................Boards Order 7 April 1815

The following excerpts are from Perez Drinkwater's letters as written to his brother (original spellings are retained to reflect the tenor of those times):

"DARTMOOR PRISON
                          Saturday Morning, May 20th, 1814
Dr. Brother
We arrived into Plymouth on the 20th of January was put on board the [prison ship] Brave on the 24th and was landed from her on the 31 and marched to this place in a snow storm. This prison is situated on one of the highest places in England and it either snows or rains the whole year round and is cold enough to wear a great coat the whiole time there is 10,000 of us here now but the French are about to go home.
This is the first time I have ever been deprived of my liberty and when I sit and think of it it almost deprives me of my sences for we have nothing else to do but sit and reflect on our preasant situation which is bad enough god knows for we have but 1 lb and a half of black bread and about three ounces of beef and a little beef tee to drink and all that makes us one meal a day the rest

of the time we have to fast which is hard times for the days are very long heir now I want to get out of heir before the war is over so that I cn have the pleasure of killing one Englishman and drinking his blood which i think I could do with a good will for I think them the worst of all the human race for their is no crimes but what they are gilty of....

Yisterday they called up 500 French men to go away their was one that had been in prison Nine years and had worn his blanket out so that he had but half of it to give those rebels and on that account they sent him back and puit him on the bottom of the books for exchamgeing, the man took it so hard that he cut his throught and was found dead between the prison dores, and a thousand other such deeds they have been guilty of since we have been confined heir in this cursed place and a mongth these rebels for I can call them nothing better and I shall never dye happy till I have had the pleasure of killing onme of them which I am determined to do if an opportunity ever offers to me to doe it....

We have plenty of creepers (insects such as bedbugs and lice) heir to turn us out in the morning, them and the Englishmen together don't let us have much peace day nor night for they are both enimyes to us and likewise to peace and the more they can torment the human rase the better they are pleased....

From your sincere friend and Brother,
PEREZ DRINKWATER

To his wife:

ROYAL PRISON Dartmoor
Oct. 12th 1814

Dear Sally

It is with regret I have to inform you of my unhappy situation that is, confined heir in a loathsome prison where I have wourne out almost 9 months of my days; and god knows how long it will be before I shall get mu Liberty again.... I cheer my drooping spirits by thinking of the happy day when we shall have the pleasure of seeing you and my friends.

This same place is one of the most retched in this habited world ... neither wind nor water tight, it is situated on the top of a high hill and is so high that it either rains, hails or snows almost the year round.... I am compeled to smugle this out of prison for they will not allow us to write to our friends if they can help it.... So I must conclude with telling you that I am not alone for there is almost 5,000 of us heir, and creepers 1,000 to one.

Give my brothers my advice that is to beware of coming to this retched place for no tongue can tell what the sufferings are heir till they have a trial of it.... This is from your even (ever) derr and beloved Husband.
PEREZ DRINKWATER

He writes to his parents with the glad news he is coming home. He also describes the massacre as he saw it two days previously:

A.D. 1815 DARTMOOR PRISON
Ap. 8th

Honoured Parents

> I have the pleasure to inform you I am in good helth and my best wishes are that when these few lines come to hand they may find you the same and all my frinds. Dowtless you have heird of the marcichre [massacre] of Dartmoor in which ther was 7 killed and 38 wounded, it was done on the 6th of this month, the soldiers fired on us when we were all in the yard about 5,000 they fired on us from all directions and after we was back in the prison they killed a number in the prison.
>
> It was one of the most retched things that ever took place amongths the savages.... I had the good fortin to escape their fury, but they killed some while begging for mercy after being wounded they likewise kicked and mangle the dead right before our faces. Pain Perry of North Yarmouth was one that was wounded but not bad [he and his parents evidently knew Perry and the fact he is said to be from North Yarmouth suggests Drinkwater's place of nativity was also that place]....
>
> I shall leave heir tomorrow morning for London and from their to Crownstad [Kronstad?] and from their to Portland ion the brig Albert of Portland I think it will be much more to my advantage than to reurn home in a corveat (corvette) as it will be some time before it comes to my turn.

He probably volunteered to help make up the crew of this vessel, as did many other Yankees at Dartmoor in order to get out sooner. He continued:

> Please to remember me to my friends and to my wife I hope that you will assist her till my return which I hope will be in 4 months.
>
> I remain your obedient son,
> PEREZ DRINKWATER

Perez did return safely home and lived to old age.

Other Journals

Anonymous (Josiah Cobb)

A Green Hand's First Cruise: roughed out from the log book of memory, of twenty-five years standing: Together with a residence of five months at Dartmoor Prison. By a Younker

Two volumes. Baltimore, Cushing and Brother 1841. Volume 1 (247 pages). Volume 2 (329 pages).

There is a copy in the Library of Congress.

Neither the author's name or that of the ship he served in are given in the text. However, the author gives a prisoner number that he says was his at Dartmoor (6632). The Library of Congress card catalogue gives the author as Josiah Cobb. A check of the information in the Dartmoor General Entry Book shows Josiah Cobb as a 19 year old seaman captured in the *Prince de Neufchatel* privateer on December 28, 1814, and received in Dartmoor on January 30, 1815. His number was 6234 and all details of his capture in the journal check with the official records. Prisoner number 6632 does not fit these details at all. Both the title page and the preface state that this is reminiscence, set down

from memory twenty-five years after the events took place. Thus in historical value it ranks behind the contemporaneously written journals. However, in descriptive details, it is far more extensive than any of the other journals located so far. It reads like a Victorian novel, which to a certain extent it is, but gives much small detail that is not available from any other source. It is the basic source apparently used by most popular authors in describing life and events at Dartmoor. Cobb could have used the Andrews journal or JYMM to jog his memory, then filled in the wealth of detail from his own recollection. He gives a detailed description of the voyage home after the war in a hired vessel, including ex-prisoners seizing the ship and changing its destination from Charleston, [South] Carolina, to Boston.
— Ira Dye

As recorded in the General Entry Books for Dartmoor Prison.

Prison number	6234
By what ship or how taken	*Leander* Newcastle
Time when	28 Dec. 1814
Place where	Lat. 36 Long. 55
Name of prize	*Prince de Neufchatel*
Whither man o' war, privateer or merchant vessel	Privateer
Prisoner's Name	Josiah Cobb
Quality (rank)	Seaman
Time when received into custody (Dartmoor)	30 Jan. 1815
From what ship and where received	HMS *Pheasant*
Place of Nativity (birthplace)	Massachusetts
Age	19
Stature (height)	5 ft. 8 ins.
Person	Stout
Visage and complexion	Oval and Dark
Hair	Black
Eyes	Grey
Marks or wounds	None
Date of supply (bedding, clothing, etc.)	30 Jan. 1815
Exchanged; Run (escaped); Died; Discharged	Discharged
Date when (Board Orders)	5 July 1815
If discharged, whither and by what order	Board's Order 16 March 1815

Joseph Valpey

Journal of Joseph Valpey Jnr. of Salem, November 1813–April 1915, with other papers relating to his experiences at Dartmoor Prison.
Valpey E.G., Editor. Michigan Society of Colonial Wars 1922 (71 pages).
There is a copy in the Library of Congress.
Joseph Valpey, 22, was captured in the *Herald* privateer on August 15, 1814. He was received in Dartmoor on October 28, 1814, and was released on April 20, 1815, having bought another man's turn to be released—a common practice. He therefore spent about six months at Dartmoor.
His descriptions of prison life convey a sense of interminableness and boredom

that must have been a major feature of the POWs' [prisoners of war] life. He describes the contacts between shipmates and Salem town-mates which served to fill in the time. He was also a prolific poet, and the poems give additional insights into the life of POWs and their attitudes. The first ten pages give a vivid description of privateering life.

— Ira Dye

As recorded in the General Entry Books for Dartmoor Prison

Prison number	4947
By what ship or how taken	*Endymion*
Time when	15 Aug. 1814
Place where	[Obscure]
Name of prize	*Herald*
Whither man o' war, privateer or merchant vessel	Privateer
Prisoner's Name	Joseph Valpey
Quality (rank)	Seaman
Time when received into custody (Dartmoor)	20 October 1814
From what ship and where received	HMS *Ackbar* from Halifax
Place of Nativity (birthplace)	Salem
Age	22
Stature (height)	5 ft. 7¼ ins.
Person	M/Size
Visage and complexion	Long/Dark
Hair	Brown
Eyes	Grey
Marks or wounds	Scar right side
Date of supply (bedding, clothing, etc.)	28 Oct. 1814
Exchanged; Run (escaped); Died; Discharged	Discharged
Date when (Board Orders)	21 June 1815
If discharged, whither and by what order	Board Order 16 March 1815

Nathaniel Pierce

"Dartmoor Prison, December 28, 1814, Plymouth near Devonshire, Nathaniel Pierce, His Book, dated at Dartmoor this 28th day of December in the year of our Lord one thousand eight hundred and fourteen 14. In No. 7 Prison S.E. and Middle Deck, England. Nathaniel Pierce of Newburyport, Mass."

Typescript copy of a manuscript in the Widener Library, Harvard University. The double spaced typescript has 48 pages.

In the Dartmoor General Entry Book his name is spelled "Pirss," however, phonetic spellings are not uncommon in these records. The details in the official records jibe closely with the journal. He was captured from the *Halifax* packet, a prize to the *Harpy* privateer, by HMS *Bulwark*. He was received in Dartmoor on December 27, 1814, and released on July 3, 1815 — one of the later prisoners to be received and one of the last to be released.

I have found his journal to be the most useful of all from the point of a late twentieth century researcher trying to see these early nineteenth century men and events through their own eyes. The journal has lots of detail, unusual insights, and to me at least, it has a distinct "sailor-like" flavor. He ends the journal on July 2, 1815, "for want of paper" and says "tomorrow I leave this depot." The General Entry Book confirms that he did.

— Ira Dye

As recorded in the General Entry Books for Dartmoor Prison

Prison number	5977
By what ship or how taken	HMS *Bulwark*
Time when	Nov. 1814
Place where	Georges Bank
Name of prize	*Cossack*, prize to *Grand Turk*
Whither man o' war, privateer or merchant vessel	Privateer
Prisoner's Name	Nat Pirss
Quality (rank)	Mate
Time when received into custody (Dartmoor)	27 Dec. 1814.
From what ship and where received	HMS *Penelope*
Place of Nativity (birthplace)	Newberry (Newbury)
Age	19
Stature (height)	5 ft. 10 ins.
Person	Stout
Visage and complexion	Oval/Fresh
Hair	Brown
Eyes	Grey
Marks or wounds	None
Date of supply (bedding, clothing, etc.)	27 Dec. 1814
Exchanged; Run (escaped); Died; Discharged	Discharged
Date when (Board Orders)	3 July 1815
If discharged, whither and by what order	Board's Order 16 March 1815

Francis G. Selman

Extracts from the Journal of a Marblehead Privateersman Confined on Board British Prison Ships 1813, 1814, 1815.
Contained in the *Marblehead Manual* compiled by Samuel Roads Jnr. Marblehead, Mass. Statesman Publishing Co. 1883 (pages 28 – 96).
There is a copy in the Library of the Essex Institute, Salem, Mass.
Francis G. Selman was the first lieutenant of the privateer *Growler*, which was captured on July 7, 1813, near Newfoundland by HMS *Electra*. The crew were taken first to St. Johns, Newfoundland, and just put in a prison ship there. After about a month he was taken to England, first to a prison ship at Portsmouth, then another at Chatham, and finally to Dartmoor where he arrived on October 8, 1814. He provides information on the deaths of prisoners of his acquaintance, and the journal includes a list of men who died at Dartmoor hospital and at Stapleton. He was released on April 27, 1815.

— Ira Dye

As recorded in the General Entry Books for Dartmoor Prison

Prison number	4436
By what ship or how taken	HMS *Electra*

Time when ....7 July 1814
Place where ....At sea
Name of prize ....*Growler*
Whither man o' war, Privateer or merchant vessel ......Privateer
Prisoner's Name ....Francis Selman
Quality (rank)...2nd Lieut.
Time when received into custody (Dartmoor) ....8 Oct. 1814
From what ship and where received...............................*Chatham* (hulk) by HMS *Leyden*
Place of Nativity (birthplace) ....Marblehead
Age 28
Stature (height) ....5 ft. 5 ins.
Person ....Stout
Visage and complexion ....Round/dark
Hair..Brown
Eyes ....Blue
Marks or wounds ....None
Date of supply (bedding, clothing, etc.) ....20 Sept. 1814
Exchanged; Run (escaped); Died; Discharged ....Discharged
Date when (Board orders)...27 April 1815
If discharged, whither and by what order....................Board Order 16 March 1815

19

Survivors

A photograph titled "Dartmoor Prisoners of 1812" was taken in 1850, we know not where. The original could not be found; only a poor quality reproduction remains.[1] The names on the print are: T. Thomas, J. Small (son), L. Clover, R. Conklin, B. Marshall, J. Deagle, B. Howard, Mrs. Small, J. Swain and G. Saunders.

On the flag displayed in the photo are the words "Sailors Rights and No Impressments," which refers a slogan stating Americans' objections to be pressed into the British Navy, one of the main causes of the war. The General Entry Book has details relating to four of these men as follows:

As recorded in the General Entry Books for Dartmoor Prison
G. Small

Prison number	4810
By what ship or how taken	*Scylla*
Time when	22 March 1813
Place where	Bay of Biscay
Name of prize	*Tigre*
Whither man o' war, Privateer or merchant vessel	Merchant
Prisoner's Name	G. Small
Quality (rank)	Seaman
Time when received into custody (Dartmoor)	7 Oct. 1814
From what ship and where received	HMS *Niobe*
Place of Nativity (birthplace)	New York
Age	24
Stature (height)	
Person	Medium size
Visage and complexion	Round/dark
Hair	Black
Eyes	Hazel
Marks or wounds	None
Date of supply (bedding, clothing, etc.)	At Chatham
Exchanged; Run (escaped); Died; Discharged	Discharged.

Date when (Board orders)..1 May 1815
If discharged, whither and by what order...................Board's Order 16 March 1815

Small's son (was his father dead?) has his hand on his mother's shoulder in the picture. During her husband's imprisonment at Dartmoor, Mrs. Small is believed to have lived in Prince Town and borne her son there.

As recorded in the General Entry Books for Dartmoor Prison
J. Deagle

Prison number..3142
By what ship or how taken ....Impressed
Time when ....22 Sept. 1813
Place where ....London
Name of prize ....
Whither man o' war, Privateer or merchant vessel......
Prisoner's Name ....James Deagle
Quality (rank)..Seaman
Time when received into custody (Dartmoor) ....11 Sept. 1814
From what ship and where received ....HMS *Freyer* from Chatham
Place of Nativity (birthplace) ....Yarmouth
Age 24
Stature (height) ....5 ft. 10¾ ins.
Person ....Stout
Visage and complexion ....Long/fresh
Hair..Brown
Eyes ....Hazel
Marks or wounds ....None
Date of supply (bedding, clothing, etc.) ....12 Sept. 1814
Exchanged; Run (escaped); Died; Discharged ....Discharged
Date when (Board orders)..28 May 1815
If discharged, whither and by what order...................Board's Order 16 March 1815

As recorded in the General Entry Books for Dartmoor Prison
L. Clover

Prison number..5392
By what ship or how taken ....*Malabar*
Time when ....17 Jan. 1814
Place where ....Calcutta
Name of prize ....*Union*
Whither man o' war, Privateer or merchant vessel......
Prisoner's Name ....Lewis Clover
Quality (rank)..Seaman
Time when received into custody (Dartmoor) ....31 Oct. 1814
From what ship and where received ....HMS *Leyden* from Chatham
Place of Nativity (birthplace) ....Jersey
Age 23
Stature (height) ....5 ft. 4½ Ins.

Person	Slender
Visage and complexion	Long/ sallow
Hair	Brown
Eyes	Grey
Marks or wounds	None
Date of supply (bedding, clothing, etc.)	31 Oct. 1814
Exchanged; Run (escaped); Died; Discharged	Discharged
Date when (Board orders)	1 July 1815
If discharged, whither and by what order	Boards Order 16 March 1815

As recorded in the General Entry Books for Dartmoor Prison
R. Conklin

Prison number	1029
By what ship or how taken	*Pelican*
Time when	14 Aug. 1813
Place where	Irish Channel
Name of prize	*Argus*
Whither man o' war, Privateer or merchant vessel	U.S. Navy Brig
Prisoner's Name	Robert Conklin
Quality (rank)	Gunner
Time when received into custody (Dartmoor)	10 May 1814
From what ship and where received	Plymouth
Place of Nativity (birthplace)	Kingsale
Age	26
Stature (height)	5 ft. 4¾ ins.
Person	Stout
Visage and complexion	Oval/fair
Hair	Light Brown
Eyes	Blue
Marks or wounds	None
Date of supply (bedding, clothing, etc.)	12 Feb. 1814
Exchanged; Run (escaped); Died; Discharged	Discharged
Date when (Board orders)	2 Nov. 1814
If discharged, whither and by what order	Board's Order

Robert Conklin was a gunner on the *Argus*, and as the date for his entry to Dartmoor coincides with the entry date of the seventeen *Argus* men accused of being British deserters (see Chapter 10), he must have been one of them.

20

The Depot's Final Days

On April 20, 1815, the first batch of Americans to be repatriated marched out of the depot for home. It was a profoundly emotional departure so soon after the massacre. There were 249 of them, all of whom had been among the first to be sent to Dartmoor. They displayed a large white flag they had made and on it was depicted the goddess of Liberty with the slogan "Columbia Weeps and We Remember." They felt they'd had a raw deal throughout their captivity and Dartmoor was remembered as an evil place. All of them were poorly clothed and some were barefooted, no clothing having been issued for nearly a year. It was therefore a sad procession that passed out under the archway to freedom, but once outside the walls they could no longer contain their joy. There was an outburst of prolonged cheering which came ringing back to the ears of their countrymen still inside the depot and who returned their cheers over and over until they were out of earshot.

At Cattedown (Plymouth waterside) they embarked on a Swedish ship the *Maria Christiana*, exactly 40 days after the Treaty of Ghent was ratified. Charles Andrews was on board still recording his everyday experiences.

Benjamin Palmer was released on April 17, by which time there was a brisk trade among the Americans selling their turn for release by desperate men who either needed the money very badly or who had nothing to go home to. He bought a black man's turn (Charles Carrol) for two pounds on the understanding the money was deposited with a turnkey and would be handed over only when he got clear of the depot, otherwise it would be given back to him. In the eight days since the first Americans left someone had evidently made an effort to clothe them because shoes were now issued to those without for the march to Plymouth. By this time hundreds of relatives had congregated at Cattedown hoping to meet with, or at least receive news of, their relatives who might still be at the depot. Benjamin Palmer was among those who, while waiting to embark, were besieged by groups of anxious people clamoring for information and plying them with food and drink. When the time came to board the cartel they discovered they were to share the voyage home with several officers who had been living on parole at Ashburton. They had little liking for them (the officers had an easy time of it compared to the prisoners at the depot, they thought). With drink flowing freely, fighting broke out, resulting in a number of men being taken off the ship to await another cartel.

The French Come Again to Dartmoor

Following his return from Elba in March 1815 Napoleon resumed his position in France, formed a government and raised an army. With all of Europe opposed to him, he assumed personal command of the French forces against the combined might of Britain and its allies. His army now had about 74,000 men, mostly volunteers and veterans, the latter termed the "Grand Moustaches" by the British soldiers. He was confronted by the Duke of Wellington, who commanded a mixed force (including Belgian and Dutch contingents) numbering 67,000 men, of whom only 24,000 were British (the victorious Peninsula Army had been sent to fight in America after the fall of France in 1814 and had not yet returned). The Prussian Marshal Blucher brought 52,300 men to the battle. The countryside of Flanders was where

French prisoners captured at Waterloo are on their way to Dartmoor, some of them for the second time, depicted in an oil painting on canvas. Spattered with mud, bedraggled and wearing torn uniforms, some wounded, all of them exhausted — they were a pitiful sight. Repatriation began after Napoleon went into exile at St. Helena in August 1815. The last of them (hospital cases when they arrived) left for home in February 1816, after which the depot closed until 1850, when it was reopened as a convict jail (courtesy of Dartmoor Prison Museum).

the once mighty Bonaparte was to be finally crushed. The Battle of Waterloo was fought on June 18, 1815, the culmination of two lesser engagements at Ligny and Quatre Bras. The victorious Duke admitted afterwards it was a "damned close run thing," a reference to the timely appearance of the Prussian Army at a critical moment in the fight.

Three weeks later more than 4,000 prisoners from those battlefields arrived at Dartmoor Depot. The roles of the French and American prisoners were now reversed; this time it was the Americans who were leaving and they repaid the favor they owed the French by handing over their various artifacts — market paraphernalia, tools and other useful items. Several of the Frenchmen had been at Dartmoor before and had collected bits of wood and other odds and ends at the roadside with which to make articles to sell at market. They were a sorry sight, having been hustled into captivity straight from battle in uniforms torn and caked in mud, many of them suffering from wounds which had received only the briefest of attention. Blood soaked bandages and pained expressions typified the survivors of a once magnificent army.

This time their stay was a brief one. Napoleon, considering surrendering to the European Powers and the United States in turn, finally plumped for Britain as the place where he could expect the most generous terms. He sent a letter from Rochefort to the Prince Regent, an excerpt of which reads:

13th July 1815

Having been exposed to the factions which distract my country and to the enmity of the greatest powers of Europe, I have ended my political career, and I come, like Thermistocles, to throw myself on the hospitality of the British people. I put myself under the protection of their laws, which I claim from Your Royal Highness, as the most powerful, the most constant, and the most generous of my enemies.

This eloquent plea (widely quoted then and afterwards in the several accounts of that event) was never answered. On July 15 he gave himself up to Captain Maitland of the British 74 gun *Bellerophon*, anchored off Rochefort, accompanied by five generals, four lieutenant colonels, and four captains. The French wars were at an end once and for all.

The Last of the Yankees Depart

At Dartmoor all the Americans had left for home and by July 14 everyone was aboard their cartel, the last to go being the Rough Allies and the Negroes. Rough and ready they may have been, but their hearts must have rejoiced at the thought of home. Earlier that month one of them had written: "The sweet smile of content was easily perceived on the countenance of all

20. The Depot's Final Days

the prison — Moll and Sue is all the talk now," which is almost certainly an understatement. Some of the cartels were taken over by their passengers in mid-Atlantic with the object of landing at ports more convenient to them, especially the black men, who did not want to be returned to the Southern states to end their days in slavery. The masters of the vessels concerned were given signed certificates absolving them from responsibility for the change in destination.

Charles Andrews recorded the wording of the certificate which was handed to the master of his cartel: "We, the undersigned, citizens of the United States of America, do hereby certify that on the second day of June 1815 at twelve meridian, being in Lat. 40.30 Long. 69.30 by mutual agreement of majority of prisoners now on board the Cartel 'Maria Christiana' bound for Norfolk, did take possession of her and directed her for the port of New York."

The Americans left behind a record of constant umbrage against authority and unrelenting rancor at the alleged injustices they suffered. In a way this was no bad thing for men imprisoned indefinitely, and in many cases wrongfully (those who had been illegally impressed by the Royal Navy for example and who later "declared" themselves). They were determined to defend their country's independence and to "bend the knee" to no man, a proud ideal that saved many of the prisoners from hopelessness and death.

The French prisoners languished on the moor while their master and idol Bonaparte was brought first to Torbay and then to Plymouth, where he was confined on board the *Bellerophon* at anchor in the sound until his fate was decided. He had pledged to be a model prisoner if the British would agree to maintain him in the style he was used to and might reasonably expect, but because he had returned from exile and caused more bloodshed, the British were taking no chances. To have kept him in Britain would have been an embarrassment, they felt. Finally, after considering the Cape of Good Hope as a possible place of banishment, it was decided instead to send him into exile for life on the remote Atlantic island of St. Helena. Napoleon was dismayed when he was told what his fate was to be. He had supposed he would obtain an honorable agreement with the British whereby he would live in relative comfort with his retinue in self-imposed exile. Instead he was transferred early in August 1815 to another Royal Navy ship, the *Northumberland*, for the long voyage into oblivion.[1]

The men he once commanded were now released from Dartmoor and by December most of them had left for France, leaving only a few sick men and the remnants of the garrison behind. By February 1816 everyone had gone home and the mighty gates of the once great bastion slammed shut, leaving the birds to nest in the cocklofts and the ghosts of more than 1400 prisoners who had died there.

Sir Thomas Tyrwhitt

Prince Town's halcyon days were now at an end and the town went into decline, despite further endeavor by the stalwart Sir Thomas. One of his major accomplishments was the formation of a railway company which built a horse-drawn tramway from Plymouth to the Dartmoor quarries. It was afterwards extended to the center of the town. The line was intended to transport granite and products of the moorland farms to Plymouth, bringing back timber, building materials, and other resources in the hope of encouraging further development. There was little interest, however, and the line closed a few years later.

Sir Thomas never married and died on February 24, 1823, at 71 years of age.

Daniel Asher Alexander, Architect

The man who designed Dartmoor Depot and supervised the building of it afterwards made his home in Exeter and went on to design the huge prison at Maidstone in Kent. He died at Exeter on March 2, 1846, and was buried at Yarmouth, Isle of Wight, at his own request. He knew the place well and had an affection for it; in fact, he had previously paid for the church tower to be heightened to act as a guide for boats approaching the harbor entrance. His body now rests in the churchyard beneath it.

Captain Thomas George Shortland

Captain Shortland joined the Royal Navy in 1785 at the age of 14. He led an active service life and took part in several actions at sea during which he earned the admiration of his superiors as an able commander and a firm disciplinarian. He served as a lieutenant on one of the ships that made up the very first convict convoy to Botany Bay in Australia and lived ashore there for some time as an assistant administrator. He took up his appointment as agent at Dartmoor in December 1813 and remained there until its closure. In April 1816 he was made captain superintendent at Plymouth, a position he held for three years. In 1825, Shortland went to Jamaica as resident commissioner and died there in 1827, twelve years after the massacre he is remembered for.

Dr. George MaGrath

Dr. MaGrath was a cut above the average. In an age when amputations were performed without anesthetics and operations took place under primitive conditions using instruments terrifying to behold, surgeons were not the most popular of men. George MaGrath, however, was a giant among them. When Dartmoor first opened in 1809 he volunteered for service there, but was passed over in favor of Dr. George Dykar. He remained at Mill Prison, Plymouth, until 1813, when he transferred to the depot. He at once made a good impression and earned the heartfelt thanks and genuine affection of Britain's most troublesome prisoners of war — the Americans. Charles Andrews, on his arrival there that year, wrote: "No pains had been spared to render the hospital convenient and comfortable and much credit is due to whoever organised it." So Dr. MaGrath got off to a good start thanks in part to his predecessor, Dr. Dykar.

During the smallpox epidemic of 1813–14, MaGrath battled heroically to alleviate the suffering even though he himself was in poor health at the time. His humane concern was again made apparent when he attended the casualties resulting from the massacre. When the Americans were still waiting for their release from Dartmoor he was the subject of a tribute of gratitude and respect written by the prisoners' representatives to the president of the United States, James Madison. They also wrote to their ambassador in England, John Quincy Adams. Exerpts from the two letters are taken from *A Prisoner's Memoires* by Charles Andrews:

> Dartmoor Prison
> March 28, 1815
>
> To His Excellency James Madison.
> Honoured and Respected Sir...
> Dr. George MaGrath, principle of the medical department for the American prisoners of war in England. It is impossible for us to speak of this gentleman in terms that will do justice to his superior professional science ... and unwearied exertions in combatting a succession of diseases of the most malignant character which prevailed amongst the prisoners....
> Dr. MaGrath's time and attention were fully occupied in the hospital and in the vaccinating of prisoners. From his exertions his health became seriously impaired but totally regardless of himself he persevered ... and was the means of rescuing many citizens of the United States from the embraces of death ... this truly great man's exertions in the cause of suffering have been rarely equalled, but never excelled.

The letter was signed by fifteen members of the Hospital Committee. Seldom has such praise been heaped upon any man by his country's foes.

The following selected passages are taken from a letter even more remarkable, having been written only three days after the infamous "Prince Town Massacre":

> Dartmoor Prison
> April 9th, 1815
>
> To His Excellency John Q. Adams.
> Sir,
> Impressed with the sense if duty which we owe to our country, and to ourselves, we respectfully solicit permission to introduce to your Excellency George MaGrath, Esq., M.D., principal of the medical department of this depot. Language is incompetent to delineate the worth and character of this gentleman, prominent in medical science, enriched by every virtue and accomplishment that can dignify and adorn human nature.... His professional skill has been peculiarly conspicuous in his successfully combatting a succession of diseases....
> Language is too impotent to describe Dr. MaGrath's unexampled endeavours to prevent the effusion of blood; regardless of the many dangers by which he was environed, he persevered amid the heavy and incessant fire of musketry in his humane endeavours to prevent the fatal catastrophe.
> His treatment of the unfortunate wounded Americans is superior to all praise, and was such to entitle Dr. MaGrath to the esteem and gratitude of the citizens of the United States. We therefore respectfully and ardently solicit that your Excellency would be pleased to honour Dr. MaGrath with your particular notice and esteem, and to convey these our sentiments to the government of the United States, for we would wish to give all possible publicity to our high sense of Dr. MaGrath and to evince to our country and the world how gratefully we appreciate the essential services we received from that gentleman.

This letter was signed by nine members of the Hospital Committee. He bought a house in Lockyer Street in Plymouth after the war and for several years ran a successful medical practice in Union Street, during which time he gained an illustrious reputation. On his death a memorial tablet was erected by public subscription in St. Andrews Church at Plymouth. It survived the World War II bombing raids when the church was all but destroyed and can be seen today mounted on the wall opposite the main entrance to the church.

> Sacred
> To the Memory of
> SIR GEORGE MAGRATH
> Doctor of Medicine. Inspector of Her Majesty's Fleets and Hospital. Commander of the Most Honourable Order of the Bath. Knight of the Royal Guelphic Order of Hanover. Knight of the Order of the Cross of Christ in Portugal. Fellow of the Royal College of Physicians, London, and Honourable Fellow of the Royal Linnia and Geological Societies, and Member of other Learned Bodies.

He was born in the year 1772 and died at Plymouth June 12th, 1837.
A Ripe Scholar and a Skilled Physician he served his Country by sea and by Land
for a quarter of a Century.
A Follower of the Immortal Nelson, his Patron and Friend.
In all things he did his duty.
As an Officer with Zeal.
As a Citizen with Dignity.
And as a Friend with Devotion.
He was distinguished by Nations for his services.

21

Mortality Rates and the Price of Victory

The average death rate at Dartmoor Depot was equal to that aboard the hulks — around 4 percent per year. This figure is misleading though, because the epidemics that broke out from time to time pushed the average higher than would fairly be expected. In 1809, for example, a measles outbreak killed a huge number of Frenchmen and later a smallpox epidemic took a heavy toll, especially among the Americans. Typhus, commonly known as "gaol [jail] fever" at that time, was prevalent and the cold, wet winters were the cause of chest complaints which often developed into pneumonia. The latter was the greater menace because the conditions that led to it were consistent.

Some prisoners helped bring about their own demise; for example those who (for whatever reason) did not possess shoes or sufficient clothing in winter. Nathaniel Pierce, an American prisoner from Newberryport, complained about the mist and cold on Dartmoor and mentions the interior of the dormitories where it was too dark to see to read or write even on a fine day. The chief surgeon of England blamed the stale, humid atmosphere in the prison blocks for the spread of the so-called "African Pox" which afflicted the Americans in February 1815. As we have already seen, the men blocked up the windows to stop the draught, something which created an unhealthy, stagnant environment. There was tragedy, too. No fewer than 60 coroner's inquests were held between April and September that year over the bodies of men "found dying in the prison," "found hanged," "found dead," etc.

The French, due to their longer period of imprisonment, suffered by far the greater number of deaths, nearly 1200, including a number of suicides, murders, and those killed trying to escape. Of the Americans 271 died, but as Ira Dye implies, there may be others; some sick cases for example were transferred to Mill Prison in Plymouth and may have died there. From his very extensive records, compiled by meticulous research over many years, we learn not only the several classes of American prisoners but the actual numbers of each class who died:

- 17 men were from the U.S. Navy.
- 92 were from privateers.
- 36 were from letter of marque vessels.
- 59 were from merchant vessels.
- 6 were U.S. Marines.
- 7 were soldiers from the U.S. Army.
- 14 were men taken off British or other foreign merchant ships.
- 39 were men who had been impressed, or had volunteered for the Royal Navy, but who refused to serve against the United States.
- 3 men whose records lack enough information to tell where they served before their capture.

By rank, 236 of those who died were seamen; two were boys. One, John Seapatch by name, was just 12 years old. Three had been passengers when they were captured. Four of the six Marines were privates.

Most fatalities among the Yankees occurred during the smallpox epidemic in the winter of 1814–15, and a third of them were black or mulatto Americans who comprised 15 percent of the population at Dartmoor. There was one murder, one suicide and nine men were killed as a result of the massacre.

The calorie yield for the rations, calculated at about 2,410 calories per day, was below what a young man needed to keep healthy. Prisoners who could not afford to buy extra rations from the daily market often deteriorated the soonest after the ones who wagered their rations and lost. Benjamin Palmer has related how a performance of *Hamlet* was staged in No. 4 Block, and refers with grim humor to the ease with which the ghost was portrayed by an inmate whose gaunt and pale features were not so very different "from the real thing!" At best the basic rations at the depot kept them alive.

Total Deaths 1809–1816

May 1809 to year end	149
1810	419
1811	88
1812	142
1813	239
1814	198
1815	220
1816 (Jan. only)	23

Total 1478

Ailments That Resulted in Death

The following are common conditions and ailments that resulted in the death of French and American prisoners of war.

Phthisis—this is an archaic name for tuberculosis. Phthisis pulmonalis (consumption of the lungs), in a general sense, is progressive emaciation.

Consumption—(wasting of the frame)—pulmonary consumption, or decline; emaciation of the body, and debility, attended with a cough, hectic fever, and generally purulent expectoration. It is also termed marasmus, tabes pulmonalis, a term formally applied (like consumption) to a disease of the lungs now known as tuberculosis, a wasting or consumption of the tissues.

Typhus—(putrid fever)—Malignant fever. A kind of continued fever, attended with great prostration of the nervous and vascular systems, with a tendency to putrefaction in the fluids, and vitiation of the secretions.

Atrophy—defect of nutrition; wasting or emaciation with loss of strength, unaccompanied by fever.

Dropsy—archaic word for edema. The dropsy is a preternatural swelling of the whole body, or some part of it, due collection of water. It is distinguished by different names, according to the parts affected, as the anasarca, or a collection of water under the skin; the ascites, or a collection of water in the belly; the hydrops pectoris, or dropsy of the breast; the hydocephalus, or dropsy of the brain.

Dysentery—inflammation of the mucous membrane of the large intestine; the chief symptoms of which are fever, more or less inflammatory, with frequent mucous or bloody evacuations; violent tormina and tenesmus. It occurs particularly during summer and autumnal months, and in hot climates more than cold and frequently in camps or prisons, in consequence of poor sanitation and hygiene and imperfect nourishment. A disease attended with inflammation and ulcerations of the colon and rectum, and characterized by griping pains, constant desire to evacuate the bowels, and the discharge of mucous and blood. When acute, dysentery is usually accompanied with high fever. It occurs epidemically, and is believed to be communicable through the medium of the alvine discharges.

Flux—a discharge; another term for diarrhea.

Pneumonia—inflammation of the lungs. Symptoms include fever, pain in the thorax aggravated by coughing, a quick, hard pulse, with more or less difficulty in breathing.

The Price of War

Between 1803 and 1814 the British captured 122,440 prisoners of various nationalities, most of them after 1805, the year of the Trafalgar battle. Out of this colossal number 10,341 died in captivity, and 17,607 were exchanged or paroled to France. As we have seen, accommodating such large numbers caused endless problems to the extent that the Duke of Wellington was specifically asked on February 3, 1811, not to send any more prisoners of war to Britain because of the overcrowding. He nevertheless sent 20,000 more between 1811 and 1812 alone.

Dartmoor Depot and the hulks represented the worst of prison life. At first the hulks were used to accommodate prisoners for whom there was no room anywhere ashore; later they became reception centers for newly captured men who were assessed and segregated according to rank and similar factors before being sent on parole or to the war prisons. Some prison ships were retained for the confinement of recaptured escapees and troublemakers. In 1814 there were an estimated 72,000 prisoners of war in Britain, the largest number at any one time.

At Dartmoor overcrowding was a problem as early as September 1809 when, only four months after opening, 6,031 men were detained in accommodation designed for just over 5,000. The following year this figure fell to an acceptable level, but by June 1811 the number gradually crept up to 6,577. It will be remembered two extra prison blocks were constructed using prison labor, but the place was still overcrowded when the Americans began arriving in April 1813, and this remained the case until mid–1814, when the French were repatriated.

Consider the number of each class of prisoner held in Britain for June 16, 1812, for which the official total figure stood at 54,517, including many innocents — women, children, ships' passengers and others. There were nearly 1600 Danish prisoners on board one of the Plymouth hulks. All of them had to be fed, clothed, housed and guarded. The sick had to be attended to and the highest percentage of these were among the officers on parole (some think it a result of dueling). The cost was colossal, as the official figures reveal. The sum expended for the maintenance of French prisoners during the war from 1803 to 1814 was £6,799,678 13s. 11d. And for 1815 was £71,995 18s. 00. The total was £6,871,674 11s. 11d.

Nearly £7m. was spent by the British with little or no assistance from the French toward the upkeep of their men. There was an enormous difference, too, in the actual cost of waging the wars: £225m. by France and an enormous £831m. by the British. The difference is partly accounted for by more than

£52m. (referred to at the time as "'Pitt's Gold'") the British paid its allies to arm and equip their armies in Europe.[1]

We have seen in this narrative the noblest of human endeavor and the blackest of deeds, the effects of which linger to this day. Hopefully the many examples of bravery and chivalry will be remembered too, so that we may all learn lessons to help make our world a better place.

22
Princetown Church and Memorials

This chapter on Princetown Church is perhaps more extensive than expected and for a good reason. The church was built by French and American prisoners and is a testimony to their presence at Dartmoor. It is a unique edifice — the only church in England known to have been constructed by prisoners of war. The beautiful stained glass window and the framed memorial certificates that adorn the pillars inside record the devotion of the American people to the memory of their forebears, through the U.S. Society of the Daughters of 1812, all of whom are descended from those who took part in that war.

The Christian faith was not neglected on the moor. Services were regularly held in barns and buildings set aside for religious purposes at nearby farms and country houses. Baptisms were often performed in the parents' homes. It has been mentioned already that the Prince of Wales had approved the building of a chapel in the district, but it was not until the prisoner of war depot was up and running that a start was made. It has always been understood that the architect for the depot, Daniel Alexander, designed the chapel and the next door parsonage, but it is now known that a Mr. Walters, foreman of works at the prison, was specifically instructed to draw up the necessary plans and put them into effect (attention was first drawn to this by Elisabeth Stanbrook, the editor of a local periodical called *Dartmoor Magazine* in the December 1996 issue).

On 10 January 1812 Agent Cotgrave received a letter from the Transport Office that read in part:

> Sir, the Lords Commissioners of the Admiralty having authorized us to erect a church together with a house for the clergyman ... direct you to order Mr. Walters to draw a plan and elevation of the said church and house which are to be executed upon the plainest and most economical style possible ... the church to contain about 5 or 600 people and the house ... a parlour, dining room, four

bedrooms, kitchen ... to be built of the moor or granite stone by the assistance of the necessary number of French prisoners so that the whole may be executed in the course of the summer.... It will be noticed that the house will be under the lee of the church and the back part may be possibly constructed with a hip roof as better calculated to resist the prevailing weather [it seems everyone had come to appreciate the vagaries of Dartmoor weather].[1]

After much bickering over Mr. Walters' plans and estimates, even sending him plans and drawings of their own as a guideline, the Transport Office wrote to Captain Cotgrave on March 29, 1812, informing him of their approval and instructing him to proceed with the work in accordance with what they considered the cheapest design.

The Church of St. Michael and All Angels is a unique edifice, having been constructed by French prisoners of war who worked up to the time they

The Church of St. Michael and All Angels is now closed as a regular place of worship (alternative amenities have been provided in the center of Princetown). It is in the care of the Churches Conservation Trust, which is dedicated to the preservation of churches of historical significance. Dartmoor weather conditions and inefficient heating arrangements wreaked havoc over a period of many years until the cost of renovation was far beyond the resources of the local ministry. Now the building and the artifacts it contains are preserved and are attracting visitors, who are duly impressed at what they see (author's photograph).

left for home in 1814. Then the American prisoners took over and completed the task. Dartmoor Prison Chapel, as it was first called, was more correctly a "chapel-at-ease" to the Church of St. Petrock at Lydford (Devon), the largest parish in England within which Prince Town then was located. It also has the distinction of being one of the highest situated churches in the country, although the term "church" only came into effect when Prince Town became an ecclesiastic parish in its own right in 1912.

Before and after the building of the church the minister or curate in charge for the area was the Rev. James Holman Mason, a well known clergyman in those days affectionately dubbed the "Bishop of the Moor." This remarkable man was born in Okehampton (Devon) and became curate at Lydford in which capacity he traveled many miles over rough moorland roads, often on horseback, in order to conduct services and perform baptisms. He afterwards joined the "improvers" on the moor by leasing and enclosing 600 acres of Duchy land near Crockern Tor on the Prince Town–Moretonhampstead road where he built a dwelling called Parson's Cottage. A cottage stands there now and is marked on the ordnance survey map as "Parsons Cottage" but the original little cottage was in ruins before the end of the 19th century. The Rev. Mason and Sir Thomas Tyrwhitt were firm friends and this probably influenced his appointment as chaplain to the Prince of Wales and his being appointed vicar of Treneglos and Warbstow in 1804 (both parishes are in North Cornwall) a position he held until 1848. The prince made him deputy rider and master forester of Dartmoor and in 1815 he accepted the post of vicar at Widecombe, a Dartmoor village where he lived and worked until he died in 1860.

When the chapel-at-ease at Prince Town opened for the first time on January 2, 1814, it was the Rev. Mason who conducted divine service, having been appointed incumbent minister by the Transport Office (which employed him directly in this capacity and paid his salary through the agent at the depot). This first service was conducted when the chapel was still under construction, and it must have been a makeshift affair, because (four months later on May 16 the Transport Office wrote to Captain Shortland to "approve of your causing the window frames of the church to be fitted and glazed and the several works are to be proceeded with as expeditiously as possible while the prisoners remain."[2]

There was no pulpit either, and another letter dated 13 August 1814 states: "The Revd Mr. Mason having informed us that a pulpit and desk now in St. Sitwells Church (St. Sidwells, Exeter) has been offered for sale at the price of £22, we direct you to purchase them, at that price, for the use of the church at Dartmoor."

It was not until November 1, 1815, that the burial facility was granted. By then the Americans had long since gone home and the few remaining French (those captured during the "Hundred Days") were the sick men in the hospital. Several writers, including the Rev. Sabine Baring-Gould, have alluded to empty wooden coffins being found years afterwards in the churchyard (doubtful), within the depot itself (definitely not) and in the prisoners' moorland burial ground (now part of the prison farm). It is known that in the late 1800s and early 1900s when the prison was considerably altered a number of empty coffins were discovered in the farm area. Curiously, some of them were found stood on end. The mystery was never solved, but the suggestion it might have been the work of "resurrectionists" (a polite term for ghoulish criminals who made their living by digging up newly buried corpses for sale to schools of surgery) or the result of amazing escapes by prisoners of war from shallow graves seem unlikely.

The register of baptisms for Prince Town provides an insight into the character of the place from April 12, 1807, onwards. On that day the Rev. Mason entered this statement on the first page of the register: "Register of baptisms at the prison of war on Dartmoor within the Parish of Lydford where Divine service has been performed from Jan. 25th, 1807, under the sanction of the Bishop of the Diocese by James Holman Mason, Vicar of Treneglos and Warbstow." Among the entries we find:

- April 12, 1807. Henry, son of Richard Badcock and Martha his wife, residing at Prince Hall, received his full baptism.
- June 7, 1807. Arabella, daughter of Daniel Lane, Gent., Surgeon at the prison of war and Margaret his wife.
- May 22, 1808. Harriet, daughter of Rose Johnson who was killed in the Trafalgar action, and Martha his wife, born March 29, 1803.

These baptisms must have been performed either at the depot or in private houses before the chapel-at-ease was built. The entry for June 7, 1807, tells us the depot was staffed to an extent that justified the presence of a resident surgeon well before it was completed. The construction of the prison and the huge stones which had to be maneuvered into place must have been a hazardous undertaking and there were probably injuries enough to keep the surgeon busy. Entries continue.

- April 2nd, 1815. Charlotte, daughter of Richard Edwards, a baker living at Prince Town, and Elizabeth his wife, was privately baptized January 18, 1812 [Richard Edwards supplied bread to the French officers at the depot].

Two French prisoners of war taken during the Hundred Days are listed as fathers of infants baptized in 1815. They were:

- September 3rd, 1815. Peter Dartmoor, son of Pierre Joseph Tollat, a French prisoner, Sergt. in the 26th Regt. and Catherine Elizabeth Eidam, his wife.
- November 19th, 1815. Catherine Elizabeth, daughter of Pascal Pucket, Sergt. of the 25th Regt. in the service of France, a prisoner at Dartmoor, and Helena his wife.

Up to the end of the year 1815 the entries mention fathers who pioneered the Prince Town and Two Bridges area and whose occupations included:

Moor stone mason (John Jeffry)
Blacksmith (John Halfyard, James Rowe
Carpenter (Nicholas Eden)
Canal man (Peter Germon)
Miner (Benjamin Gill)
Tailor and turnkey at the prison (John Tozer)
Butcher (John Dunning)
Prince Town brewery (William Robins)
Interpreter at Dartmoor Depot (John Moore)
Weaver (Thomas Wright)
Steward at the prison of war (John Arnold)
Carter at the prison of war (George Challacombe)
Slater at the prison of war (William May)
Innkeeper (John Ellis)
Turnpikeman (John Hannaford)

Also mentioned are a cordwainer (shoemaker) of the Derby Militia, a bandsman of the South Devon Militia, and other militiamen belonging to the West Essex (1810), East Kent (1810), Royal Cheshire (1813), Monaghan (1813), and the 12th Regiment of Foot.

What a colorful picture they represent of Prince Town's past! There was even a "sailor, residing at the prison"—one wonders how that came about. Nearly all the above-mentioned names are familiar today in the vicinity of Dartmoor and its borders.

The church has had more than its fair share of misfortune. The bells that should have been installed never arrived. Peace came in 1815 just when they were due and they were diverted to the Dockyard Church of St. Nicholas at

Plymouth, which was destroyed by enemy air raids during World War II. In 1868 the building was completely gutted by fire and nearly all the internal fittings put in by the Americans were destroyed. Some renovations were carried out in 1899, but because of financial restraints the work was so badly done that by 1905 the east wall was in danger of collapse. The wall and the east window had to be rebuilt. It was then that the pastor, the Rev. Heathcote-Smith, made an appeal to the American people for help, suggesting this might take

The American memorial window was commissioned and paid for by the National Society of United States Daughters of 1812 on behalf of the American people and in response to an appeal from the Rev. Heathcote-Smith in 1908. The newly installed window was unveiled by Mrs. Gerry Slade, president of the society, on June 3, 1910 (author's photograph).

22. Princetown Church and Memorials

The flags of three nations hang in the church. The first American flag was donated by the National Society of United States Daughters of 1812 in 1925 but was replaced in 1982 by a new, larger flag that had been flown from the Capitol Building in Washington before being sent to Princetown. The flags of France, Britain and the U.S. hang side by side in the chancel (photograph by James Stevenson).

the form of a memorial window to be inserted in the wall. On June 7, 1908, the *New York Herald* published his appeal and the cause was taken up by the National Society of United States Daughters of 1812. Their president, Mrs. Gerry Slade, thought it appropriate to put the matter to the national board of the society, as a result of which a memorial committee was set up. She obtained details of the dimensions and arranged for Messrs. Mayer and Co. of Berlin, London, and New York to prepare and supply the beautiful stained glass window which is there today. Beneath the window proper is an inscription:

> To the Glory of God in Memory of the American Prisoners of War who were detained in the Dartmoor War prison between the years 1809–1815 and who helped to build this church, especially of the 218[3] above men who died here on behalf of their Country.
>
> Dulce est Pro patria Mori

When Mrs. Slade unveiled the window on June 3, 1910, the comment was made that credit would not be claimed by the society alone but would reflect on the American nation. By 1960 the window was in need of some restoration and the society again came to the rescue by paying for the work to be done.

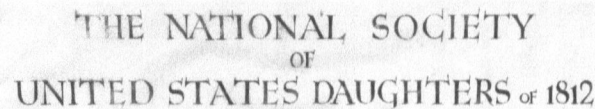

This "Certificate of Importance" indicates the vast scale of the organization that has given so much to perpetuate the memory of their forebears who were imprisoned at Dartmoor. This is framed and mounted on one of the columns in the main body of the church (photograph by James Stevenson).

In 1925 it supplied an American flag to hang in the church. In 1982 a second, larger flag was given with the kind assistance of United States Senator William V. Roth, who, prior to the flag being dispatched, arranged for it to be flown over the Capitol Building in Washington. It now hangs alongside the national flags of France and Great Britain. Five years later (1987), the society visited again and placed a plaque to mark the 175 years that had elapsed since the start of the War of 1812.

There are no rich legacies or endowments to maintain the church and Dartmoor weather has taken its toll. Dartmoor cold, frost and wet rotted the floorboards, damaged the stonework, and rendered the tower unsafe. On one occasion the author examined the west (inside) wall of the tower and noted huge patches of green and black algae clinging to its damp surface (a vivid example of what the old prisons must have been like when the French and Americans were in residence). Princes and governments have in the past donated substantial sums for its upkeep, but because of its exposed location and the winter storms, a constant battle has to be fought to keep up appearances.

The church had to close in 1994 through lack of funds to carry out the necessary repairs. After being offered unsuccessfully for sale, there was a real danger it would have to be partly demolished to make it safe, leaving perhaps the foundations and the walls as a memorial to its historic past. Fortunately that did not happen and today the church is in the care of the Churches Conservation Trust, a body established by Parliament and the Church of England to preserve churches of historical or architectural interest. The building has been renovated at a cost of more than £200,000; the church and artifacts it contains will be preserved for posterity.[4]

The Memorials at Dartmoor Prison

In July 2003 renovation work at the American Memorial Cemetery at Dartmoor Prison was completed and two specially commissioned plaques were installed to supplement the historic obelisk. Of the several thousand American prisoners who were interned at Dartmoor during the War of 1812 there are 271 known to have died, mainly from disease. As previously described, French and Americans were buried outside the prison walls without ceremony or headstones to mark where they lay.

In 2003 after years of neglect the American cemetery was completely cleared

The American obelisk and memorial plaques are shown on their newly refurbished site. The plaques bear the name, rank, origin and the date of death of every one of the 271 known to have been buried here (photograph by James Stevenson).

The new memorial plaques; one features an American Navy officer (*top*) and the other a privateer (*above*). The privateersmen far outnumbered any other service. The plaques were commissioned and installed with funds raised in the United States and by American servicemen stationed in the U.K. (photographs by James Stevenson).

22. Princetown Church and Memorials 209

24 Mai

1809 - 2009

En ce jour du bicentenaire de l'arrivée des premiers prisonniers de l'Empire à Princetown et en présence de l'adjointe du Lord Lieutenant du Devon, Lady Kitson, de l'Ambassadeur de France à Londres, S.E. Monsieur Gourdault-Montagne et du Gouverneur de Dartmoor prison Mr T. Corcoran, se sont réunis dans cette église, des citoyens et des élus britanniques et français, des officiers de la Royal Navy et de la Marine Nationale Française, le Commandant, des officiers et des marins de l'aviso « Premier maître L'Her », le Consul Général de France et des Consuls Honoraires de France et d'Allemagne en Grande-Bretagne, des descendants de l'enseigne de vaisseau Jean George Rühl, né à Nancy le 2 juillet 1786, pris sur le « Basque » au large de Bayonne le 13 novembre 1809, prisonnier sur parole de 1809 à 1814, des habitants et des écoliers de Princetown.

En particulier, sont venus de France, Mme Renée Pensec et son petit-fils Yann Mével descendants de Jean-Marie Jadé né à Douarnenez, Finistère, le 11 mars 1768, matelot sur le « Variscite », pris le 12 avril 1809 dans le golfe de Gascogne, décédé à Princetown le 6 juin 1814, M. et Mme Bougeloc et M. et Mme Lucas, collatéraux de Jean Per, né à Portsall, Finistère, le 10 octobre 1782, matelot sur le « Volontaire », pris le 4 mars 1806 au Cap de Bonne-Espérance, décédé à Princetown le 30 juillet 1813, Mme Renée Le Bars descendante de Jean-René Bolloré, né à Douarnenez, Finistère, le 9 mai 1781, décédé à Princetown le 31 janvier 1812.

Ensemble nous avons rendu hommage aux soldats et marins de l'Empire et célébré

La Liberté, L'Egalité, La Fraternité.

M. Alain Sibiril - Consul Honoraire de France à Plymouth

A French certificate records the commemoration ceremony held in May 2009. On yet another column in the church is a framed certificate designed by Alain Sibiril, consul for France at Plymouth. It records, in French, the bicentenary of the arrival of the first French prisoners of war at Dartmoor Prison and the notables who attended. It is an impressive list. The captain, officers and men of the French warship *Premier Maitre L'Heure*, berthed at Plymouth, paraded and provided a guard of honor at the French memorial after a service in the church. In particular the certificate records the names and residences of five French descendants of prisoners who were held at Dartmoor and who made a special journey to Princetown to attend. It was without doubt a spectacular landmark in Princetown's colorful history (photograph by James Stevenson).

of vegetation and debris, the obelisk scrupulously cleaned and two memorial tablets installed to the rear and on either side of the obelisk. The work was instigated by American Navy personnel based at St. Mawgan in Cornwall and completed by the prison Works Department. An American spokesman expressed gratitude to former Dartmoor Prison governors John Lawrence and Graham Johnson for their support, with special thanks to Works Department employee Adrian Kelly, who dismantled and completely relaid the stonework around the cairn, which had fallen into disarray since first constructed in 1866. It is now a pleasing sight together with the grassed area with seating and a flagpole.

A commemorative arch is at one end of the cemetery, paid for by the U.S. Daughters of 1812. It was formally opened in a ceremony in 1928. In 1987 the group again visited the church and the American cemetery and left its metal badge to be affixed to the obelisk.

The scene at the French memorial on May 24, 2009, the occasion of the bicentenary of the first French prisoners of war transferring from the Plymouth hulks to Dartmoor and the opening of Dartmoor Prison. French sailors parade to pay homage to those prisoners who died and a guard of honor prepares to salute them. In the foreground are several dignitaries, including the French consul general (based in London), the French naval attache (also from London), and the governor of Dartmoor Prison. A service of remembrance followed when wreaths were laid, among others by direct descendants of French prisoners of war who traveled from France especially for the ceremony (photograph by Tracey Elliot-Reep).

Funds were raised for the new memorial plaques mainly through the efforts of Burton Showers, former treasurer of the United States Society of the War of 1812 in Illinois (himself a U.S. Navy veteran of World War II) with other societies lending their support. United States servicemen based in the United Kingdom also made contributions for the new memorials. They were made and inscribed by H.H.L. Perfitt, a Norfolk family firm of traditional stonemasons founded in 1830 that has manufactured memorials for Britain's Royal Air Force as well as American Air Force veterans now in place all over Britain. The stone they chose for this project came from South Africa and is called roughback granite. It is a natural dark gray color with a plain texture, unlike Cornish granite which tends to be speckled. The highly polished surface shows up the silver coated names and details of every man who died to perfection together with the engraved figures and the "Stars and Stripes." Each slab weighs 1.5 tons and measures 9 feet (2.74 m) in width by 4 feet 6 inches. (1.37 m) high, and it took two days to unload and put in place. The lettering was done by a specialist engraver who spent 10 working days to finish the job. The result is a pair of commemorative headstones of which both the Americans and Messrs. Perfitt can be proud.

On August 17, 2003, a dedication service was held at the memorial attended by representatives of all three American armed services and Dartmoor Prison officials. The national flags of both countries were hoisted followed by prayers and speeches. The high point of the ceremony was the unveiling of the two headstones bearing the names of all 271 prisoners who died.

On May 24, 2009, an impressive ceremony took place to commemorate the bicentenary of the opening of Dartmoor Prison and the arrival of the first French prisoners of war. The French consul general from the French Embassy in London was accompanied by the French naval attaché and they were supported by the deputy lord lieutenant of Devon, the lord high sheriff of Devon, the governor of Dartmoor Prison, several lord mayors from the surrounding towns, and French family members who are direct descendants of some of the prisoners of war who were incarcerated at Dartmoor. The French warship *Premier Maitre L'Her* berthed at Devonport and provided a guard of honor and a contingent of sailors in support.

The first American prisoners of war arrived in April 1813, and preliminary arrangements are in hand for an American observance of this anniversary, the details of which are not available at this writing, but rest assured it will be equally encouraged and supported by the British. The memorial obelisk and its surrounds have again undergone renovation work and are in pristine condition for whatever may take place.

Is There a Ghost at Dartmoor Prison?

Over a hundred years ago a convict working in the American cemetery had a strange experience, not the only one of its kind. The cemetery at the rear of the prison contains the bones of French and American prisoners of war who died in captivity during the Napoleonic Wars and the War of 1812. They lie in separate mass graves, each of which is surmounted by a memorial stone in the form of an obelisk with an inscription commemorating their deaths. Jock O' Parkhurst was the name under which a former British Army officer, who went astray and served part of his sentence on the "Moor," wrote about his life in prison. This is how he described a strange event.

> I myself was employed in the American graveyard for several weeks cutting the grass and weeding the path. One day I saw an old grey-haired lady — a very old lady she seemed — kneeling before the memorial stone. I looked around for the

The little old lady at the American memorial, who was seen at close quarters by a convict but disappeared when a warder was summoned. Proof of her presence lay on the memorial — a fresh bunch of roses (courtesy Dartmoor Prison Museum).

officer, thinking he might speak to her. He was outside on the road. I went to tell him and he came back with me, but the old lady had gone. We looked in every direction. Then he recommended me to report sick when we returned to the orison. I went back to the stone and there on the ground we saw a bunch of red roses — roses freshly cut. I wonder of anyone else has ever seen the Old Lady of the American Graveyard.

There have been other sightings of figures over the years, imaginary or by honest mistake. In a place like Dartmoor Prison with its long history and where sad and often macabre events have occurred, it is perhaps what you would expect. However, this sighting happened in broad daylight, in the open and a long way off the public highway. An old lady would not be capable of making off so quickly as not to be seen. The writer was certainly sober and necessarily of sound mind to have placed on record what he experienced in such lucid terms. The mystery remains.

Epilogue

An anonymous writer relates his experience visiting the prison:

I walked out of the prison one cold February morning when the outlines of the walls were blurred by a Dartmoor mist; a heavy dew lay about the mossy stones and birds were trilling their morning song. The damp, moisture-laden air muffled my footsteps and I marvelled at the perfect quiet that prevailed in an establishment where hundreds of convicted men lay sleeping. Outside the Old Chapel I stopped; was that a babble of foreign tongues I could hear beyond the doorway? I sensed a restless murmuring within those dark confines where the Romans, King Dick Crafus and the Rough Allies lived all those years ago, and in my mind I could hear distant drumbeats and heavy boots crunching in unison along the old Military Walkway. Sharp commands broke the brittle early morning stillness I thought, and through the gloom I imagined the shapes of men pulling a cart on which were a number of rough boxes, sliding and jolting as they made their way from the old hospital towards the burial ground outside; pillars of smoke arose from the cookeries and there was a clanging of pots from within where the cooks were already at work; water gurgled in the waterways; it all seemed very real to me.

My reverie was shattered by the squawking of the jackdaws that throng the prison (which the convicts of long ago said were the reincarnation of old lags) and I walked on. The ancient stone wall curves towards the gateway, undulating in graceful vertical waves, caused by the passage of time and the innumerable repairs it has undergone; but its shape, height, and the encompassing barrier it represents is much the same as it always was. These are the stones that reverberated to the sound of muskets when the Americans were shot down; yells of reproach and the screams of wounded men echo down the years. The way out lies over the very ground where they fell, desperate men who were not criminals, but soldiers and sailors taken in battle amid cannon fire and the waving of standards; then I passed through the gateway where a poor Frenchman cut his own throat after failing to produce his bedding and was refused his release because of it.

Outside the prison, the tower of the Church of St. Michael and All Angels stands tall among the trees, having weathered almost two centuries of Dartmoor storms. It is a monument to the men of America and those who served Napoleon. Stone by stone they built it and hopefully it will survive many more years, a lasting testament to the futility of war and the hope of peace for every nation.

Appendix 1

Those Who Died

The details of every man who died are recorded on the memorial plaques and reproduced here. In order: surname, Christian name, rank, date died, birthplace.

ADAM	William	Seaman	15 Mar. 1815	Massachusetts
ADAMS	James	Seaman	06 Nov. 1814	North Carolina
ADAMS	John	Sailing Master	03 Dec. 1814	Boston, MA
ADAMS	Robert	Seaman	05 Feb. 1815	Unknown
ADAMS	William	Seaman	24 Apr. 1815	North Carolina
ADDIGO	Henry	Marine	23 Dec. 1813	New York
ALLAN	Asha	Seaman	14 Nov. 1814	New Bedford, MA
ALLEN	Archibald	Seaman	03 Mar. 1815	Massachusetts
ALLEN	John Baptist	Seaman	21 Nov. 1814	Africa
ALMENO	Jose	Seaman	03 Nov. 1814	Carthagena, Bolivia
AMOS	Peter	Passenger	18 Feb. 1815	Martha's Vineyard, MA
ANDERSON	Jacob	Seaman	26 Jan. 1815	Portland, ME
ANDREWS	Joshua	Seaman	21 Nov. 1814	Ipswich, MA
APPLETON	Daniel	Seaman	04 Jan. 1814	Ipswich, MA
ARCHER	Daniel	Prize Master	14 Jan. 1814	Salem, MA
AUBURY	Martin	Seaman	17 Feb. 1815	Carthagena, Bolivia
BABB	Benjamin	Seaman	29 Jan. 1815	Barrington, England
BADSON	Jacob	Seaman	22 Mar. 1815	Boston, MA
BAILEY	Moses	Seaman	17 Feb. 1815	Pennsylvania
BAKER	Charles	Seaman	30 Jan. 1815	Virginia
BALDWIN	John	Seaman	05 Dec. 1814	Boston, MA
BARNETT	James	Mate	08 Dec. 1814	Pennsylvania
BARON	Thomas	Servant	08 Nov. 1813	Norfolk, VA
BARRY	Peter	Seaman	20 Nov. 1814	Salem, MA
BATEMAN	John	Seaman	23 Nov. 1814	Baltimore, MD
BEAN	William	Seaman	28 Nov. 1814	Virginia
BECK	William	Seaman	18 Jan. 1815	New Hampshire
BELLOA	Darius	Seaman	25 Jan. 1815	Rhode Island

BIRCH	Peter	Seaman	13 Mar. 1815	Philadelphia, PA
BISLEY	Horace	Seaman	11 Apr. 1813	Rockhill, NH
BLASDON	Philip	Soldier	17 Jan. 1815	New Hampshire
BOARDBY	Samuel	Seaman	29 Mar. 1815	Baltimore, MD
BODGE	Daniel	Marine	16 Jan. 1815	Arundel, England
BRAY	Isacher	Seaman	20 Nov. 1814	Cape Ann, MA
BRIEN	Lewis	Seaman	05 Nov. 1814	North Carolina
BRISSONS	John	Seaman	24 Jan. 1815	Baltimore, MD
BROWN	George	Seaman	11 Feb. 1815	Pennsylvania
BROWN	William	Seaman	20 Jul. 1815	New York
BROWN	Charles	Seaman	17 Feb. 1815	Virginia
BURBIDGE	Henry	Seaman	25 Dec. 1814	Washington
BURLEIGH	Henry	Seaman	02 Dec. 1814	Newmarket, England
BUTLER	John	Seaman	23 Feb. 1815	Pennsylvania
BUTTS	Joseph	Seaman	02 Dec. 1814	New York
CAMPBELL	Henry	Seaman	22 Mar.1815	Delaware
CAMPBELL	James	Seaman	07 Apr. 1815	New York
COMPICHI	St. Yago	Seaman	16 Jan. 1815	Carthagena, Bolivia
CARSON	John	Seaman	16 Oct. 1814	New Orleans, LA
CARTER	Daniel	Seaman	06 Oct. 1814	Virginia
CATERET	James	Seaman	11 Nov. 1814	Maryland
CHANDLER	Simon	Seaman	25 Oct. 1814	Massachusetts
CHULT	David	Seaman	03 Mar. 1815	Massachusetts
CLARK	Simon	Seaman	24 Jan. 1815	North Carolina
CLERK	William	Seaman	21 Oct. 1813	Newport, RI
COFFEE	Ramos	Seaman	04 Dec. 1814	New York
COLE	John	Seaman	26 Nov. 1814	Baltimore, MD
COLEMAN	William	Seaman	05 Nov. 1814	North Carolina
COLLINS	John	Seaman	08 Oct. 1814	Philadelphia, PA
CONGDON	James	Seaman	11 Nov. 1814	Rhode Island
CONKLIN	Ventus	Seaman	23 Jun. 1815	New York
COOK	Benjamin	Seaman	06 Apr. 1814	Baltimore, MD
COOMBES	James	Seaman	20 Mar. 1814	Wiscasset, MA
COOPER	Thomas	2nd Mate	08 Nov. 1814	Massachusetts
CORNISH	Charles	Seaman	10 Jan. 1814	Maryland
CURREN	Nathaniel	Gunner	01 June 1815	Salem, MA
CUSSAR	James O.	Seaman	07 Dec. 1814	New York
DAVENPORT	John	Seaman	10 Jun. 1815	Easthaven, CT
DAVIS	James	Seaman	26 Feb. 1814	Savanna, GA
DEBATES	Amos	Seaman	18 Nov. 1814	Hamburg, Germany
DENHAM	Silas	Seaman	14 Nov. 1814	Boston, MA
DENNING	Joseph	Seaman	12 Apr. 1815	Massachusetts
DEVINAS	John	Seaman	12 Apr. 1815	Salem, MA
DIAMOND	William	Seaman	23 Jan. 1815	Rhode Island
DILLAIN	William	Marine	10 May 1814	New Guernsey
DILNO	Benjamin	Seaman	30 Mar. 1815	Massachusetts
DYER	Jonathan	Seaman	11 Mar. 1815	Cape Cod, MA
EDGAR	William	Seaman	28 Jan. 1814	New Jersey
ERWIN	William	Hospital	14 Mar. 1815	Cumberland, MA

EVANS	Edward	Seaman	05 Jan. 1815	Virginia
FERNALD	William	Prize Master	23 Jan. 1815	Kiny, MA
FISHER	Charles	Seaman	06 Apr. 1815	Delaware
FLETCHER	William B.	Seaman	16 Jul. 1813	Marblehead, MA
FLOWERS	John	Seaman	06 May 1815	Boston, MA
FOGERTY	Archibald	Seaman	18 Mar. 1815	Massachusetts
FOWLER	Joshua	Seaman	30 Jan. 1815	Boston, MA
FRANCIS	John	Seaman	15 Apr. 1815	New Hampshire
FREELY	Henry	Seaman	20 Jan. 1814	Pennsylvania
FULFORD	Joseph	Seaman	27 Jan. 1815	North Carolina
GARDNER	Jeremiah	Seaman	01 Mar. 1815	Rhode Island
GARDNER	Timothy	Seaman	15 Jan. 1815	Rhode Island
GATWOOD	James	Seaman	17 Feb. 1815	New Hampshire
GAYLER	James	Seaman	03 Dec. 1814	North Carolina
GENNIFON	Michael	Seaman	12 Nov. 1814	Baltimore, MD
GIBSON	William	Seaman	22 Oct. 1815	New York
GLADDING	William	Gunner	14 Mar. 1815	New Jersey
GLODDING	Joseph	Seaman	14 Mar. 1815	Rhode Island
GREAVES	Thomas	Seaman	23 Feb. 1815	Boston, MA
GREY	John	Seaman	26 Apr. 1815	Richmond, VA
GWYNN	Josh	Seaman	22 Feb. 1815	Salem, MA
HALL	Thomas	Prize Master	18 Apr. 1815	Maryland
HARMAN	Isaac	Quartermaster	09 Nov. 1814	Massachusetts
HARRIS	Lamen	Seaman	05 Mar. 1814	Massachusetts
HARRIS	William	Seaman	24 Nov. 1814	New Hampshire
HARRISON	Samuel	Seaman	08 Jan. 1815	North Carolina
HART	James	Seaman	08 Jul. 1814	Connecticut
HAWLEY	Frederick	Seaman	05 Feb. 1815	Wilmington, DE
HAYCOCK	Joseph	Gunner	20 Mar. 1815	Portland, MA
HAYWOOD	John	Seaman	06 Apr. 1815	Maryland
HENDERSON	Alexander	Seaman	27 Dec. 1814	Connecticut
HENRY	James	Seaman	03 Jul. 1814	New York
HENTY	Jacob	Seaman	16 Apr. 1815	Salem, MA
HENY	Daniel	Prize Master	25 Jan. 1815	Salem, MA
HOBDAY	Francis	Marine	24 Feb. 1814	Gloster, MA
HOLBROOK	Ebeneezer	Seaman	09 Mar. 1815	Massachusetts
HOLDING	Henry	Seaman	06 Mar. 1815	Boston, MA
HOLFORD	Elisha	Seaman	05 Jan. 1815	New York
HOLSTEIN	Richard	Seaman	25 May 1814	Virginia
HOPSON	John	Seaman	14 Mar. 1815	North Carolina
JACK	John	Seaman	14 Mar. 1815	Baltimore, MD
JACKSON	Thomas	Cook	06 Jun. 1814	New York
JACKSON	Thomas	Seaman	07 Apr. 1815	New York
JARVIS	Thomas	Seaman	25 Jan. 1815	Marblehead, MA
JENKINS	Nathaniel	Seaman	21 Feb. 1815	Baltimore, MD
JENNINGS	John	Seaman	22 Feb. 1815	Martha's Vineyard, MA
JOHANNES	John	Seaman	08 Jan. 1815	St. Thomas
JOHNSON	John	Boatswain	01 Feb. 1815	Rhode Island
JOHNSON	Joseph	Seaman	06 Apr. 1815	Connecticut

JOHNSON	William	Seaman	09 Mar. 1815	Philadelphia, PA
JOHNSON	William Alexander	Seaman	02 Nov. 1814	Charleston, NC
JONES	George	Seaman	30 Apr. 1814	New Orleans, LA
JONES	Isaac	Seaman	23 Jan. 1815	Boston, MA
JONES	James	Seaman	27 May 1815	New York
JONES	Stephen	Seaman	04 Nov. 1814	New York
JONES	Thomas	Cook	23 Feb. 1815	Baltimore, MD
JOSE	Emanuel	Seaman	25 Nov. 1814	Portugal
JOSEPH	Pedro	Seaman	25 Feb. 1815	Guadalupe, Mexico
KELLEY	John	Seaman	29 Mar. 1815	Marblehead, MA
KING	Uriel	Seaman	03 Feb. 1815	Massachusetts
KITRE	Dumpy	Seaman	23 Dec. 1814	North Carolina
KNABBS	William	Seaman	26 Feb. 1815	Baltimore, MD
LACKEY	Joseph	Seaman	04 Feb. 1815	Massachusetts
LAMB	Anthony	Seaman	22 Nov. 1814	Connecticut
LARKIN	Amos	Seaman	29 Jan. 1815	Beverly, MA
LARKIN	Louis	Seaman	30 Sep. 1814	Connecticut
LAWSON	James	Steward	05 Jan. 1814	Africa
LEE	Richard	Seaman	19 Jun. 1815	Marblehead, MA
LEE	Richard Robert	Seaman	20 Jan. 1815	Massachusetts
LEMAN	Ambrose	Seaman	24 Oct. 1814	Carthagena, Bolivia
LILLEY	Samuel	Seaman	16 May 1815	Boston, MA
LIPPART	Thomas D.	Prize Master	09 Mar. 1815	Pennsylvania
LONG	Joseph	Seaman	29 May 1815	Massachusetts
LOUIS	John	Seaman	05 Aug. 1814	New Orleans, LA
LOVELY	Placid	Seaman	01 Nov. 1814	New Orleans, LA
LOVERIDGE	William	Seaman	06 Apr. 1815	New York
MAN	Jabez	Seaman	06 Apr. 1815	Boston, MA
MARCH	Jesse	Seaman	05 Feb. 1815	Massachusetts
MARSHALL	Benjamin	Seaman	27 Mar. 1815	Maine
MARSHALL	John	Seaman	08 Apr. 1815	New Bedford, MA
MARSHALL	Solomon	Seaman	20 Nov. 1814	Massachusetts
MARTIN	Manuel	Seaman	22 Sep. 1814	New Orleans, LA
MEADS	William	Seaman	24 Jul. 1815	North Carolina
MENDOZA	Cesar N.	Seaman	25 Oct. 1814	Carthagena, Bolivia
MENIIIO	John	Seaman	18 Nov. 1814	Baltimore, MD
MILLER	Edward	Seaman	23 Feb. 1815	New Jersey
MILLER	Richard	Seaman	20 Nov. 1814	Pennsylvania
MILLS	William	Seaman	24 Mar. 1815	New Jersey
MINGO	Albert	Civilian	25 Oct. 1814	New Orleans, LA
MISTA	William	Seaman	13 Feb. 1815	Virginia
MITCHELL	Ezekiel	Seaman	12 Jan. 1815	Massachusetts
MITCHELL	Reuben	Gunner	11 May 1815	Maryland
MONTE	Charles	Seaman	21 Feb. 1815	San Antonio, TX
MONTGOMERY	John	Seaman	24 Feb. 1814	New York
MOORE	George	Seaman	29 Mar. 1815	Boston, MA
MORE	Henry	Seaman	04 Jan. 1814	New York
MORRELL	Jacob	Seaman	27 Apr. 1815	Massachusetts
MURRAY	James	Seaman	17 Oct. 1813	Maryland

NASH	Daniel	Seaman	14 Feb. 1815	Vermont
NORTON	Edward	Seaman	29 Sep. 1814	Massachusetts
OSBORNE	John L.	Seaman	24 May 1815	Newbury Port, RI
PACKER	William	Seaman	28 Nov. 1814	Barnstable, MA
PALMER	Joseph	Seaman	17 Nov. 1814	Portsmouth, NH
PARISH	Samuel	Seaman	01 Apr. 1815	Virginia
PARKER	Thomas	Seaman	05 Nov. 1814	Delaware
PASS	Samuel	Seaman	12 Mar. 1814	Unknown
PAUL	Jonathon	Seaman	09 Mar. 1815	Massachusetts
PECK	Thomas	Seaman	15 Mar. 1815	Connecticut
PERIGO	Joel	Seaman	24 Nov. 1814	Connecticut
PERKINS	John	Carpenters Mate	03 Nov. 1814	New Hampton, IA
PETERS	Aaron	Seaman	14 Jan. 1815	Rhode Island
PETERSON	Jacob	Seaman	04 Nov. 1814	Rhode Island
PETERSON	John	Seaman	01 Jun. 1815	Albany, NY
PETERSON	Lawrence	Seaman	08 Jan. 1815	Unknown
PETTINGALL	Joshua	Seaman	07 Oct. 1815	Salem, MA
PINKHAM	Jacob	Seaman	25 Sep. 1814	Massachusetts
POLLAND	John	Seaman	23 Nov. 1814	Brazil
PORTER	Gideon	Seaman	22 Mar. 1815	Newport, RI
POTTER	John	Seaman	05 Oct. 1815	Philadelphia, PA
POWSLAND	Edward	Seaman	08 Jun. 1815	Beverly, MA
QUEENWELL	Peter	Seaman	27 Jan. 1815	Dartmouth, England
RANSON	Joseph	Seaman	01 Mar. 1815	Philadelphia, PA
RAYSDEN	John	Seaman	14 Feb. 1815	New York
READ	David	Seaman	14 Nov. 1814	Wiscasset, ME
READ	William	Seaman	03 Jun. 1815	New Hampshire
RENNABEN	Benjamin	Seaman	16 Nov. 1813	New Orleans, LA
RICKS	Thomas	Seaman	22 Jan. 1815	New York
ROBERSON	James	Seaman	01 Apr. 1815	Massachusetts
ROBERTS	John	Seaman	12 May 1815	Baltimore, MD
ROBINSON	Samuel	Seaman	15 Feb. 1815	Boston, MA
ROBINSON	William	Seaman	18 Apr. 1815	Philadelphia, PA
ROGERS	Luke	Seaman	13 Nov. 1814	North Carolina
ROMEL	Francis	Seaman	07 Feb. 1815	San Sebastian, Spain
ROTH	James	Seaman	29 Dec. 1814	Connecticut
ROWLINSON	Thomas	Seaman	26 Nov. 1814	Virginia
SALISBURY	Joseph	Civilian	13 Mar. 1815	Newport, RI
SAUL	Francis	Seaman	20 Oct. 1814	Unknown
SAUNDERS	William	Seaman	16 Jan. 1814	Massachusetts
SAWYER	Jacob	Seaman	25 Oct. 1814	Providence, RI
SCHEW	Richard	Seaman	08 Feb. 1814	New York
SEAPATCH	John	Civilian	07 Feb. 1815	Massachusetts
SHAW	William	Seaman	17 Oct. 1814	Philadelphia, PA
SHELDON	Smith	Soldier	19 Jan. 1815	Rhode Island
SHERRIDEN	Henry	Seaman	24 Jan. 1815	New York
SIMMONS	Thomas	Seaman	20 Jan. 1815	New Bedford, MA
SIMONDS	David	Seaman	22 Jan. 1815	Massachusetts
SIMONDS	Ebeneezer	Seaman	12 Jan. 1815	Newburyport, MA

SIMONDSON	Isaac	Seaman	20 Nov. 1814	New York
SMART	William	Seaman	05 Dec. 1814	Virginia
SMITH	Andrew	Seaman	05 Mar. 1815	Maryland
SMITH	Nicholas	Seaman	09 Jan. 1815	Richmond, VA
SMITH	Richard	Seaman	14 Apr. 1815	Salem, MA
SMIDES	Rich	Seaman	06 Mar. 1815	New York
SNELL	Shadrach	Fifer	16 Mar. 1815	Rhode Island
SQUIBB	Silus	Seaman	18 Mar. 1815	New London, CT
STACEY	Stephen	Seaman	16 Mar. 1815	Marblehead, MA
STANWOOD	Timothy	Seaman	20 Mar. 1815	Newburyport, MA
STEEL	John	Seaman	15 Dec. 1814	Maryland
STONE	John	Seaman	05 Jan. 1815	Arundel, England
STOVE	Lewis	Seaman	21 Nov. 1814	Connecticut
STROUT	John	Seaman	20 Jan. 1815	Portland
STUDDY	Richard	Seaman	03 Nov. 1814	Virginia
SUTTON	Martin	Seaman	22 Feb. 1815	New Bedford, MA
TAYLOR	David	Seaman	19 Jun. 1815	Philadelphia, PA
THOMAS	Abraham	Seaman	23 Jul. 1814	Connecticut
THOMAS	John	Seaman	25 Oct. 1814	Unknown
THOMPSON	Henry	Seaman	21 Feb. 1815	New York
THOMPSON	Thomas	Seaman	16 Jun. 1815	New York
THOMSON	William	Cook	18 Apr. 1815	Haiti
TIMERMAN	Matthew	Seaman	26 Sep. 1814	New York
TOBY	Elisha	Seaman	09 Mar. 1814	Massachusetts
TOMKINS	Abraham	Seaman	03 Nov. 1814	New York
TOPHOUSE	Samuel	Soldier	11 Feb. 1815	Washington
TREMERIN	Joseph	Seaman	04 Jun. 1815	Philadelphia, PA
TUCKER	James	Seaman	28 Apr. 1815	Long Island, NY
TURNER	David	Seaman	17 Mar. 1815	Boston, MA
TURNEY	John	Seaman	05 Apr. 1815	Massachusetts
TUTTLE	French	Seaman	24 Nov. 1814	Massachusetts
TYREN	William	Seaman	25 Feb. 1814	North Carolina
VAUGHAN	Nathaniel	Seaman	31 Aug. 1814	Newport, RI
WASHINGTON	John	Seaman	06 Apr. 1815	Savanna, GA
WEST	George	Seaman	27 Jan. 1815	Baltimore, MD
WEST	George	Seaman	27 Jan. 1815	Delaware
WHITTAN	John	Seaman	18 Jan. 1815	Portsmouth, VA
WILLIAMS	Charles	Seaman	09 Mar. 1815	New London, CT
WILLIAM*	Edward	Seaman	21 Mar. 1815	Virginia
WILLIAMS	John	Seaman	14 Jan. 1815	Connecticut
WILLIAMS	Joseph	Seaman	01 Feb. 1815	Martha's Vineyard, MA
WILLIAMS	Samuel	Seaman	15 Mar. 1815	Massachusetts
WILLIAMS	Thomas	Seaman	20 Mar. 1814	Connecticut
WILLIAMS	William	Seaman	27 Oct. 1814	Georgetown, SC
WINDYER	Joseph	Seaman	06 Jan. 1815	Marblehead, MA
YOUNG	William	Seaman	21 Jan. 1815	Massachusetts

* Edward William from Virginia should read "Williams." This matches the General Entry Book listing. Also, there is one other discrepancy and that is the death of an

American prisoner which has not been recorded on the memorial plaques. Our informant is none other than Charles Andrews (*A Prisoner's Memoires*, pages 133–134), who wrote how a fellow prisoner killed himself and was buried on the moor. He relates how he procured a slate and planted it on his grave with the following inscription:

Here lies
JOHN TAYLOR
A NATIVE OF THE CITY OF NEW YORK,
Who committed suicide, by hanging himself in prison No. 5, on the evening
Of the first of December, 1814.

Appendix 2

Chronology of Dartmoor Prison

1772.	Tavistock-Moretonhampstead-Ashburton Road Act passed.
1785.	Sir Thomas Tyrwhitt joins "improvers" and establishes Tor Royal.
18 May 1803.	Treaty of Amiens ends, war with France renewed.
1805.	Transport Office proposes prisoner of war depot in Devonshire.
20 March 1806.	Sir Thomas Tyrwhitt lays Dartmoor Prison foundation stone.
22 May 1809.	First French prisoners arrive at Dartmoor Depot.
November 1809.	Outbreak of measles epidemic. Nearly 500 prisoners die during winter.
1811–1812.	Two extra prisons completed to cope with overcrowded conditions.
2 April 1813.	First 250 American prisoners arrive from Plymouth hulk *Hector*.
16 October 1813.	"Romans" removed from Dartmoor to Plymouth hulks.
22 December 1813.	Captain I. Cotgrave leaves and is replaced by Captain T. Shortland.
Winter 1813–1814.	Severe winter. Snow to top of prison walls. Water supply frozen.
February 1814.	American government allows prisoners 1½d. per day. Americans admitted to daily market to buy tobacco and soap. Colored men segregated to No. 4 block. "King Dick" Crafus rules.
March 1814.	American government allows further 1d. per day. All Americans permitted to attend daily market.
11 April 1814.	Napoleon abdicates. French war ends.
20 June 1814.	All the French have been repatriated from Dartmoor. Napoleon exiled to Elba. British decide to transfer all American prisoners (except the officers) to Dartmoor.
24 December 1814.	Treaty of Ghent. War of 1812 ends.
26 February 1815.	Napoleon returns from Elba. War resumed — the "Hundred Days."
13 March 1815.	HBMS *Favourite* arrives from the United States with ratification of the Treaty of Ghent.

4 April 1815.	The "Bread Riot." Fresh bread issued after confrontation with guards.
6 April 1815.	The "Prince Town Massacre." Nine Americans die as a result and many are wounded when guards open fire.
19 April 1815.	First batch of American prisoners leave for home.
18 June 1815.	Battle of Waterloo. Napoleon defeated.
1–4 July 1815.	Over 4,000 French prisoners arrive at Dartmoor, many for the second time, straight from the battlefields.
15 July 1815.	Napoleon surrenders to Captain Maitland on HBMS *Belepheron*, and the French wars finally end.
24 July 1815.	Last of the Americans leave for home—the colored men and "Rough Allies."
August 1815.	Napoleon leaves Plymouth for exile on St. Helena.
December 1815.	All French prisoners have left Dartmoor except for the sick in the hospital.
February 1816.	All prisoners gone home. The garrison leaves. The gates are locked.

For the next 34 years the prison remained empty. Various ideas were considered for utilizing the facility, including a suggestion that orphans from the streets of London be housed there. Albert, the Prince Consort, thought it a suitable location for the confinement of convicts (transportation was coming to an end and the existing British jails were full). Both possibilities were rejected. In 1846 the British Patent Naphtha Company leased the place and installed retort stokers for the production of gas and oils from peat. It was a short-lived project and the company went into liquidation shortly afterward.

In 1850 work commenced, using convict labor, to convert some of the old prison blocks at Dartmoor for use as a penal establishment after all. Despite several threats of closure, because of its remote location and expensive running costs, Dartmoor Prison has survived. Today it still plays an important part in Princetown's economy and the confinement of convicted men. Sir Thomas Tyrwhitt would have approved.

Chapter Notes

The Public Record Office is the guardian and custodian of the National Archives. The term "Public Record Office" no longer officially applies but is still used by researchers to avoid confusion with other countries' establishments. Thus the correct postal address is: National Archives, Kew, Richmond, Surrey, TW9 4DU, England.

Every document is catalogued and a code number is applied. The various sources are abbreviated: for example ADM refers to Admiralty (Royal Navy) papers. FO refers to Foreign Office (Government) documents and so on.

In a reference such as "Public Record Office, Kew, ADM 98/143," the ADM is Admiralty papers, 98 is the class number and 143, the paper number. So with the information ADM 98/143 it is possible to locate the piece that you want, i.e. paper no. 143 in class 98 of Admiralty papers (ADM) at Kew.

Introduction

1. Modern research has concluded the king in fact was not mad at all but was subject to bouts of porphyria, an illness that causes stomach cramps, delirium and confusion in the mind much like insanity.

2. The two extra prisons were built by French prisoners who volunteered for the work and were paid a daily wage. This has led to a misunderstanding that the depot was built by the French prisoners of war, but, as we shall see, it was constructed by a private company.

Chapter 1

1. Pixies are mythical and mischievous little elves.

2. Lord Warden of the Stannaries was a post of historic importance which entailed convening and enforcing decisions of the Stannary Court. This body was made up of elected representatives of the tin mining industry mainly in Cornwall but including Dartmoor. Among other duties, the court settled disputes and punished wrongdoers within the industry.

3. Black Rod is a senior officer in the House of Lords. He is responsible for security, controlling access to and maintaining order within the House and its precincts.

4. This was never done; a lease was substituted but the scene was set for building Dartmoor Prisoner of War Depot. In addition to several of the farms and inns on the moor, many properties in Princetown, including the present day convict prison at Dartmoor, still pay an annual leasehold rent to the duchy.

5. HBMS: His Britannic Majesty's Ship.

6. W. Branch Johnson, *The English Prison Hulks* (London: Christopher Johnson, 1957), p. 86.

7. "Essay Toward a History of Plymouth," p. 79.

Chapter 2

1. Public Record Office, Kew, ADM 98/143.
2. The outer wall still stands, a truly mammoth work approximately one mile in length.
3. A perch is a volume of stone wall. 1 Perch = an area 16.5 feet long, 1.5 feet high and 1 foot thick (altogether just under 1 cubic yard).
4. Public Record Office, Kew, ADM 1/3774.
5. Public Record Office, Kew.
6. There is no trace of the foundation stone today.
7. The dead man was Jean-Pierre Masse from Concarneau, a sailor on *Le Scorpion*, taken at Trafalgar.
8. A full account of this discovery, together with a report on the bicentenary commemoration ceremony held at Dartmoor by the French in conjunction with Dartmoor Prison's governor and staff, can be found in the illustrated book *Rendezvous in Princetown* written and produced by Alain Sibiril, Monique Sibiril and Trevor James (copies may be obtained from the author).

Chapter 3

1. The prison farm is now closed and has been returned to the duchy, which leases it to private landowners.

Chapter 5

1. Included in "Instructions to Agents" from the Transport Office.
2. There follow instructions for lashing up hammocks to allow free circulation of air within the prisons, which are to be kept locked and all windows left open during the prisoners' absence.
3. Public Record Office, Kew.

Chapter 6

1. How did ordinary sailors know how to construct a ship, a necessary requirement for building such perfectly accurate models? The answer is simple and straightforward. Ships were often damaged either by storm or during a battle and hundreds of miles from the nearest port (which might not be a friendly one anyway). Repairs had to be carried out by the crew either at sea or by running their vessel aground onto a beach. Therefore among the ship's company were always at least two shipwrights who supervised the work during which sailors learned exactly how a ship was constructed, thus enabling them to produce the beautiful models we see and admire today.

Chapter 7

1. The author acknowledges the invaluable help he received from the Leicester Lodge of Research at Freemasons Hall, Leicester, which not only assisted in every way, but kindly gave permission to use material from "French Prisoners' Lodges" by the late W. Bro. John T. Thorp, a founding member of the lodge.
2. The author is grateful to the late Ron Chudley, retired *Western Morning News* (a Plymouth daily paper) journalist of Exmouth (Devon) for drawing his attention to it and for providing a possible explanation for the unusual circumstances surrounding it.
3. The author has made inquiries to United Grand Lodge of England without success.

Chapter 8

1. West Devon Record Office, Coxside, Plymouth, England.
2. See *The Marches of a Militiaman: An Account of Life in the 1st Devon Militia* by anonymous.

Chapter 9

1. Images on pages 84 and 85 provided by Public Record Office, Kew, ADM 1/3774.
2. He was not eligible for parole, therefore the only purpose in being sent to Dartmouth on discharge was to board a cartel for America, probably on exchange.

Chapter 10

1. The cooks boiled the meat or fish and vegetables in nets for each mess. The fat that rose to the surface of the cauldrons congealed when cool to be skimmed off and sold to other prisoners to be spread on bread, a highly prized and nourishing addition to their diet. This was a recognized "perk" for cooks in the Royal Navy at that time but caused much resentment among prisoners of war at Dartmoor.

2. The Transport Office instructions were that the prisoners should be permitted to inspect their provisions before they were issued. On one occasion the entire batch of daily bread was rejected and the contractor heavily fined. It happened in October 1812 after a sample of the bread was sent to the authorities in London; retribution was swift and uncompromising, as the following letter from the Transport Office to Captain Cotgrave (the agent) makes clear: "I am directed to acknowledge the receipt of your letter of the 29th instant with the sample of bread therein referred to ... and to acquaint you that they have ordered [a fine] of £500 to be imposed on Mr. Cock for his breach of contract, and have given him notice that his contract will cease on 31st January."

3. For much of what follows the author is indebted to the late Ira Dye, writer, researcher, and author of *The Fatal Cruise of the Argus* (United States Naval Institute, Annapolis, Maryland, 1994).

4. At the time of writing the headstone requires attention, as the detail has become badly eroded. A fund has been set up to have the entire inscription renewed and, true to form, the National Society of the Daughters of 1812 have already made a generous donation.

Chapter 11

1. Each man already got one and a half pence per day (× 32) = 48d. The new allowance = 1d. extra per day (× 32) = 32d., for a total of 80d. (12 pence = 1 shilling and 20 shillings = £1-0-0). The sum 80d. = 6s. 8d., which is exactly one third of £1-0-0, and therefore £2-0-0 per six men = 6s. 8d. each.

Chapter 16

1. The full report and relevant letters for this (first) Royal Navy inquiry are to be found at the Public Record Office, Kew, under Reference ADM 1/836.

2. The prisoners appointed a committee of ten men to prepare a summary of their version of events, taken from statements made by those who were involved.

3. The full transcript of the above main inquiry conducted by Francis Seymour Larpent and Charles King are to be found at the Public Record Office, Kew, under Reference FO 5/111 53146.

4. Public Record Office, Kew, under Reference FO 5/111.

5. From public records at Kew, Surrey, England, Reference FO 5/107/189.

6. Henry Clay, speaker to the House of Representatives, and Albert Gallatin, secretary to the Treasury, were signatories to the Treaty of Ghent.

7. From public records at Kew, Surrey, England, Reference FO 5/107 282.

Chapter 17

1. This charge was made by officers at Dartmoor Depot as well as Royal Navy officers who captured them. In fact, these same navy officers also took captured vessels as prizes, just as the privateers did. It was a case of extreme disappointment when, after the Battle of Trafalgar, a number of French prize ships foundered and sank in a storm.

2. It was estimated by Lloyds (the shipping insurers) the Americans captured 1,175 British ships during the war, less 373 recaptured (*Command of the Ocean: A Naval History of Britain 1649–1815* by N.A.M. Rodger, Penguin Group, 2004, page 569).

3. An indication of the optimism and confidence of the owners!

Chapter 18

1. The titles and locations of the journals written by former prisoners of war at Dartmoor are quoted by Ira Dye. Today most of them can be found on the Internet.

2. This prison also organized boxing matches. Benjamin Palmer describes one match that was so vicious and gruesome he had to leave. Brown tells us that after the war Dick Crafus was well-known in Boston as an instructor in pugilism.

3. This must have been the expedition that resulted in the Battle of New Orleans in January 1815, which ended in disaster for the British, some of whose finest soldiers were annihilated by a smaller American force lying in wait for them. The war had officially ended and neither side knew.

4. These were the sentiments of every American and with some justification. Their young nation had more than held its own against one of the most powerful countries in Europe. All the same, the contents of the treaty provided for nearly every contentious issue to return to the status quo.

5. His full name was Benjamin Franklin Palmer.

6. "2/-" is another way of saying 2 shillings.

7. Sent to Plymouth for interview by a Mr. Smith.

8. Of course it is, and after reading it one can understand why. In any case he has done no more than record events as they happened and in the spirit one would expect from a man who was subjected to the sufferings he describes.

9. The correct date was the second of April 1813 and in any case Andrews did not go to Dartmoor until July 1, as the General Entry Book tells us (pages 9–10).

10. List is a selvedge of a piece of fabric. A selvedge is the woven edge of a piece of fabric to prevent it from unraveling. The shoes therefore must have had list straps as fasteners (page 23).

Chapter 19

1. The photo originated from the United States Navy Museum, Annapolis, Maryland. I have contacted the museum and asked for a copy of the original photo, but after much searching no trace of it could be found, although it is confirmed it was in their collection some time ago.

Chapter 20

1. He died on St. Helena on May 5, 1821. He had stated a preference for burial in France near the River Seine; otherwise, if the British should dictate he remain on the island, which they did, he chose the Valley of Geranium, since renamed the Valley of the Tomb, as his last resting place. He was laid to rest there until 1841, when he was exhumed and brought home to Paris, where his wish to lie beside the Seine was honored. His tomb is now a national monument.

Chapter 21

1. The figures vary depending on which sources are consulted, but nevertheless these give a good idea of the enormous expenditure.

Chapter 22

1. Public Record Office, Kew, reference not recorded.

2. The phrase "while the prisoners remain" is a reference to the cheap labor provided by the French prisoners whose repatriation was imminent. By June 20, the French had all gone and there was much still to be done. It fell to the Americans to finish the work.

3. The number is now known to be 271.

4. At the time of writing, efforts are being made to raise the necessary funds to renovate the memorial window yet again. The U.S. Daughters have already made a contribution. (For more information visit the trust's Web site, www.visitchurches.org.uk.)

Bibliography

Abell, Francis. *Prisoners of War in Britain 1756–1815*. London: H. Milford/Oxford University Press, 1914.

Andrews, Charles. *A Prisoner's Memoires of Dartmoor Prison*. 1815. Printed for the author in New York.

Atholl, Justin. *Prison on the Moor: The Story of Dartmoor Prison*. London: John Long, 1953.

Baring-Gould, S. *Devonshire Characters and Strange Events*. London: Bodley Head, 1908.

Beckett, Ian W. *The Amateur Military Tradition*. Manchester: Manchester University Press, 1991.

Blackburn, Julia. *The Emperor's Last Island*. New York: Pantheon, 1991.

Brachen, C.W. *History of Plymouth and its Neighbourhood*. Plymouth, England: Underhill, 1931.

Branch Johnson, W. *The English Prison Hulks*. London: Christopher Johnson, 1957.

Bryant, Arthur. *Years of Victory 1802–1812*. New York and London: Harper and Brothers, 1945.

Cherry, Bridget, and Nikolaus Pavsner. *Buildings of England*. Exeter, England: Devon, 1989.

Chudley, Ron. *Our Brothers the Enemy*. Exmouth, England: published privately.

Cronin, Vincent. *Napoleon*. London: HarperCollins, 1994.

Crossing, William. *One Hundred Years on Dartmoor*. Exeter, England: Devon, 1987.

_____. *Princetown: Its Rise and Progress*. Brixham, Devon, England: Quay, 1989.

Devon Record Office (Exeter, England). *Princetown Massacre*. Devon Quarter Sessions. (Inquest reports on two men who died later). Bundle for Exeter, 1815, Box 284. Bundle for Michaelmas, 1815, Box 285.

Dickinson, M.G. "Princetown Massacre (Footnote to Baring Gould's Account)." *Devon and Cornwall Notes and Queries*, Vol. 6, p. 248. Devon Record Office, Exeter, England, 1908.

Dictionary of American Biography. First published New York: Charles Scribner's Sons.

Douglas, David C., and George W. Greenaway, eds. *English Historical Documents*. London: E. Methuen, 1981.

Dye, Ira. *The Fatal Cruise of the Argus*. Annapolis, MD: Naval Institute, 1994.

Endle, Rufus. *Dartmoor Prison*. Cornwall, England: Bossiney, 1979.

Evans, Rachel. *Home Scenes of Tavistock and Its Vicinity*. London: Simpkin and Marshall, 1846.

Halevy, Elie. *History of the English People in the 19th Century*, Vol. 1. London: E. Benn, 1924.

Hamilton-Williams, David. *The Fall of Napoleon*. London: Brockhampton, 1999.

Harris, John. "Essay Toward a History of Plymouth." 1806. Two volume typescript, Plymouth Local Studies Library; original volumes held by Plymouth & West Devon Record Office, Plymouth, England, accession numbers 219/1 and 219/2.

Harris, Vernon. *Dartmoor Prison Past and Present*. Plymouth, England: William Brendon and Sons, 1875.

Haswell, Jock. *The British Army: A Concise History*. London: Book Club Associates, 1975.

Hickey, Donald R. *The War of 1812*. Chicago: University of Illinois Press, 1989.

Hill, H.S. "Princetown: Its History and its Prisons." Three articles in the *Western Daily Mercury*, Plymouth, England, April 1869.

Horne, Alistair. *Napoleon: Master of Europe 1805–1807*. London: Weiderfield and Niclolson, 1979.

Horsman, Reginald. *The War of 1812*. New York: Knopf, 1969.

The Marches of a Militiaman: An Account of Life in the 1st Devon Militia. Copy at Public Record Office, Clare Place, Coxside, Plymouth, England.

Mellish, J. *Description of Dartmoor Prison with an Account of the Massacre at the Prison by a Former American Prisoner*, 1815.

Openheim, M.M. *Maritime History of Devon*. Devon, England: University of Exeter, 1968.

Oxford Dictionary of National Biography (updated yearly), England.

Palmer, B.F. *Diary of Benjamin Palmer, Privateersman*. Printed for the Acorn Club by Tuttle Morehouse and Taylor, 1914.

Rhodes, A.J. *Dartmoor Prison*. London: John Lane, Bodley Head, 1933.

Richardson, Albert Edward, and Charles Lovett Gill. "Princetown: The Work of Sir Thomas Tyrwhitt and Daniel Alexander," *Regional Architecture of the West of England*. London: Ernest Benn, 1924.

Rowe, Samuel. *A Perambulation of Dartmoor*. London, England: Hamilton Adams, 1848.

Thomson, Basil. *The Story of Dartmoor Prison*. London: William Heinemann, 1907.

Thorne, R.G. *The House of Commons 1790–1820 (History of Parliament Trust)*. London: Secker and Warburg, 1986.

Thorp, John T. *French Prisoners' Lodges*. Leicester, England: George Gibbons, 1900.

Transactions of the Devonshire Association. Available at Exeter City Library, Exeter, Devon, England.

Walker, J. *British Economic and Social History 1700–1980*. London: Macdonald and Evans, 1981.

Walrond, Col. H. *Historical Records of the 1st Devon Militia*. London: Longmans, Green, 1897.

Woollacombe, L. *Princetown and Its Prison* (2d ed.). Exeter, England: James Townsend, 1935.

Periodicals

The Times. London.

Trewman's Exeter Flying Post. Exeter, Devon, England. (Closed in 1927.)

The Western Mercury. (Now incorporated in the *Western Morning News*, Plymouth, Devon, England.)

Western Morning News. Plymouth, Devon, England.

Index

Numbers in **_bold italics_** indicate pages with photographs.

Alexander, Daniel 24, 27–30, 33, 190
Allen, Lt. William Henry 93, **_94_**–95
American Depot 111, 171
Andrews, Charles (seaman, merchant vessel) 168–70
Argus **_93–94_**, 96, 97–99

battle of New Orleans 82
Bienfaisant 23, 31, 69; *see also* Freemasons Lodge
Bouverie, Hon. E. 24, 25
Le Brave 88
Brown, Benjamin (clerk, privateer) 159–162

cachot ("black hole") 43, 53–55, 113
Le Caton (hospital ship) 23
cemeteries **_41_**–42
Cheshire Militia 48
Cobb, Josiah (seaman, privateer) 179
Crafus, Richard ("Big Dick") 108
criers 91–92, 129

Delphey, Midshipman Richard 94, 95
Derbyshire Militia 131
"detenues" 37
Drinkwater, Perez (3rd lieutenant, privateer) 177–178
Duchy of Cornwall 15–16
Duckworth, Adm. Sir John 140
emergency rations 38
escapes 43, 75, 115–118
Europe 23
exchange of prisoners 77

El Firme 21, 23
Freemasons 68–69, **_71_**, 73
Freemasons Lodge **_70_**, 72

Ganges 23
Generaux 23
Grand Army 7

Hector 21, 23, 88, 96, 167, 168

"Instructions for Agents" 58
Isbell Rowe & Company 30

King, Charles 143
King George III 7

Lancashire Militia 48
Larpent, Francis Seymour 143
Little, George (prizemaster, privateer) 173–175

MaGrath, Dr. George 123, 132, 137–138, 145, 191–192
Maples, Capt. R.N. John Fordyce 93
market 38, 54, 63, 104
Mason, the Rev. James Holman 201–202
massacre 131–132, **_133_**, **_134_**, 135, 137–138; first inquiry 140–142; second inquiry **_143_**–147, 149
memorials **_205_**, **_208_**–209, **_210_**–211
military walk **_34_**
militia 14, 34, 44; corruption 49; duties 47; massacre 78, 81, 114, 135
Mill Prison, Plymouth 18, 31, 32, 191

Napoleon 7, 18, 37, 56, 77, 105, 125, 188–189
Norman Cross 18, 20, 27, 111
Nottinghamshire Militia 48

L'Oiseau 23

Palmer, Benjamin (seaman, privateer) 163–166
Panther 23
Plume of Feathers 17
Prince of Wales 15, 17, 20, 24, 30, 199, 201
Prince Regent 7–8, 149–150
Princetown Church 199, **_200_**, 203, **_205_**, 206–207

231

prison   34–39
prison ships (hulks)   8, 13, 19–21, *31*, 32, 37, 47, 49, 69, 78–*80*, 194
privateers   *86*, 153–155

rations   43, 52, 57, 59, 60, 87, 130
Romans   37, 48, 66, 100
Rough Allies   *110*, 111, 123, 130, 132, 174, 188
Royal Navy   18, 27, 28, 37, 49, 52, 83, *84–85*, 90, *93*, 106

San Nicolas   21, 23
San Rafael   21, 23
San Ysidro   21, 23
Shortland, Capt. Thomas   101, 104, 106, 116, 123, 130, 135, 140, 143, 147–148, 190

Shropshire Militia   49
Somerset (1st) Regt. of Militia   121
Staffordshire Militia   48
Stapleton   18, 20, 111, 171–173, 181

Transport Office   20, 24, 27
Treaty of Amiens   13, 18, 37, 44, 82
Tyrwhitt, Sir Thomas   15, *16*, 17, 26, 31, 111, 190

West Ropery (Devonport dockyard)   18–19

Yankees   4, 14, 91, 101, 106, 107, 118–120, 126, 195

www.ingramcontent.com/pod-product-compliance
Lightning Source LLC
Chambersburg PA
CBHW051220300426
44116CB00006B/650